OUSMANE SEMBÈNE

INTERVIEWS

CONVERSATIONS WITH FILMMAKERS SERIES
PETER BRUNETTE, GENERAL EDITOR

Credit: Associated Press

OUSMANE SEMBÈNE

INTERVIEWS

EDITED BY ANNETT BUSCH
AND MAX ANNAS

UNIVERSITY PRESS OF MISSISSIPPI / JACKSON

www.upress.state.ms.us

The University Press of Mississippi is a member of the Association of American University Presses.

Manufactured in the United States of America

First printing 2008

∞

Library of Congress Cataloging-in-Publication Data

Ousmane Sembène: interviews / edited by Annett Busch and Max Annas.
p. cm. — (Conversations with filmmakers series)
Includes index.
ISBN 978-1-934110-85-0 (cloth: alk. paper) — ISBN 978-1-934110-86-7 (pbk.: alk. paper) 1. Sembène, Ousmane, 1923–2007—Interviews. 2. Motion picture producers and directors—Senegal—Interviews. I. Busch, Annett. II. Annas, Max.
PN1998.3.S397A3 2008
791.4302′ 33092—dc22

2007046866

British Library Cataloging-in-Publication Data available

CONTENTS

INTRODUCTION

> *"I am really unable to talk about my life—I don't know my life. I've traveled a lot and this is the life that I have lived, but that doesn't mean that I know myself."*
>
> *(Greer interview).*

IN 2003, THE LONDON MAGAZINE *Black Filmmaker* presented a profile of the man with the pipe and posed the question: "Ousmane Sembène: The World's Greatest Filmmaker?" In this particular context the question might seem affirmative, maybe provocative. For a white European or American audience it is certainly surprising as Ousmane Sembène's films haven't been around very much in many countries of the world since his debut *Borom Sarret* in 1963. This fact itself asks questions about how their distribution in the West was carried out. However, for an African audience the question of whether Sembène was the greatest filmmaker would sound purely rhetorical or close to ideological.

Sembène is one of sub-Saharan Africa's leading intellectual figures, who has apparently easily transformed classical postcolonial thinking towards a progressive position that continuously demands Africa's real independence, while criticizing the achievements within the first two decades of independence as an actual "step backwards." Outside of the African continent, especially in the United States and Great Britain, a growing and interconnected community has emerged that incorporates Sembène and his work in a predominant aesthetic, political, and academic discourse. These communities, mainly African American and African British, have made use of Sembène to build bridges between the mother continent and the Diaspora. Film theorists and curators—like Manthia Diawara, June Givanni, Frank N. Ukadike or Professor Samba Gadjigo (Sembène's official biographer)—have been systematically promoting the (academic) reception of African films—particularly on the institutional level and in postcolonial studies—through festivals and conferences.

As a matter of fact, there is hardly any other film director worldwide whose reputation is similarly dependent on the composition of a national as well as continental audience. But there might be also only few artists who have consciously challenged these different receptions. So Sembène has often talked differently to African journalists (that is to say, more seriously and factually) than to European journalists. These differences are obviously due to the nature of the questions posed to him as well as the knowledge that the respective interviewer has about African heroes and everyday politics. But Sembène leaves no doubt that his films and their meaning change according to the spectator's identity, positioning, and background. That has earned him accusations of being arrogant. Nor was he concerned with ingratiating himself or acting as a dogsbody for the entertainment industry. Rather, he claimed that in Africa cinema had something of the evening school about it. It had an important role to play in social development but it had to find the right site of struggle.

In France, where the African community is rather divided, it is the circles of the political left, although white, who dominate the presentation and interpretation of Sembène's films. In particular around the film journal *CinémAction*, founded in 1978 by Guy Hennebelle and edited by him until his death in 2003, a circle of film academics and journalists emerged (Albert Cervoni, Catherine Ruelle, Daniel Serceau, amongst others), who commented systematically and regularly on film productions from the African continent from the very beginning, having the colonial and neocolonial role of France always very much in mind. It was only later that *Cahiers du Cinema* joined in.

Within these circles Serge Daney played a crucial role. He was likely one of the very few film intellectuals in Europe who successfully refused, already in the 1970s, to position himself within the aesthetic versus political debate led by left cineastes, instead underlining the universalistic potential of cinema. Thus he formulated a vision of *Ceddo* as it could certainly not have been articulated in an interview situation and follows a perception of the film that Josie Fanon, for example, was far from being interested in:

> By habit and laziness, racism too, whites always thought that emancipated and decolonized black Africa would give birth to a dancing and singing cinema of liberation, which would put them to shame by confirming the idea that, no way around it, blacks dance better than they do. The result of this "division of labor" (logical thought/body language) is that the Western specialists of recent African cinema, too preoccupied with defending it through political solidarity or misguided charity, have failed to grasp its real value and originality: the oral tradition, storytelling. Are these "stories told otherwise?" Yes, but in a cinema that is literal (but not metaphorical), discontinuous (not homogenous) and verbal (not musical). This basis in speech, not music, is what already characterized the early films of Ousmane Sembène, Oumarou Ganda, and Mustapha Alassane, as well as those created in exile by Sidney Sokhona. The same is still true for the most recent—and most beautiful—film by Sembène, shot in 1977 and entitled *Ceddo*.

And further on, he writes:

> Between the beginning and the end of the story told by *Ceddo*, what has changed is the status of speech. In the beginning, it is clear that we are in a world *where no one lies*, where all speech, having no other guarantor than the person who produces it, is speech of "honor." When he films these people who will soon be reduced to silence, Sembène first insists on restoring their most precious possession: their speech. It's an entirely political calculation. For what the defeat of the *Ceddo* signifies is that African speech will never again be perceived by whites (first Muslims, then Christians) as speech, but instead as babble, chatter, background noise "for poetic effect" or, worse, "palavers." Now, what Sembène brings before us, beyond archeological concerns (which we are too ignorant of Africa to evaluate) is African speech in so far as it can also have the value of writing. Because one can also write with speech.[1]

Ousmane Sembène's status in Africa cannot be overestimated. He is, and is seen as, many things in one. He was one of the great artists of African independence; his novels described this process from the perspective of the working class, whose consciousness-raising was for Sembène a crucial element in the emancipation from French colonialism. In 1946, Sembène participated as a young member of the worker's union in the legendary strike of rail workers on the route between Dakar and Bamako. He later incorporated this crucial event in his novel *God's Bits of Wood*. In the 1960s, he was one of the pioneers of African cinema, experimenting with documentary and fiction until he discovered the classical one-and-a-half to two-hour fiction movie as his favorite format. He published some film projects between book covers as well as in films, although twice he developed the film material first.

After his film *Guelwaar* (1992) Sembène waited eight more years before he produced two new productions within a few years. He is the "Oldest of the old" (L'Ancien des Anciens) amongst African filmmakers. His decision to favor films over literature was a reaction to the ongoing illiteracy on the continent. Sembène neither avoided a fight against the corrupt state nor an argument with poet-president Senghor whom Sembène considered nothing more than a good French man. No continent other than Africa has born or can present an artist who combines such an intellectual capacity with this form of political influence.

And hardly any other artist from that continent had the opportunity to work on so many historical fractions. After formal independence from Europe, Sembène identified first the constructions of African elites and later the new dependency of African countries through development aid from the North as signifiers of evil. For Sembène these two problems are interlinked. In *Mandabi* (book 1966, film 1968) he portrays a poor man wandering around. The man has received a money transfer from Paris but is not able to exchange it into cash since he is not in possession of an ID. Ignorant officials leave him to deal with the problem on his own. This helplessness is no longer visible in *Guelwaar* (film 1992, book 1994). A village divided by religious conflict comes together to organize a transport of food aid, just to pour the grain in the dust. "If your neighbour's house catches fire, you help him to extinguish. And you also help him to rebuild the house again," Sembène comments. "But after that, you will have to work and earn money yourself again. And the neighbour will have to complete the rebuilding of his house on his own. But in Africa this does not happen. People rely on being helped here. . . . You have to realise that those who rule cannot rule without outside help. And the debts, which exist because of this situation, do no good at all. At the moment you can witness the re-colonization of francophone West Africa—a re-colonization by the most legal means you can imagine. Private French companies, for instance, begin to control the big cities' water and energy supplies, communication and TV stations. And what is left? Nothing" (Wolpert).

Sembène entered the film business as an established novelist. He joined the French army in the Second World War and lived in France between 1948 and 1960 where he worked at Citroën and the docks of Marseille. He became familiar with Marxism, became a member of the KPF and started writing in 1956, first in French and later in Wolof, the language of Senegal's majority. He published five novels and five short story anthologies. In 1961–62, he studied film in Moscow since he was not satisfied with publishing in Wolof. His potential to influence society through the written word was quite limited due to widespread illiteracy. It has been mentioned that the move towards film was therefore a compromise. But anyone who considers these films and their effectiveness can discover quite easily that Sembène entered the medium without compromise.

Borom Sarret (1963) was his debut film that gave hope to many. Sembène tells the story of a carretero who dashes around Dakar with his skinny horse, transporting what is there to transport, in a manner in which he strictly takes sides. At that time, the ideology of optimism was visible throughout the recently made independent/decolonized African countries. However, this movie, which was less than half an hour long, was not supposed to fit into the demands of the ruling class since ordinary people—the working class—could literally not buy anything for themselves from independence. At the end, the carretero is robbed of his cart and therefore his tools when a suit-wearing man persuades him to drive to a formerly European part of the city called Plateau, which he was not allowed to enter with his cart. While the rich man leaves him without paying, the police officer does the "dirty work." The carretero will not be able to feed his family anymore. The perpetrators and victims are clearly identified.

At that time, filmmaking in the sub-Saharan context was risky and adventuresome. Although France was already prepared to establish and use francophone Africa through cultural imperialism as a sales market dumping ground, the practice was not yet working. Dakar was then a city in search, on departure toward something great. The genre-spreading "Festival Mondial des Art Nègres" brought a variety of artists from all over the world who left diverse traces, and suddenly the city on the peninsula became the capital of African culture. Musicians from the whole of West Africa played in its clubs; Star Band was *the* musical institution of the country that later went on to produce the really big combos like Baobab and Nr. One de Dakar, as well as the young Youssou N'Dour. Several activists already joined in the 1950s to make films and support each other. That is how Paulin Soumanou Vieyra's *Afrique sur Seine* (1957) evolved, which is generally identified in film history books as the first sub-Saharan African movie. Besides Vieyra and Sembène, films were regularly produced throughout the 1960s by the likes of Aboubacar Samb-Makharam, Mahama Johnson Traore, and Djibril Diop Mambety.

Mambety's approach differed from that of Sembène. Mambety's *Badou Boy* (1970) can be read as a replica of *Borom Sarret*. It also describes an odyssey through Dakar in which the main character, a teenager without a cent in his pocket, visits the same places as Sembène's carretero. The boy's gestures are reminiscent of Jacques Tati and he self-confidently appropriates these places where he is not supposed to belong such as the quarter of the rich. Between Sembène and Mambety there has been a subliminal rivalry that was never put in words: on one side Sembène with his realistic view on material conditions in his environment; on the other, a loud poetic attitude whereby Mambety, no less political, portrays the everyday concerns of Dakar. However, while the disciplined worker Sembène creates an oeuvre which continuously grows, Mambety withdrew, frustrated with cinema after *Touki Bouki* (1973). He only reappeared on screen in the 1990s with *Hyènes* (1992), an opulent adaptation of a Duerrenmatt piece, *The Visit*, and two lively forty-minute films, *Le Franc* (1995) and *La petite vendeuse du Soleil* (1998), dedicated to the strength of survival of the "petits gens." Here again Mambety is pretty far from being analytical and is rather close to clownery and fairytales, but he is nevertheless amidst description of the harsh reality. Mambety and Sembène were the only protagonists of these days of the beginnings of African cinema who have been shown over the decades at the big festivals.

The Burkinian director Idrissa Ouedraogo even commented in the 1990s that each African film made is a miracle since its individual story of production with all the organizational and financial problems is almost impossible to measure. But he said that at a time when European

TV broadcasts had only just discovered "African" film and while more African films were being produced than ever before or after. The metaphor of the miracle obviously does not consider the Herculean effort that lies behind every African film—even today. Some of Sembène's colleagues literally died of exhaustion. Aboubacar Samb-Makharam (1934–1987) or Djibril Diop-Mambety (1945–1998) are just two examples. Several filmmakers on the continent quit at one stage due to the fact that the conditions of production were too hard and sometimes even too humiliating.

Mandabi (1968), Sembène's first long feature-film, was generated at a time when there wasn't any real or reliable chance to think of a dimension of cinema between Sahara and South Africa. The FESPACO (Festival Panafricain du Cinema et de la Television de Ouagadougou) in Burkina Faso's capital Ouagadougou, only took place for the first time one year later, annually awarding the best African film in alternation with the JCC (Les Journees Cinematrographiques de Carthage, since 1966) in Tunis. In *Mandabi*, Sembène portrays Senegalese bureaucracy as pure self-indulgence, no official understanding his job as something that should serve the people. For Sembène it signified that after independence the representatives of power may have changed, but not necessarily the circumstances within society.

Emitai (1971) was Ousmane Sembène's first attempt to write African history in cinema in an African way. In 1942 the French army wanted to force a male village population in the south-Senegalese Casamance to serve in the army—and thus serve a country to which the majority of the people there only nominally belonged. The women are the most radical in their attempt to resist the project by refusing to deliver rice to the army. Not for the first time—but for the first time articulated so clearly—Sembène is putting women in the main focus; not only as components but also as agents of power, struggle, and even war. This was poorly understood by the conservative societies on the continent. However, for Sembène, it was the beginning of a continuity that continued until his death in 2007.

Xala (1974) is a strong attack on the elites of their countries. The protagonist is as corrupt as his environment and has just found his third wife. Just before the wedding he is made deeply insecure by a curse, the xala. He can no longer get an erection—and this happens just before he gets married to a young lady. The search for the reason behind the xala transforms into an absurd comedy from which the protagonist cannot benefit. The fact that, of all possible people, it was the once-rejected beggar who turns out in the end to be responsible for the curse underlines Sembène's visible understanding of class differences.

Within his most productive decade, Sembène also produced his best film: *Ceddo* (1976). He turns the certainties on which Senegalese society was built upside down. Within the seventeenth century, Islamic and Christian crusades were indistinguishable in their unconditional attempt to convert people to their faith. Competition led the Imam to finally hand his rivals over to the slave traders. Sembène's most impressive film also has the strongest score. Manu Dibango, who at that time had already reached his most creative period, delivers an Afrobeat-like soundtrack whose delayed beats unconditionally underline the victims' pain within the religious power play.

Sembène never really had a productive relation to music. For a long time, music played a minor role in his films or was not present at all. With *Ceddo* he changed that policy. After Manu Dibango, other established stars of West African pop music such as Ismael Lo, Baaba Maal, Yandé Codou Sene, and Boncana Maiga were responsible for the score. Nevertheless this did not necessarily lead to something remarkable which seems to be due to Sembène's indifference towards this medium. One exception was Ismael Lo's composition for the massacre in *Camp de Thiaroye*, gloomy sounds dominated by a trumpet, in such a way that the memory of the image is inseparably linked to music, and vice versa. "I tried to figure out their life context, the context in which they were living. It is the trumpet that structures the day of the soldiers" (Pfaff).

In *Camp de Thiaroye* there are actually more fusions within the sound collage, the precisely positioned singsong of different languages and dialects of the tirailleurs, signifying their education and also their origin in all the different colonized areas of West Africa, the swelling rattle of cutlery that leads into the protest march, the repeating melody of a harmonica that suggests tidbits of "Lili Marleen." And the gramophone plays a further key role. "Diatta owns a gramophone. A recording on this dead apparatus contains all that music which one could play on it. The images contain textures of sound, which don't need to be played to be heard. Later on, Albinoni will play from his hut and we will envision the image of the record player. Later on—when an African American GI visits Diatta—records will pass hands, and, while a piece of Charlie Parker is playing, names will be dropped: Langston Hughes, Paul Lawrence Dunbar, and Marcus Garvey. But their naming only evokes the Harlem Renaissance, the 'Black Atlantic' (Gilroy) where these overtones are already created."[2]

However, it took quite a few years before *Camp de Thiaroye* was produced. After *Ceddo*, Sembène focused on his favorite project, *Samory*, a film in two parts, altogether of three hours duration. It is a portrait of the Mandingo Chief who resisted the French as well as the English army and united West Africa. Samory Touré is known as the ancestor of former Guinean president Sekou Touré. The film was supposed to be Africa's first big-budget production. Sembène gave nonstop interviews and even announced that he would retire once the project was finalized. But *Samory* did not materialize and thereupon has been a taboo issue. Many years of work on an unrealized film and possible exhaustion led to the gap of twelve years between *Ceddo* and *Camp de Thiaroye*—and this within Sembène's most creative time.

Camp de Thiaroye (1988) is a sort of continuation of *Emitai*. Similarly, it deals with a massacre for which the French army is responsible. After the end of the Second World War demobilized African soldiers that fought within the French army in Europe against Germany are being re-barracked. The soldiers are awaiting the promised pay and resist half-heartedly after it fails to come. Nevertheless, the French commanders are not satisfied with such an unresolved situation and order tanks to kill all the Africans. As in many other films by Sembène, *Camp de Thiaroye* is drastic in its representation. And it is unreconciling towards France. Not one French franc went into the production itself and Sembène realized an idea—which remains a dream for many African filmmakers until today—producing a film without any European money. *Camp de Thiaroye* is a Senegalese-Algerian-Tunisian co-production and is thus an example of financing within the south-south-axis. For his last two movies, *Faat-Kine* (2000) and *Moolaadé* (2004), Sembène also tried to find as many collaborators on the African continent as possible. This becomes particular visible in *Moolaadé*, a pan-African production, which involved technicians and actors from several West African countries. It was also the first film Sembène produced completely outside of Senegal.

In *Guelwaar* (1992) Sembène deals once more with the ambivalence between Islam and Christianity. The old fighter Guelwaar has died but has unfortunately been buried in the wrong grave. And while the family of the dead tries to find his corpse, Sembène's story enters the web of corruption and nepotism that is primarily based on the act to embezzle international aid goods. In the end, the village is united again when people attack a truck full of grain from Europe. In this film Sembène goes further than previously: for the first time he focuses not on the representation of reality in Senegal itself or on rewriting history. Instead, in *Guelwaar* he encourages people to take over their own destiny: "Resist the aid that does not help you anyway!"

It took another period of eight years before Sembène's next film entered theaters. He was well over seventy years of age and therefore no one would have been really surprised if he had just retired from cinema. Instead *Faat-Kine* (1999) opened a new chapter in Sembène's work—his feminist era began. Faat-Kine runs a successful petrol station in Dakar, her husband has run away, and she is raising her two children with the help of her mother. Sembène creates the image of a manless society. It is not that men are not present, but rather that they have no role to play. They do not contribute to the well-being of society nor to the family. In the end, as soon as Faat-Kine celebrates her and her children's success the men come skulking in like the undead in a zombie film by George A. Romero.

During the promotion for this film Sembène didn't tire of highlighting in interviews the importance of the work of women for the existence and development of African societies, and his view that it is men who have to change.

In *Moolaadé* (2005) he even radicalizes this creed. The day before the old women with their long knives visit the young girls, the mothers agree on a compact to resist this tradition in order to prevent their daughters from being circumcised. This dispute soon divides the whole village. While the women try to understand the different arguments and develop either this or the other position, thus positioning themselves either in favor of or against the rebels, the men quickly hide within the fortresses of tradition and religion. With *Moolaadé*, Sembène expresses distinctly his view that changes within Africa will only be achieved through the battles led by women. Therefore he calls them heroes of everyday life.

However, Sembène is too experienced to confine himself to only one kind of perception. Maybe one can identify his distinct feminism as a mirror he shows to African men. But towards the rest of the world, he showed more solidarity towards the male population of the African continent. "Nobody can deny that we have a lot of wars going on; brothers killing brothers; we have a lot of diseases and catastrophes," he said in an interview. "But on the other hand, we have a majority of individuals, both men and women, who are struggling on a daily basis in a heroic way and the outcome of those struggle leaves no one in doubt. This is a struggle whose purpose is not to seize power, and I think the strength of our entire society rests on that struggle. And it is because of this struggle that the entire continent is still standing up" (Greer).

The assembled collection of interviews represents a mixture of texts published in European and North American film magazines, of academic conversations, and albeit too small, an exemplary sample of interviews carried out by African journalists. Many of the newspapers and magazines from the African continent, as well as publications within Europe that were made by Africans in exile and focused on a predominantly African audience, no longer exist and are poorly preserved in archives. But throughout the chronological and diverse composition of conversations, Sembène's opinions and manner of speaking itself turns out to be a kind of oral history of African cinema and postcolonial politics. "African cinema is itself a matter of questions and questioning, an ongoing questioning that never merely accepts the supposed givens of African reality. . . . To say that African cinema is a questioning cinema is also to say that it continually moves and changes." That is how Teshome H. Gabriel puts it in his foreword to Frank Ukadike's compilation *Questioning African Cinema*, where Sembène is conspicuously absent from the table of contents but very often and allusively present in the interviews with the other African filmmakers.[3] Ukadike finally took Sembène's refusal in 2002 to do another interview as a "blessing in disguise" as his absence opened up more space for a new generation. He is certainly right that Sembène's oeuvre has been extensively questioned like no other director from the continent. But having it assembled in such a dense way, even readers who might be quite familiar with Sembène's speeches might see lots of new details, facts, contradictions, dreams, Marxist inclinations, observations, and more.

Two important elements of Sembène's standards can be found across all of these interviews. He evaluates the role of France in the postcolonial process mercilessly. In spoken word he equates France with foreign aid and corruption in Senegal and other African countries. And in conversation with Bonnie Greer he calls the politicians of francophone Africa "alienated" and claims France is responsible for Africa's dividedness and its not being politically and culturally united. Pan-Africanism is the second constant in Sembène's speeches. He refers to George Padmore and W. E. B. Du Bois and demands the collaboration of African states on all levels under the aegis of abandonment of funds of the so-called aid from the North. Still in 1978, in conversation with Pierre Haffner, Sembène demonstrated a persistent optimism that in "Africa all is possible." He related this sentence to the development of African cinema that has been sustained since then by a few brave protagonists, but the attitude accords quite precisely with the postcolonial optimism which Sembène never implicitly shared. Later on, Sembène will appear more and more pessimistic in the interviews. To his biographer Samba Gadjigo, he speaks about Africa as a continent of 800 million voiceless people and states that, "in this century, a people who cannot speak of itself is bound to disappear." So a whole continent would disappear if these people won't find their own voice? "No! We cannot and we should not [allow that]." Sembène always saw himself in precisely this process, to communicate with people and to give them a voice to be part of things. That becomes most beautifully obvious in the interview with Samba Gadjigo when he says: "Culture is political, but it's another type of politics. You're not involved in culture to be chosen. You're not involved in its politics to say 'I am.' In art, you are political, but you say 'We are. We are' and not 'I am.'"

Most of the interviews deal with the issues his films address and the reception of the films from all sorts of angles, or with Sembène's biography. But hardly anyone talks to Sembène about his work with actors, the development of his scripts, the adoption of music, the meaning of a certain montage, or the collaboration with a seasoned team. The number of texts that are taken from film magazines and journals is small, a fact that just serves to further indicate that African cinema has not yet arrived within the consciousness of the West, although Sembène worked for that his whole life.

For advice and help in the very right moment, thanks go to Olivier Barlet, Arianna Bove, Erik Empson, June Givanni, Henriette Gunkel, Monique Hennebelle, Marie-Hélène Gutberlet, Susanne Lang, Elizabeth Lequeret, La Médiathèque des Trois Mondes, Olaf Möller, Catherine Ruelle, Florian Schneider, Lutz Semmler, and Erika Richter.

AB
MA

Notes

1. Serge Daney, "*Ceddo* (O. Sembène)," *Cahiers du Cinéma*, October 1979, p. 53. English translation at http://home.earthlink.net/%7Esteevee/Daney_ceddo.html.
2. Marie-Hélène Gutberlet, *Auf Reisen: Afrikanisches Kino*, Frankfurt: Stroemfeld, 2004.
3. Nwachukwu Frank Ukadike, *Questioning African Cinema: Conversations with Filmmakers*, Minneapolis: University of Minnesota Press, 2002.

CHRONOLOGY

1923	Born in Ziguinchor, Senegal, on January 1. His father, a fisherman, belonged to the small ethnic group of the Lebou and was a French citizen.
1937	Retaliates against a French teacher who has hit him and is expelled from school. Moves to Dakar.
1944	Joins the French army.
1946	Demobilization in Baden-Baden and return to Senegal. Joins a construction union and witnesses the general strike that paralyzes the colonial economy for a month.
1947–48	Takes part in the historic strike of the railway workers on the Dakar-Nigerline, which lasts from October 1947 to March 1948.
1948	Moves to France. Finds a job in the docks of Marseille.
1950	Becomes member of the French Communist party.
1956	Publishes first novel: *Le docker noir* (*The Black Docker*, 1987).
1957	Novel: *O pays mon bon peuple*.
1958	Travels to China and Vietnam.
1960	Senegalese independence. Poet Leopold Sedar Senghor is the first Senegalese president. Novel: *Les bouts de bois de dieu* (*God's Bits of Wood*, 1970). Sembène returns to Senegal.
1961–62	Training at Maxim Gorki film school in Moscow.
1962	Short story collection: *Voltaique*.
1963	*Borom Sarret*, Sembène's first film, is produced. It wins first prize at the Tours Film Festival.
1964	Short film: *Niaye*. Novel: *L'Harmattan*.
1965	Two collections of short stories, *Vehi-Ciosane* and *Le mandat* (*White Genesis* and *The Money Order*, 1972), are produced.

1966	Film: *La Noire de . . .* The film is presented at the Festival Mondial des Arts Nègres in Dakar and wins the Jean Vigo Prize at the Tanit d'Or Carthage Film Festival.
1967	Member of the Jury in Cannes and Moscow.
1968	President of the Jury at the Carthage Film Festival. *Mandabi* is produced; it is Sembène's first full-length film in Wolof, his native language.
1970	Short film: *Tauw*. It wins the Golden Lion Prize at the Addis Ababa Film Festival.
1971	Film: *Emitai*. It wins the Golden Bear at the Moscow Film Festival. Monthly magazine *Kaddu* (*Letter*) founded.
1972	Sembène shoots material about African sports during the Olympic Games in Munich but, due to the events of Black September, this footage is never released.
1973	Novel: *Xala* (*Xala*, 1976).
1974	Film: *Xala*. It wins the Karlovy Vary Special Prize.
1976	Film: *Ceddo*. It wins a special prize at the Los Angeles Film Festival.
1980	President Leopold Sedar Senghor is succeeded by Abdou Diouf.
1981	Novel: *Le dernier de l'Empire* (*The Last of the Empire*, 1983).
1987	Short story collection: *Niiwam* (*Niiwam and Taaw*, 1992).
1989	Film: *Camp de Thiaroye* (co-directed with Thierno Faty Sow). It wins a special jury prize at the Venice Film Festival.
1992	Film: *Guelwaar*.
1993	Novel: *Guelwaar*.
2000	Film: *Faat-Kine*. Abdou Diouf loses his bid for election, which marks the end of socialist rule in Senegal after forty years.
2001	Leopold Sedar Senghor dies at the age of ninety-five.
2004	Film: *Moolaadé*, wins Un Certain Regard Award at the Cannes Film Festival.
2007	Dies in Dakar on June 9.

FILMOGRAPHY

1963
BOROM SARRET (*CHARRETIER / WAGONIER / CART DRIVER*) (Filmi Domirev / Les Actualités Françaises)
Producer: **Ousmane Sembène**
Director: **Ousmane Sembène**
Screenplay: **Ousmane Sembène**
Cinematography: Christian Lacoste
Editing: André Gaudier
Cast: Abdoulaye Ly (The Wagoner), Albourah (The Horse)
16 mm, Black & White
22 Minutes

1964
NIAYE (Filmi Domirev / Les Actualités Françaises)
Producer: **Ousmane Sembène**
Director: **Ousmane Sembène**
Screenplay: **Ousmane Sembène**
Cinematography: Georges Caristan
Montage: André Gaudier
Music: Fatou Casset, Keba Faye
Cast: Serigne Sow (Griot), Astou Ndiaye (Griotte), Mame Dia (Mother), Moudou Sene (Soldier)
35 mm, Black & White
35 Minutes

1966
LA NOIRE DE . . . (*BLACK GIRL*) (Filmi Domirev / Les Actualités Françaises)
Producer: André Zwobada
Director: **Ousmane Sembène**
Screenplay: **Ousmane Sembène**
Cinematography: George Caristan
Editing: André Gaudier
Music: Air populaire senégalais
Cast: Thérèse N'Bissine Diop (La Bonne, Duana), Anne-Marie Jelinek (Madame), Robert Fontaine (Monsieur), Momar Nar Sene (Young Man), Toto Bissainthe (voice)
35 mm, Black & White
65 Minutes

1968
MANDABI (*THE MONEY ORDER*) (Filmi Domirev / Comptoir français du Film)
Producers: Jean Maumy, Paul Soumanou Vieyra
Executive Producer: Robert de Nesle
Director: **Ousmane Sembène**
Screenplay: **Ousmane Sembène**
Cinematography: Paul Soulignac
Editing: Gillou Kikoine
Sound: Henry Moline
Cast: Mamadou Gueye (Ibrahima Dieng), Isseu Niang (Second wife), Serigne Ndiaye (The Imam), Serigne Sow (Maissa), Moustapha Touré (Shopkeeper)
35 mm, Color
86 Minutes

1970
TAUW (Broadcasting Film Commision / National Council of the Church of Christ)
Producers: Paulin Soumanou Vieyra, Herbert F. Lowe
Director: **Ousmane Sembène**
Screenplay: **Ousmane Sembène**

Cinematography: Georges Caristan
Editing: Mawa Gaye
Music: Samba Diabara Samb
Cast: Amadou Dieng, Mamadou M'Bow, Fatim Diagne, Coumba Mané, Yoro Cissé, Mamadou Diagne, Christophe Colomb
Documentation
16 mm, Color
24 Minutes

1971
EMITAI (*GOD OF THUNDER / DIEU DU TONNERRE*) (Filmi Domirev)
Producers: Paulin Soumanou Vieyra, Myriam Smadja
Director: **Ousmane Sembène**
Screenplay: **Ousmane Sembène**
Cinematography: Georges Caristan
Editing: Gilbert Kikoine
Music: Manu Dibango
Cast: Robert Fontaine (Le Commandant), Ibou Camara (The villager), Michel Renaudeau (The Lieutenant), Pierre Blanchard (The Colonel) Andoujo Diahou (The Sergeant)
35 mm, Color
96 Minutes

1974
XALA (*IMPOTENCE*) (Filmi Domirev / SNCP)
Producer: Paulin Soumanou Vieyra
Director: **Ousmane Sembène**
Screenplay: **Ousmane Sembène**
Cinematography: Georges Caristan
Editing: Florence Eymon
Music: Samba Diabara Samb
Cast: Tierno Leye (El Hadji Abdou Kader Beye), Miriam Niang (Rama), Douta Seck (Gorgui), Younousse Seye (The second wife), Seune Samb (The first wife)
35 mm, Color
117 Minutes

1976
CEDDO (*OUTSIDERS*) (Filmi Domirev)
Producer: Paulin Soumanou Vieyra
Assistance: Fatima Diaw
Administrator: Robert Loko
Director: **Ousmane Sembène**
Screenplay: **Ousmane Sembène**
Religious consultant: Imam El Hadji Abdoulaye Sarr & Reverend Père Henri Gravrand
Cinematography: Georges Caristan, Orlando Lopez, Bara Diokhane, Seydina O. Gaye
Editing: Florence Eymon, Dominique Blain
Sound: El Hadji Mbow, Moustapha Gueye
Music: Manu Dibango, Chorale St Joseph de Cluny-Dakar conducted by Julien Juga ("Make It Home Someday" by Arthur Simms)
Cast: Tabata Ndiaye (Dior Yacine), Mamadou Ndiaye Diagne (Ceddo), Mamadou Dioum (Biram Ngone Tioub), Mustapha Yade (Madior Fatim Fall)
35 mm, Color
111 Minutes

1988
CAMP DE THIAROYE (*THE CAMP AT THIAROYE*) (SNCP / SATPEC / ENAPROC/ Filmi Domirev / Filmi Kajoor)
Producers: Mustafa Ben Jemja, Ouzid Dahmane, Mamadou Mbengue
Directors: **Ousmane Sembène**, Thierno Faty Sow
Screenplay: **Ousmane Sembène**, Thierno Faty Sow
Cinematography: Smail Lakhdar-Hamina
Editing: Kahena Attia-Riveil
Sound: Rachid Bouafia, Hachim Joulak
Music: Ismael Lo
Cast: Ibrahima Sane (Sergent Diatta), Mohamed Dansoko Camara (Corporal Diarra), Sikiri Bakara (Pays), Jean Daniel Simon (Capitain Raymond), Pierre Orma (Capitain Labrousse)
35 mm, Color
147 Minutes

1992
GUELWAAR (Filmi Domirev / Galateé Films / FR 3 Film Production, Channel Four, WDR)
Producers: Jacques Perrin, **Ousmane Sembène**
Director: **Ousmane Sembène**
Screenplay: **Ousmane Sembène**
Cinematography: Dominique Gentil
Editing: Marie-Aimée Debril
Music: Baaba Maal
Cast: Omar Seck (Major Gora), Ndiawar Diop (Barthélémy), Mame Ndoumbe Diop (Nogoy Marie Thioune), Isseu Niang (Véronique), Miriam Niang (Hélène), Tierno Ndiaye (Guelwaar)
35 mm, Color
115 Minutes

2000
FAAT-KINE (Filmi Domirev, Agence de la Francophonie, Canal + Horizon)
Producer: Wongue Mbengue
Director: **Ousmane Sembène**
Screenplay: **Ousmane Sembène**
Cinematography: Dominique Gentil
Editing: Kahena Attia-Riveil
Music: Yandé Codou Sene
Cast: Venus Seye (Faat-Kine), Mame Ndoumbe Diop (Her Mother), Tabara Ndiaye (Amy Kasse), Awa Sene Sarr (Mada), Ndiagne Dia (Djip)
35 mm, Color
120 Minutes

2004
MOOLAADÉ (Filmi Domirev / Centre Cinematografique Marocian, Direction de la Cinematografie Nationale, Cinetelefims, Films de la Terre Africains)
Producer: Bertrand Michel Kaboré
Director: **Ousmane Sembène**
Screenplay: **Ousmane Sembène**

Cinematography: Dominique Gentil
Editing: Abdellatif Raiss
Sound: Denis Guilhem
Music: Boncana Maiga
Cast: Fatoumata Coulibaly (Collé Gallo Ardo Sy), Maimouna Hélène Diarra (Hadjatou), Salimata Traoré (Amasatou), Dominique Zeida (Mercenary)
35 mm, Color
120 Minutes

OUSMANE SEMBÈNE

INTERVIEWS

A Historic Confrontation in 1965 between Jean Rouch and Ousmane Sembène: "You Look at Us as If We Were Insects"

ALBERT CERVONI/1965

DURING THE COURSE of a confrontation considered today as "historic" between Jean Rouch and Ousmane Sembène, taken down by Albert Cervoni, some formulations were pronounced that since then have become classics with regard to direct cinema, ethnology, and African cinema. We've reproduced large excerpts of this original interview. This has allowed us to reestablish some of the formulations in their original precision. Since then, Sembène has refused to make any commentary on Rouch's cinema.

OUSMANE SEMBÈNE: *Will European cinematographers, you for example, continue to make films about Africa once there are a lot of African cinematographers?*

JEAN ROUCH: This will depend on a lot of things but my point of view, for the moment, is that I have an advantage and disadvantage at the same time. I bring the eye of the stranger. The very notion of ethnology is based on the following idea: someone confronted with a culture that is foreign to him sees certain things that the people on the inside of this same culture do not see.

From *CinémAction* 81 (1996). Translated from the French by Muna El Fituri.

OUSMANE SEMBÈNE: *You say seeing. But in the domain of cinema, it is not enough to see, one must analyze. I am interested in what is before and after that which we see. What I do not like about ethnography, I'm sorry to say, is that it is not enough to say that a man we see is walking, we must know where he comes from, where he is going.*

JEAN ROUCH: You are right on this point because we have not arrived at the goal of our knowledge. I believe as well that in order to study French culture, ethnology having to do with France must be practiced by people on the outside. If one wants to study Auvergne or Lozere, one must be a Briton. My dream is that Africans will be producing films on French culture. As a matter of fact, you have already started. When Paulin Vieyra did *Afrique sur Seine* (*Africa on the Seine*) his purpose was indeed to show African students, but he was showing them in Paris and he was showing Paris. There could be a dialogue, and you could show us what we ourselves are incapable of seeing. I am certain that the Paris or Marseilles of Ousmane Sembène is not my Paris, my Marseilles, that they have nothing in common.

OUSMANE SEMBÈNE: *There's a film of yours that I love, that I've defended and will continue to defend. It's* Moi, un Noir. *In principle, an African could have done it, but none of us at the time had the necessary conditions to realize it. I believe that there needs to be a sequel to* Moi, un Noir, *to continue—I think about it all the time—the story of this young man who, after Indochina, does not have a job and ends up in jail. After Independence, what becomes of him? Has something changed for him? I don't believe so. A detail: this young man had his diploma, now it so happens that most delinquent youth have their school diplomas. Their education doesn't help them, doesn't allow them to manage normally. And, finally, I feel that up to now two films of value have been made on Africa: your* Moi, un Noir *and* Come Back Africa, *which you do not like. And then there's a third one, of a particular order, I'm talking about* Les Statues Meurent Aussi (Statues Die Too).

JEAN ROUCH: I would like you to tell me why you don't like my purely ethnographic films, those in which we show, for instance, traditional life?

OUSMANE SEMBÈNE: *Because you show, you fix a reality without seeing the evolution. What I hold against you and the Africanists is that you look at us as if we were insects.*

JEAN ROUCH: As Fabre would have done. I will defend the Africanists. They are men that can certainly be accused of looking at black men as if they were insects. But there might be Fabres out there who, when examining ants, discover a similar culture, one that is as meaningful as their own.

OUSMANE SEMBÈNE: *Ethnographic films have often done us a disservice.*
JEAN ROUCH: That is true, but it's the fault of the authors, because we often work poorly. It doesn't change the fact that in today's situation we can provide testimonies. You know that there's a ritual culture in Africa that is disappearing: griots die. One must gather the last living traces of this culture. I don't want to compare Africanists with saints, but they are the unfortunate monks undertaking the task of gathering fragments of a culture based on an oral tradition that is in the process of disappearing, a culture that strikes me as having a fundamental importance.

OUSMANE SEMBÈNE: *But ethnographers don't collect fables and legends only of the griots. It is not solely about explaining African masks. Let's take, for example, the case of another one of your films,* Les Fils de I'Eau. *I believe that a lot of European viewers didn't understand it because, for them, these rites of initiation didn't have any meaning. They found the film beautiful, but didn't learn anything.*
JEAN ROUCH: While filming *Les Fils de I'Eau,* I thought that by seeing the film European viewers could do just that, go beyond the old stereotype of blacks being "savages." I simply showed that just because someone doesn't participate in a written culture doesn't mean they do not think. There's also the case of *Maitres Fous,* one of my films that provoked heated debates among African colleagues. For me, it testifies to the spontaneous manner in which the Africans shown in the film, once out of their milieu, get rid of this industrial and metropolitan European ambiance by playing it, giving it as spectacle. I believe, however, that problems of reception do come up. One day, I showed the film in Philadelphia at an anthropological congress. A lady came to see me and asked: "can I have a copy?" I asked her why. She told me she was from the South and . . . she wanted to show . . . this film to prove that blacks were indeed savages! I refused. You see, I gave you an argument.

In agreement with the producers, the showing of *Maîtres Fous* has been reserved for art houses and cinema clubs. I believe that one should not bring such films to an audience that is too large, ill-informed, and without proper presentation and explanation. I also believe that the unique ceremonies of the people in *Maîtres Fous* make a primordial contribution to world culture.

Ousmane Sembène: For Me, the Cinema Is an Instrument of Political Action, But . . .

GUY HENNEBELLE/1969

OUSMANE SEMBÈNE could be described, especially since *Le Mandat*, as one of the foremost figures in African cinema. We caught up with him in 1969.

GH: *How did you come to work in cinema?*

OS: At least you can say that I did not enter the profession by the large door. I was born in Zinguinchor, in Senegal, in 1923, in a family which was not rich. I practiced thirty-six trades. I was a fisher, mason, mechanic, and then a docker on the port of Marseilles for nearly six years. I was involved in an important trade-union activity there. I also started writing my first books there: *Black Docker* in 1957; *Oh Country, My Beautiful People* in the same year; *God's Bits of Wood* in 1960; *Voltaique* in 1962; *L'Harmattan* in 1964; and *Vehi-Ciosane* in 1965, for which I got first prize in the Festival of Negro Arts in Dakar. And finally I wrote *Le Mandat* in 1966, which I made into a film.

GH: *Why did you give up literature for cinema?*

OS: I realized that with a book, especially in Africa where illiteracy is known to prevail, I could only touch a limited number of people. I became aware that film, on the contrary, was likely to reach broad masses. At

From *L'Afrique Littéraire et Artistique*, no. 7 (1969). Translated from the French by Anna Rimpl. Reprinted by permission by Monique Martineau Hennebelle.

this point I addressed requests for different scholarships in order to receive a cinematographic foundation degree. The first country to answer me in a favorable way was the Soviet Union. I spent one year at the Gorki studio in Moscow where I received, under the direction of Mark Donskoi, a teaching practicum.

GH: *Back in Africa, how did you begin making your first films?*
OS: In 1963, the Malian government asked me to make a documentary on the Empire of Songhays. Then I had to find money. That remains a problem today, but at the time it was even more difficult. There had only been a few African films made: *Afrique-sur-Seine* and *Me*, by Paulin Vieyra, *Aouré* and *The Ring of King Koda*, by Mustapha Alassane, and *Grand Magal à Touba* by Blaise Senghor. This is pretty much all, I think.

I founded a modest house of production in Dakar: Filmi Domirev whose means were, and still are, extremely weak. In co-production with Les Actualités Françaises, directed by André Zvobada (an author from Morocco who directed films like *La septième porte* in 1947 and *Captain Ardant* in 1952), I then realized *Borom Sarret*, my first true short film. It is the story of a cartman who is, to some extent, the taxi driver of a horse-drawn cart. Confronted by a rich customer in a residential district prohibited to such a type of vehicle, a cop stops him, makes a complaint, and seizes the cart. Relieved of his livelihood, the poor fellow remains sadly in his place. His wife entrusts the guardianship of their children to him and leaves, while saying to him, "We will eat this evening. . . ." For this film I got the first work prize at the Festival of Tours in 1963.

GH: *Then you made* Niaye *in 1964. More complex than* Borom Sarret, *the story of this film is more difficult to follow. Can you summarize it?*
OS: In the film a bard sits in a tree, in the village square, and observes the life of all. In fact, he tells its history. The chief of the village, married and father to a family, had an incestuous relationship with his own daughter whom he made pregnant. The whole village knows his crime and disapproves of it but nobody dares to rebel against the authority of the chief. The ridiculed wife, no longer able to support this double dishonor, commits suicide by taking poison. Then the son returns, traumatized from a colonial war that he was forced to partake

in. His arrival disturbs the life of the village because he dreams of nothing else but military marches, battles, parades, and shootings.

Instigated by the cousin of the undignified chief, a conspiracy is plotted. The cousin, who has coveted the throne of the chief for a long time, benefits from the madness of the ex-soldier by bribing him and inciting him to kill his father, which he does. The notable ones accommodate the new chief with favor, and furthermore he receives recognition from the French administration. All is apparently returned to order, but the bard, nauseated by such hypocrisy, leaves the village. The young mother also goes away with her baby. At one moment, she even decides to get rid of it, but when she sees the vultures, which resemble planes in the neighborhoods, she is dissuaded from committing the crime. She leaves for a new destiny.

GH: *You then made* La Noire de . . . *?*

OS: Yes. It is a short feature film or a long short film, since it lasts fifty-five minutes. This film tells the dramatic adventure of a young Senegalese woman in France who is taken on for the holidays by her employer, the technical co-operators of Dakar. Grown lonely in Antibes and treated with hardness and contempt by her "Madam," the girl (played by Thérèse Mbissine Diop) ends up committing suicide in the bathtub.

GH: *Why this uncomfortable duration: one hour—is this too long or too short?*

OS: I know, but there were several reasons to do that. The most important one: I started to make this film without the authorization of the National Center of the French Cinema. However, as it was a co-production between Domirev (Dakar) and Les Actualités Françaises, it needed one. Due to a vicious circle I could not obtain authorization because I did not have the professional card since to obtain one it is necessary to have already made a film or to have been assistant (which I did not want to be). Finally we realized that by presenting *La Noire de . . .* as a short film (less than one hour) it would be easier to regularize the situation with the CNC.

In the beginning, i.e. in the time of the scenario, the film was meant to be about one hour and a half. So I cut all the color scenes. . . .

GH: *But do some remain?*
OS: Some do indeed remain but only in certain versions; in particular that which was presented at the Algerian cineclub at the time of the Pan African retrospective. But there was one more: at the beginning of her stay in Antibes, the girl saw all in pink. All was perfect: she had so much dreamed to go to France! Little by little, reality appeared to her, and she sunk into it. Thus I passed into the black and white.

GH: *You have had a professional card since?*
OS: *La Noire de . . .* got various prizes: the Jean Vigo in France, the best prize for full-length films in the Festival Mondial des Arts Nègres of Dakar, and the Gold Tanit in Carthage in 1966. That facilitated things.

But our situation—that of scenario writers in Black Africa is really uncomfortable. I always repeat that African cinema cannot depend eternally on the "goodwill" of the French. On the one hand this is because that can hold surprises for us, on the other hand, because it is not normal. All that returns to the general problem of the neocolonialism which we are in with the complicity of our governments. We are enclosed in a web of contradictions. Under these conditions it is necessary to act as well as possible. I will not wait, sitting on a chair, for my country to take in hand all its economic and political destinies.

The crafty ones criticize me for working with French money. It was indeed with an advance on receipts from Malraux (30 million AF) that I could make *Mandabi* (total cost: 150 mio). I answer that indeed it is a contradiction. But I did not have the choice: between two contradictions, it is necessary to choose the smallest evil. I had two solutions: to take this money which enabled me to find a French producer and to make my film, or to not accept this money and not make a film. It is very clear, very simple, like two and two make four. If an African country had proposed a budget to me I would have accepted it with joy. That was not the case. I take the money where I find it. I am ready to make an alliance with the devil if this devil gives me the money to make films. But I will not disavow any of my political convictions. Moreover I was subjected to no pressure. My screenplay was not discussed. This form of co-production is quite satisfying. But I repeat myself when I say that it is necessary that Africa (especially Black Africa) decides as soon as possible to take in its own hands its cinematographic destinies.

GH: *How much did* La Noire de . . . *cost?*
OS: Ten million.

GH: *Before we come to* Mandabi*, could you tell us something about the situation of distribution in French-speaking Africa?*
OS: It is a permanent scandal. All the movie theatres of our countries are the property of two French monopolies: the COMACICO and the SECMA. The first holds eighty-four of them and the second fifty-six. The few African cinema owners are forced to bypass the COMACICO or the SECMA to supply themselves. Those two companies establish the programming to their liking, notwithstanding the local censures. What I criticize, among other things, about these two companies (as do the majority of my colleagues) is that they do not contribute to the development of the African cinema. They have never financed even one African film. To distribute *Mandabi*, the COMACICO initially proposed a ridiculously tiny sum to me. Recently I managed a little more serious agreement, but for multiple reasons this is far from giving me complete satisfaction. I am a convinced advocate of pure and simple nationalization of the distribution and circulation as it is the case in Algeria for example. This is the only way to change things. If we don't assume ownership of our own distribution, we can hardly work safely. . . .

GH: *Does this mean that Africa's assumption of responsibility for distribution would be a solution?*
OS: Of course this is not obvious. One risk for example (it is the more probable hypothesis) is the creation of mixed societies between one of the aforementioned trusts and the States where some straw men will be named as directors. One could start to produce African films perhaps, but one can fear that it will be in the Egyptian manner: consumer or prestige films. This is why I suggest that the really committed engaged cineastes, those really politicized and eager to make films of value, gather themselves in an association; a little in the manner of the Brazilian cineastes with the cinema "novo." They succeed, in spite of the nature of their government, to make engaged films–protests, if not revolutionary films—which are not like commercial "chanchadas" of the time before. This is an example to be followed. We African cineastes must have the courage to be us. The Pan African Union whose foundation was provided

in Algiers at the time of the Festival of the Culture, and which will be officially created in Addis-Adeba, is undoubtedly a good thing but, you understand, all of them will take part: the "moderate ones" and the "revolutionaries." It is a first step, but it is necessary to go further. This is why I intend to try and cause a regrouping, which is different from African cineastes and which intends really to make an engaged cinema, a political cinema, a cinema of handing-over in question.

GH: *How would you summarize your position? What kind of cinema do you want to make exactly?*
OS: What is interesting for me is exposing the problems my people have to face. I am not a leftist intellectual. Moreover I am not an intellectual at all. I regard the cinema primarily as a political instrument of action. I stand, as I've always said, for Marxism-Leninism. I am for scientific socialism. However, as I always continue to specify, I am not for "socialist realism," nor for a "cinema of signs" with slogans and demonstrations. For me revolutionary cinema is something else. And then I am not naive to the point that I believe that I could change Senegalese reality with only one film. On the other hand, if we managed to set up a group of cineastes who all make a cinema directed in the same direction, I believe that then we could influence a little bit of the destinies of our country. You asked me before why I gave up literature for the cinema: it is for this reason precisely. I think that the film, more than the book, can crystallize an awakening within the masses. I am personally inspired much by the example of Brecht. I believe that *Mandabi* is a Brechtian film.

GH: *What was your reason for making* Mandabi*?*
OS: The same one as for *La Noire de . . .* I guess that it does not supply anything to tackle colonialism now, since this colonialism (except, of course, in Angola, Mozambique, and elsewhere) has died. That becomes a lullaby which is used to prevent our people from becoming aware of current realities, of the engagements of today. The enemy in 1969 is foreign neocolonialism, but also the local bourgeoisie, who become accomplices of them for their greatest interest. Africa is currently the theater for a fight between classes, which has become increasingly acute. This is why in *La Noire de . . .* I denounce two things: neocolonialism (indeed why

does this treatment of the Africans continue?) and the "new African class" (generally made up of bureaucrats and a certain form of technical assistance). In *Mandabi* I denounce, in a Brechtian manner, the dictatorship of the bourgeoisie over the people. This bourgeoisie, which could be called transitional, is a special bourgeoisie that is not so much made up of possessors (but it comes, it comes) as by intellectuals and administration. This bourgeoisie uses its knowledge, its position, to keep the people under its power and to increase its fortune.

GH: *Some did remark that* Mandabi *was less incisive than* La Noire de . . . *Do you agree and recognize that indeed it is less resounding, although, paradoxically, it is made in a better way then* La Noire de . . . *?*
OS: It is difficult for me to answer. The situations are different. The action in *La Noire de . . .* goes on in an apartment between three antagonists. The framework of this film was thus more limited than that of *Mandabi*, where I show a lot of things. I believe that the difference comes from there. But personally, I prefer *La Noire de . . .*, because the whole film depends on only one person. My work on *La Noire de . . .* was at the same time more difficult and more agreeable: my camera did not leave Thérèse Moissine Diop. I had in front of me a face that had to translate what I wanted to express.

GH: *Isn't the plasticity of* Mandabi *greater than in* La Noire de . . . *in which the psychological meanderings of the personages are only outlined?*
OS: They speak very little in *La Noire de . . .* and yet the film develops according to a psychological evolution. At least, I think so.

GH: *Did some accuse you of expressing reverse racism in* La Noire de . . . *?*
OS: No, I do not see it: if I had been Spanish or Portuguese, I could have called my film "The Spanish of . . ." or "The Portuguese of . . ." The color of the skin is only additional in this business. In France, the Blacks, the Portuguese, the Maghrebians are exploited in the same way.

GH: *Why didn't you replace the monologue of the maid by dialogues which would have perhaps allowed you to avoid the slight explanatory redundancy that one notes here?*

OS: "La Noire de . . ." is not an intellectual. She is illiterate. She speaks little with her entourage because she finds herself confined in an apathetic and limited universe. She locks herself in a defensive dumbness. In ruminating only on her misfortune, she hardens her position of refusal.

GH: *It was also said that you had wrongly dramatized the situation, and that suicide did not exist in Africa?*
OS: The film relies on various authentic facts, which I read in *Nice-Morning* in July 1958. It is from there that I wrote the novel, which appeared in *Voltaique*, since I made the film by adapting the novel. There is no exaggeration. For example, there really exists in Dakar a "market with maids" as I show it in my film. The situation that I decry in *La Noire de . . .* remained, roughly speaking, the same.

GH: *How long was the making of* Mandabi*?*
OS: Five weeks. The preparation required two months and half for me. The actors are not professionals because I do not believe that a professional actor can put himself in the skin of the unemployed. Many people did agree to appear voluntarily.

GH: *Why did you make this film in color?*
OS: Me, I didn't warm to it at all. On the contrary, I was very afraid.

GH: *Afraid of what?*
OS: I was afraid to fall into folklore. But friends like Paulin Vieryra and Aboubacar Samb reassured me and insisted that I accept the arguments of my producer, who absolutely wanted to turn it in color. But still now, I am not happy with it: I find that the processes now are not satisfactory under the African sky. Furthermore, the color has constrained me to look after the clothing of my characters particularly, so that I've been criticized sometimes that I equipped them too well whereas they are unemployed. This reproach does not hold because everyone gets dressed like that in Dakar. It is Boussac fabric which is not expensive at all.

GH: *How do you conceive the question of the language?*
OS: Wolof is spoken by 85 percent of the Senegalese population. It could well have been set up in national language instead of in French.

With regard to films, the language constitutes a fundamental problem. Many African films in French sound false. It is the case for example for the French version of *Mandabi* in which my heroes have the appearance of "a bamboulas." (Because I had, after the contract, to make two versions simultaneously: one in Wolof and the other in French.)

GH: *In a Senegalese newspaper you answered many reproaches, which had been addressed, by way of the press at* Mandabi. *Could you summarize these criticisms and your answers?*
OS: Recapitulate . . .

GH: *Pessimism: Why did you have to show shantytowns?*
OS: It is curious how some spectators do not want to look at the truth shown on the screen. There are shantytowns in Senegal.

GH: Mandabi *will create a bad opinion of Senegal abroad!*
OS: Some would like the truth to be masked in order to preserve the legend of the good, honest, and hospitable Senegal. One noted the same phenomenon at the time of the beginnings of neorealism in Italy: certain Italians also did not want the misery in the cities or the underdevelopment of Mezzogiomo to be shown.

GH: *There is a disproportion between the amount of the postal order and the hopes which lie on it!*
OS: Yes, because the women of Ibrahim Dieng did not really know the exact sum of the *postal order* and this becomes the symbol of Fortune. As for *La Noire de . . .* I did not invent the anecdote: it is authentic.

GH: *I would have encouraged polygamy by showing two co-wives who get along perfectly!*
OS: I am not against polygamy but I did not intend to deal with this problem in this film. That would have hurt the unit of action.

GH: *Ibrahim Dieng suffers his misfortunes like a disease. He does not react!*
OS: Indeed, I wanted shown a Senegalese who, as many other people would have done, remains passive in a situation that he believes fatal, whereas we know that it is not. It is an absurd attitude which has to be

fought against. This is why I want to make a militant cinema that causes an awakening in the spectators. It cannot give ready-made solutions. At most, I can suggest directions. A film is only useful if it allows debates between spectators after it.

GH: *My criticism would be coated with chocolate!*
OS: However, I believe that the significance of *Mandabi* is very clear since it ends in a call for a change. I already said, in addition, that I did not want to make a cinema of signs. And then, although there is for us in Senegal a certain liberty to criticize left, there nevertheless exists, there, as elsewhere, a censure.

GH: *I would have enlarged reality!*
OS: No. They were angry that I showed my hero belching "coarsely." It is like that in reality.

GH: *What do you think of the cinema of Jean Rouch?*
OS: My position with regard to my friend Rouch is known: I do not like his cinema. I am opposed to his work in which I find that he looks at us, us Africans, like insects. Perhaps I will make an exception for *Moi, un Noir*.

GH: *What is the exact significance of the mask during and at the end of* La Noire de . . . ?
OS: This mask constitutes in *La Noire de* . . . an essential element. At the beginning one sees the child who is playing with this mask as he would any object because these objects originally had in Africa an ordinary utility. For this child the mask does not have more importance than any other toy. The maid, who noticed the interest of her owner in these kinds of things, buys it for the kid and offers it to him, only aiming to please him. It is a certain African mania that I denounce there in passing. Later, at the peak of her despair, the maid takes back this African gift, which constitutes her only bond with Africa. When the co-operator brings back the mask and the bag of the maid, who committed suicide, to her mother, he appropriates the mask although its significance for him is totally

different than at the beginning. For me the mask is not a mystical symbol as it could have been to our previous ancestors but a symbol of unity and identity and the recuperation of our culture. Today, the mask has become an article of export for tourists. You find it in Africa's airports and the worst thing is that Africans themselves encourage that.

GH: *Who are your favorite cineastes?*

OS: To be honest, I do not know. In all styles, cinema has to be fundamentally original.

We Are Governed in Black Africa by Colonialism's Disabled Children

GUY HENNEBELLE/1971

THE SENEGALESE DIRECTOR Ousmane Sembène, often called "the pope of the African Cinema," presented his third long film *Emitai* (in color) during the last Moscow Festival. Here he is talking to us before the preview of this film which illustrates the period of the anticolonial resistance around 1942 in Casamance (a region near Guinea-Buissau).

GH: *Could you please tell us how you got into cinema?*

OS: Born in 1923 in Ziguinchor (the capital of Casamance), I have tried out a variety of different jobs. I was a fisherman, mason, mechanic, docker at the harbour of Marseille (over a period of ten years). I wrote books: *Docker Noir* (*The Black Docker*), *Oh pays, mon beau people* (*Oh my country, my beautiful people*) in 1947, *Les bouts de bois de Dieu* (*God's bits of wood*) in 1960, *Voltaique* in 1962, *L'Harmattan* in 1964, *Vehi-ciosane* in 1965 (first novel award at Black Arts Festival) and *Le Mandat* in 1966 (from which I made a film with the same title). In all these works I am trying to give an idea about the life of my people. One day I realized that because of illiteracy, which predominates Black Africa with a rate of 90 percent, literature would never allow me to reach the masses. This is the reason

---

From *Les Lettres Françaises*, no. 1404 (1971). Translated from the French by Julien Enoka-Ayemba. Reprinted by permission of Monique Martineau Hennebelle and Corlet Editions Diffusion S.A.R.L.

I chose the cinema and stayed for one year at the Gorki Studio in Moscow under the direction of Donskoi. Back in Africa in 1963, I made a documentary (which is not well known) about the Songhay Empire for the Malian government, then two short cuts *Borom Sarett* and *Niaye*. After this I made *La noire de . . .* which won the Prix Jean Vigo and the Tanit d'Or award in Carthage in 1966. In this film I was denouncing the French neocolonialist, the new African bourgeoisie, his accomplice, and above all, the new black slave trade. But because it is always easier to attack foreign countries, in the following film *Le Mandat* (special award of Venice in 1968) I tackled the dictatorship of our valueless bourgeoisie over the Senegalese people. Again I picked up the same topic for a short cut (also in color) which I was asked for from the Ecumenical Council of the American Churches (I am taking the money from where I can get it): *Tauw*. This is the story of a young twenty-year-old unemployed man in Dakar. I might remake the short cut (shot in 16 mm) into a long film.

GH: *Why* Emitai?

OS: For many reasons:

1) In order to get out of the city where I have been doing all my films until now.

2) In order to show another tribe than the Wolofs (here the Diolas).

3) And mainly to convey a national feeling to the people. In fact, in contrast to the Maghrebian bourgeoisies for example, the black African bourgeoisies are not trying to develop a national culture. We are ruled by people whom I call the "disabled children of the French imperialism." In "L'Afrique de l'Ouest bloquée" Samir Amin explained why we were ruled by cultural bastards: our bourgeoisies do not have sufficient economical resources. They are only agents on the periphery of the occidental neocolonialism.

4) Finally, there might be a possible fourth reason: I myself was a soldier at the age of fifteen. I joined the army at an early age because in those days it was the only way to leave in dignity. Thus, I wanted to get even . . .

GH: *What initial idea did you start with?*
OS: My first thought was to evoke the stance of a Senegalese female hero, named An Sitoe (Aline Sitoe for the French), who during the Second World War had led a battle against the army which had confiscated the rice in the villages in the name of a successful war. But while doing biographical research I realized that the legend had veiled the historical truth and that it was difficult to separate one from the other. And then the mysticism of An Sitoe made me sick, me who am an Atheist and Marxist. So I have decided to remove An Sitoe from her role as main character. But I kept the idea to illustrate on screen the anticolonial resistance of the Diolas during this period. In the film I did not want to point out the exact date the incidents happened. This was around the years 1942, 43, 44. We do not know if this was when de Gaulle came to power in Senegal or in France. What I wanted to suggest is that for us Africans there was no fundamental difference between the two regimes. We were always colonized subjects. Certainly, the methods have changed a little bit but the objectives were always supposed to maintain the French empire. This we could easily observe after the liberation of France: With blood the African demands were suffocated in Thiaroye in Senegal, Grand Bassam in Ivory Coast, Setif and Guelma in Algeria, in Madagascar and without talking about Indochina.

GH: Emitai *is also a kind of homage to the women?*
OS: The film starts with the kidnapping of young men who are being recruited by force. We then witness a village being attacked because of having refused delivering the three hundred tons of rice according to the regulations. The soldiers employed by the French win easily against the Diolas peasants only equipped with chassepots. In order to force the women to give (because first of all rice is their property: it is them who had cultivated and hidden it), the French colonel exposed them to the sun. During this time the men were talking to the fetishes (You can find both Muslims and Christians among the Diolas but the fetishist basis remains fully or partly). I will not talk about the story in detail. You have to watch the film. I wanted to oppose the propensity of men to subordination (under the cover of the god's desires) to the strong desire of human resistance of women. The title *Emitai* means "God of Thunder."

GH: *How did the shooting go?*
OS: I rewrote the story three times. It was only in the last stage that I chose the three parts: time, place, and action. I did not have a precise script, only a story of about twenty pages. My team was very reduced. The shooting in total took seven weeks but spread out over one year in the village Dimbering. I had five hours of last rushes. The photography was assured by the Senegalese cameraman Georges Caristan. The budget approached about 500 million of ancient francs. This is the first entirely Senegalese production in the history (of long films).

GH: *How did you achieve the collaboration with the village people?*
OS: I had to fight against a particular disbelief in the beginning: the people feared not being paid according to the agreements. But little by little the cooperation was turning out to be good, mainly with the women who were much more obedient than the men. They were trained by Thérèse M'bissine Diop (the lead actor of *La noire de . . .*). I only had to give explanations when needed depending on the situation. I felt a bit uncomfortable about the language because while I speak Wolof, Mandingue, and Bambara, I only understand a little bit of Diolas. I did not have professional actors, only Robert Fontaine (the French commanding officer) and Thérèse. I am emphasizing that the way I used the Diola costumes and rituals is only fairly accurate. You have to know that the Diola believe in a multitude of gods. Gods who can subdivide in smaller subordinate gods. If you are not satisfied with your god, I can get rid of him.

The Diolas were not pleased when they saw me moving their fetishes but I explained that I had a personal and secret agreement with the fetishes who exceptionally authorized my behavior. I did not want to record all the ceremonies of the chef Djiméko's burial (on the occasion of a real burial) because I believe this would have been immoral. For the Diolas, accustomed to living with death, the burial . . . You feast and you fornicate . . . You also talk with the dead person carried by four men. To answer yes, he moves forward, to answer no he moves backwards. If he hesitates, he swings. I paid attention not to lead into exoticism and folklore. I wanted to suggest that these practices belong to a *culture*. I am sure that even Africans will not entirely understand this film deeply rooted in the Diola culture. At any rate, I am determined to show the film only in the original version, with French or English subtitles. I will not have the same experience again as with *Mandat* (which existed in two versions: Wolof and French).

GH: *With* Emitai *you are showing that, in this case, religion takes part of the culture of a people. But while elevating it you also seem to criticizing it. It appears to me that there is a certain ambiguity.*

OS: Although I respect all the faithful, I am personally an opponent to all religions. They are opium. This is particularly true in Senegal. During the period of passive resistance against the colonization, the religions were able to sometimes maintain the flames of the popular resistance, but in my film the fetishes rather animate to resign. I am against all people giving an idyllic picture of Africa before the arrival of the whites. It is right that they significantly aggravated the situation on one hand. During the colonial period, it was a usual strategy to impute all our illnesses to colonialism because the fundamental contradiction was between the colonialists and colonized. Today, it is between the people and the local bourgeoisie supported by the neocolonialists. The meaning of my film is that it belongs to the people to decide about their own destiny, not the gods. In addition, *Emitai* is as well, I think, a film against the negritude, which has become a hoax ideology.

GH: *How could you define your conception of the cinema?*

OS: My concern is to make the problems faced by my people public. I view cinema as a political weapon. I own to the Marxism Leninism ideology. But I'm again a "cinema de pancartes" (cinema of placards). I do know well I will not be able to change the Senegalese reality with one film. But I think a group of cineastes can help to awaken. I know very well that I'm used like an alibi by Senghor who can say abroad: "Look how liberal I am: I let Sembène make subversive films." It is a contradiction that I am trying to use to the best. I would like to clearly denounce all the African bourgeoisies betraying our peoples but it is a quite dangerous scheme. I don't want to make intellectual films but shoot popular films addressing the masses. I like a cinema addressing the people like the Brazilian cinema *novo*. Cinema should as well be an entertainment. Concerning this, I have a project of making a portrait of

Samory, a hero of the resistance against the French Takeover. (See *Histoire de l'Afrique* by Djibril Tamsir Diane and Jean Suret). It will last five hours und will be collectively directed.

GH: *What do you think about the Black African Cinema in 1971?*
OS: At the level of the *distribution*, we notice that two French trusts, COMACICO and SECMA are still doing well. They have followed a new tactic of taking a maximum of African cineastes on their command. My dream is the absolute nationalization of all the Film Theaters, even though I know this will not be easy at all. At the level of *production*, we still have the same financial difficulties. Concerning the *creation*, I think the African cinema is splitting into two directions: the commercial and the militant. It is "normal."

GH: *A word about Rouch?*
OS: No, I don't want to talk any more about this dear Rouch. I have said his cinema does not suit us at all. *Petit à Petit* is just the most overwhelming of all. As to his shared anthropological system, it means that everyone shows his a__. I am not interested in it.

GH: *You attacked the left European critique in Carthage . . .*
OS: I was wrong, I think. What's annoying me is the reliance of the African readers on the French press and the French critique. *Le Monde* is Gospel's truth for them. But this happens because of the lack of an African critique. We can't impute this to the French critique. We need an African one.

Filmmakers Have a Great Responsibility to Our People

HAROLD D. WEAVER/1972

OUSMANE SEMBÈNE is the director of *Mandabi* (*The Money Order*), the first African feature film to be theatrically exhibited in the United States. French critic Guy Hennebelle characterizes Sembène as "the pope of African cinema" and "the father of Senegalese cinema." He describes Sembène as a filmmaker who "pursues his own way while zig-zagging between the contradictions of the Senegalese regime, French neo-colonialism, and the cactuses on the desert of African cinema." The following interview was done by Harold D. Weaver, Jr., former Chairman of the Department of African Studies at Rutgers University, and was translated by Carrie Moore. It took place in 1972 on the occasion of Sembène's participation in the 15th Annual Meeting of the African Studies Association.

CINEASTE: *What message do you have for the Afro-American community regarding your recently-released film* Emitai (God of Thunder)?

OUSMANE SEMBÈNE: I think that what I want to do first of all is to give them an exact idea of Africa, a better idea of Africa, so they can learn of other African ethnic groups. Each ethnic group has a culture and I would compare the Diola, who are a minority in Senegalese society, to the Afro-Americans, who are a minority among whites. They have a culture and they must do everything to save it because that culture is

---

From *The* Cineaste *Interviews*, edited by Dan Georgakas (Chicago: Lake View Press, 1983). Reprinted by permission of Harold D. Weaver.

what makes their personality. I think that knowing Africa better will solidify their personality with that new black personality now emerging in American society because we all have the same cultural matrix.

CINEASTE: *What did you set out to do in* Emitai? *What were your objectives?*

SEMBÈNE: My first goal was to make this film a school of history. From ancient times in Africa—dating back to the medieval period—we know stories of resistance. During the period of colonialism it would appear that there were no struggles for national liberation, but that's not true. I can show that during this period not a single month passed when there was not an effort of resistance. The problem was there was no communication among the people. There were scattered struggles, even individual struggles, but they were stifled. If people had known about it before, we would have been free now for a long time. But today, with filmmaking, we can learn from each other.

For example, we are thirsty to know all about the Afro-American movement. We know that in the Civil War there were black batallions which participated. We know that Afro-American mothers have done everything to raise their children. We also know of great Afro-American writers. And if one day they can bring these facts to the screen, you can imagine the number of people who are going to realize all of this. That's why I think *Emitai* is important. That's also why we think that, for us, filmmaking has to be the school, and that filmmakers have a great responsibility to our people.

CINEASTE: *Would you elaborate on your comments of last night in which you compared the behavior of the French colonialists in Africa with the present-day politicians and administrators of constitutionally independent Africa?*

SEMBÈNE: We have to have the courage to say that during the colonial period we were sometimes colonized with the help of our own leaders, our own chiefs, and our own kings. We mustn't be ashamed of our faults and our errors. We have to recognize them in order to fight them. In recent years there have been many, many coup d'etats in Africa but not a single one of these military people fought for the liberation of Africa. At the time when there was an awareness developing in Africa, it was these military men who were killing and imprisoning their own brothers, mothers, and sisters. In the majority of the African countries the leaders and heads of state are heads of state with the consent of the French. Most of their personal guards are former French military officers and their personal advisors are French.

I can give you two striking examples. When the Gabonese people wanted to overthrow their government, France sent soldiers, but the soldiers came from Dakar and Abidjan. And not too long ago in Madagascar the French became tired of their former chiefs, so when the people were struggling to overthrow the president, France declared she was not going to intervene. We have another example, Gilbert Youlou, in the Congo. When the people wanted to overthrow him, he telephoned De Gaulle who said, "No." If De Gaulle had said, "Yes," Youlou would still be the president. This is to explain to you the totality of things taking place in Africa and the kind of thing I wanted to show in the film.

CINEASTE: *One thing that impressed me about* Emitai *was the importance of women in the act of resistance to colonialism. Women are thought of by many Americans to have a subordinate role in Africa. Did you set out intentionally in* Emitai *to point out the important role of women in Africa, both historically and currently?*

SEMBÈNE: First of all, I have to say that the story of *Emitai* is based on an actual event. The person who led the struggle, all by herself, was a woman—and a woman who was sick. The colonialists killed her, but they didn't kill her husband. I can give you an example of the strike of Thies, I can give you an example of the birth of the R.D.A.,* I can even talk of recent times under Senghor. In 1963 the women left the indigenous quarter called the *medina* to overthrow Senghor. On their march the men also came and in front of the palace they killed more than one hundred and fifty people. I think it's a white man's vision that says that our women have never participated in our struggle. In fact, the participation of women in the struggle has several levels, including the raising, the socializing of children, and preserving our culture. It's a fact

* The Rassemblement Democratique Africain, founded in 1946 by Felix Houphouet-Boigny of the Ivory Coast, was one of the foremost interterritorial nationalist movements involved in agitating for independence from France during the postwar years.

that African culture has been preserved by the women, and it's thanks to them that what has been saved has been saved. They're also less alienated and much more independent than the men. All of this means that we mustn't neglect the participation of women in the struggle. It is true that at the present time we have a lot of "sophisticated" girls, but these are girls in the city, and most of the time it's not their fault because they don't have any symbols or points of reference. All of their symbols, all of their criteria for beauty, come from the Western world. Based on that, the Europeans always accuse the African women of being alienated. But you have to live with an African family in their own household to see—they have paid all the expenses of colonialism.

CINEASTE: *How did you intend to show the traditional political leadership in* Emitai?

SEMBÈNE: There are two things in *Emitai* concerning traditional chiefs; in the tradition, what has been preserved is for them a democracy. You can't be a chief by birth. One is a chief because one is worthy, a man who is respectable. In their gathering in the film each elected person must speak. The chief is not a chief in the Western sense—he's the spokesman. He's only the chief when there's a need, he's not a chief all the time. I think it's a democracy. Another thing is that the chief, as the chief, can't decide anything as regards the women. You see that in the film. They can't decide anything even though they are all elected.

CINEASTE: *What do you mean they can't decide anything as regards the women?*

SEMBÈNE: I mean that they're chiefs and from a European point of view they ought to have been able to decide to give up the rice. But they knew that it was up to the women to decide that, they could not, and the only thing they could do was to all go to war. But they couldn't bring anybody else into it—that's another form of democracy within a certain specific ethnic group. There are ethnic groups in Africa where the kings and chiefs decide. There are also a lot of ethnic groups like mine, for instance, where there are no kings or chiefs. The fellow is elected, he doesn't earn any money, he doesn't have anything more than the rest of them, and, commonly, they call him the servant of the people.

CINEASTE: *You mentioned earlier the role of the military in contemporary Africa—the negative tradition, the anti-African tradition out of which it has come. What specifically did you intend to show in* Emitai *about the soldier?*

SEMBÈNE: Those soldiers, who were mercenaries, were called "*tirailleurs.*" France recruited them by force and gave them minimal instruction, a small salary and a rifle, and they obeyed. They started by conquering their own families, by participating in the colonization of their own homes and villages. With the development of colonialization they were everywhere. Behind two whites there were thirty soldiers with rifles, but not a single one of them had the idea to revolt. At no moment in history did they rebel—neither for the people nor out of their own personal humiliation. Colonialism just levelled them down and now, during independence, it's they—having been formed by the French army or the British army—who make the coup d'etats and who assume the leadership. And they are worse today because they're fascists. Therefore, what I wanted to show with the soldiers was that the past and the present are the same. We see the sergeant, for example, as an obedient dog. He doesn't even have a name; his name is Sergeant, like a dog.

CINEASTE: *The term "fetish" is mentioned in the film from time to time. Is that your term or is that the translation? In terms of describing religious practices, is there any particular reason it is simply not called "religion" or "traditional religion"?*

SEMBÈNE: It is the sergeant who uses the term and who explains it—you have put yourself into his mentality because he is the man who has been "educated." There are two words that we use everyday which the Western world has imposed upon us concerning our own religion and culture. When we talk about an African culture or dance we say "folklore" and when we talk about our religion we talk about "fetish," and that is exactly why I put that in the sergeant's mouth. It pleases me that you noticed it, because I have it repeated several times. But the others never say "fetish," they always say "we are going to consult our gods."

CINEASTE: *Personally, I am very sensitive about words like "fetish," "chief," and "tribe."*

SEMBÈNE: The old men in the group never talked about Senegal. They always said "we the Diola" because they identified with something.

CINEASTE: *The final question on* Emitai *related to movement in the film. I would like you to comment on the tempo, the movement of the film and how it actually relates to the nation state Senegal, with its diversity of languages. I just want a little bit of explanation on something you said earlier.*

SEMBÈNE: The Diolas are a minority in Senegal, they speak a language that the others don't understand, so the sub-titles are in French. They majority of the people who go to see the film, first of all, don't speak Diola, and they have problems reading sub-titles. In order to have them better understand the film, then, it was necessary to have a slowness which was, however, not *too* slow—and that's why I adopted that particular approach. I also worked a great deal on the decor. Each shot includes something which lets them see for themselves that their country is very beautiful, that we are not showing them the countryside of France, that our trees are just as pretty as others—even the dead trees can be pretty. But to come back to the question of language, I think it is very important when you make a film of similar ethnic groups to work on the musicality of the words so they will have a very precise and very clear tone so that the people who see the film are not shocked, so their ears are not shocked by the sound. That's why I worked so much on this tempo, which is a little slower than that of *Mandabi*. This problem of language is one of the problems confronting filmmakers in Africa.

CINEASTE: *The major problem or just one of the problems?*

SEMBÈNE: One of the problems. I think given the fact that there is such a diversity of languages in Africa, we African filmmakers will have to find our own way for the message to be understood by everyone, or we'll have to find a language that comes from the image and the gestures. I think I would go as far to say that we will have to go back and see some of the silent films and in that way find a new inspiration.

Contrary to what people think, we talk a lot in Africa but we talk when it's time to talk. There are also those who say blacks spend all of their time dancing—but we dance for reasons which are our own. Dancing is not a flaw in itself, but I never see an engineer dancing in front of his machine, and a continent or a people does not spend its time dancing. All of this means that the African filmmaker's work is very important—he must find a way that is his own, he must find his own symbols, even create symbols if he has to. This doesn't mean we are rejecting others, but it should be our own culture.

CINEASTE: *You were talking earlier about the music of the wind. Would you explain what you mean by that?*

SEMBÈNE: The whites, for example, have music for everything in their films—music for rain, music for the wind, music for tears, music for moments of emotion, but they don't know how to make these elements speak for themselves. They don't feel them. But in our own films we can make the sensation of these elements felt, without denaturing the visual elements, without broadcasting everything to the audience.

I'll give you an example, even two. In *Emitai,* when the women are forced by the soldiers to sit out in the sun, the only sound you can hear is the sound of the rooster and the weeping of the children; however, there was also wind. I did not look for music to engage the audience. I just wanted to show, by gestures, that the women are tired, their legs are tired, their arms are burdened—one woman has the sun shining in her eyes, another two are sleeping. All this is shown in silence, but it is a silence that speaks. I could have had a voice coming from the outside, but I would have been cheating. Instead, for example, there were the two children who were walking along to bring water to the women. When they crossed the woods, you couldn't see their legs, but you could hear, very clearly, the dead leaves underfoot. For me, this represents the search for a cinema of silence.

Another example: in the Sacred Forest, life continues because there is a fire and the wind is blowing. I didn't try to bring in any music, so when the empty gourd falls it makes a noise. In that case, the silence is very profound. I think all of this indicates a search on our parts, a search for African filmmaking. And I'm sure that we are on the way to creating our own cinema because we often meet as African filmmakers to discuss our films with enthusiasm, to look for the best way to transmit our message.

European filmmakers often use music which is gratuitous. It's true that it is pleasant to hear but, culturally, does it leave us with anything? I think the best film would be one after which you have to ask yourself, "Was there any music in that film?" Today there are films that you could sell with music, such as *Shaft*. You remember the music, but maybe you don't remember the images or the message. In that case I would say it was the musician who was the filmmaker.

CINEASTE: *I became very much aware of your own sensitive use of music in* Borom Sarret*—it was very obvious, very overt, there. When the cart driver goes between the European borders and the medina, it becomes very obvious how you switch back and forth between the indigenous music of the medina and European traditional music, which they call "classical" in the European quarters.*

SEMBÈNE: *Borom Sarret* was my first film and I didn't have the awareness that I have now, but I wanted to show the European area and the Africans who lived in the European life-style. The only music I could relate to them was the classical music, the minuets of the eighteenth century, because they're still at that mentality.

CINEASTE: *Regarding your reason for making* Tauw, *you are quoted as having said, "This is the basic problem of Africa, there is a terrible gulf between young people's aspirations and their accomplishments." Would you elaborate on that?*

SEMBÈNE: All young people in the world (and I think this is true) have an aspiration to surpass, or to measure themselves in relation to, something that is great—to surpass what their fathers have done. But in Africa today the youth are completely sacrificed. For example, since I made *Tauw* approximately a year ago, the situation in Africa has become worse—for the simple reason that they don't have any work. And when I say that they don't have any work, I'm only talking about the men, I'm not even talking about the women who are the majority of the Senegalese population of four million. The majority of them are under twenty-five years old and there are perhaps only about one-third of them who go to school, and even their future is uncertain.

CINEASTE: *I would like you to explain another quote attributed to you—"We must understand our traditions before we can hope to understand ourselves." Many Afro-Americans feel the same way, but I'm curious about your own interpretation of what that means.*

SEMBÈNE: That is, we must understand our traditions, our own culture, the very depths of it. In African languages the word culture does not exist.

They say that a man is educated, he is very well brought up, or he is from a very agreeable society. Therefore, culture is just a mental approach to a pleasant society. Culture itself, then, is like the hyphen between a man's birth and his death.

The Europeans say that our old men are good, but we never say that a man is good, we say that he is a man of culture. We mean that he is from an agreeable society and has an elevated sense of humanity. It has nothing to do with weakness. You can be present at meetings of old men where for hours they don't say anything to each other, they just sort of joke around. But in the process of joking they say what they want to say. A man of culture for us is one who has the key word for every situation. And you can go anywhere you want to and you'll always find the same attitude—you can't be a witness or a judge where we are as long as the community doesn't recognize you as one. You can have all kinds of diplomas and not be invited to participate; and the greatest humiliation for a man in Africa is never to be called upon at difficult times. For us, then, one is not automatically a judge. Sometimes when there is a public discussion, and there is a foreigner or stranger in the area, they'll invite him—but he has to be a respectable stranger. After having exposed all the facts they ask him what he thinks, posing the question this way: "In a similar situation where you're from, how do you resolve this problem?" And depending on what he says and his manner of expression, we know whether or not he is a man of culture. So in Africa there is no man of culture in the European sense of that word. Culture for us means an honorable man, a man worthy of your faith and whose word means something. For example, if an old man sends a young person to see another old man, sometimes he sends along an object of value. He gives to the young person an object that would be recognized and he says, "Here, take this and tell the other that I sent you."

CINEASTE: *One key problem the black filmmaker faces in the United States is that there are only white distributors. This appears to be the case in many parts of Africa also, including your own country. How does this affect which films are shown?*

SEMBÈNE: I am very happy you posed that problem because it is a problem for the whole third world—and we consider the Afro-American community to be a colony within American society. So, faced with the same problems, we're looking for a solution. We think that instead of innundating the African market with films made by whites, there's a place for films made by Afro-Americans. But there is no immediate solution. If Afro-Americans were rich enough to buy all of the theaters here they'd have the control, but I don't think that's going to happen. Likewise, in Africa—Francophone Africa and Anglophone Africa—distribution is in the hands either of the French, the British, or the Lebanese. At the moment, we are trying to find a means of resolving this problem. Perhaps if we could get the Afro-American filmmakers and the African filmmakers together, it might be possible—by beginning on a small scale—to distribute our own films on the African continent and with Afro-American distributors. But we mustn't forget that while the cinema is an art, it's also an industry, and the problem that you pose concerns the industrial side of filmmaking. It could probably only be solved by the formation of a group which shares the same ideology. I don't mean ideology in a political sense, but in the sense of having the same interests.

CINEASTE: *At Cannes, in 1970, in a conversation with the man who is responsible for distribution in Kenya, he indicated to me that there was no real interest in the distribution of Afro-American films there, that they were primarily interested in cowboy films.*

SEMBÈNE: That's the same answer we get from the French or from our African leaders because they have a complete ignorance of the role of films. We think that, little by little, we are changing this mentality which says that a cowboy film is the only kind of film that the African public likes. I think that it's up to African filmmakers to fight to change this defective distribution. The African public is now beginning to appreciate our films, so saying that it is a cowboy film that the African public prefers is not really telling the truth. For instance, there is a public now prepared to receive Afro-American films in Ghana, Nigeria, Tanzania, Kenya, etc. For the African public the most well-known actors are Sidney Poitier and Harry Belafonte, and I'm sure a film like *Super Fly* would have the largest box-office of any film in Africa. So you can see that it's not really a question of a preference for cowboy films, it's just that those distributors and certain government leaders who deal with distribution prefer cowboy films.

But I think that with the Pan-African Federation of Cineastes [FEPACI] we are now beginning to change things. The Federation is now recognized by the Organization for African Unity and the Arab League and our films are beginning to circulate on the African continent. My own method has been that each time I go into an African country, I show my film and afterwards discuss it with the audience and with the government officials. For example, *Mandabi, La Noire de . . .* , and *Borom Sarret* have been all over Africa. And other films made by Africans are circulating. Of course, overall distribution is still in the hands of foreign interests. There is not a single African who controls distribution outside of countries like Guinea, Mali, or Nigeria, and since in these cases it's the government which controls distribution, they take all the films made by Africans. Upper Volta also controls its film distribution and they take all the African films. While this is something very positive, it's still insufficient because there is no coordination between the various states, so what we're working for now is that coordination. Next year we're supposed to have a meeting of filmmakers and the report that I'm supposed to give is on the problem of distribution (films being distributed, their ability to gain income, their tax, and to forsee a general distribution plan). We think that what we're going to ask for is within the reach of our governments so we're sure that in the future we'll accomplish our goal—that's what we're working for.

CINEASTE: *Have you seen any of the new films being produced about black Americans and, if so, are there any that you have liked?*

SEMBÈNE: I saw *Sounder* and, when I saw it, I wondered if it had been written by a white man or a black man. When I was told it had been written by a black man, I was very happy. I don't know if it's his first, second or third film, and I don't know how much money he had to make it, but I sense a man who loves his people and who, by means of this story (even though it is limited), wants to tell us something. I don't know about his childhood but I know that he loves his family and I know that he is respected. It's a film that I would like for all fathers to see. And the woman who plays the mother is the best Afro-American actress I've ever seen. I don't know if this film has been sub-titled or dubbed into French but I'm going to recommend that it be invited to Africa. I'm sure that if this film is projected for an African audience, they will forget that it takes place in America. The only thing which did not please me about the film is that I'm sure that in 1933 there were an enormous amount of racial problems in the U.S. But even if this problem isn't brought out, the film gives a sense of a respectful family just as it exists within us in Africa.

The other film I saw was *Black Girl*, the new film by Ossie Davis which also deals with the family in America. It shows that within the family it's possible to have all kinds of hate, all kinds of lowness, but it's still the family. I think that we need to explore the inner workings of the family, and in this film we have four generations tied together: the grandmother, the mother of the daughter, and another younger girl. A moral problem is raised because the grandmother is living common-law; the mother didn't have a husband, but she worked and raised her children, and even raised a girl who was not her own child, she succeeded; and the only man in the film has a lot of money and thinks that love can be bought. If we compare the man in *Black Girl* to the man in *Sounder*, and compare the children in *Sounder* to the children in *Black Girl*, we'd have a complete universe. And that's the kind of film that I like to make, because it's the kind of film that teaches us to read and to know and to enhance our sentiments. We mustn't forget that for centuries they've been working to destroy us. We're everything except moral men—we're gangsters, drug addicts, criminals, as if we had no parents. So I think that films like this are useful.

CINEASTE: *I would like to ask one final question. What is your next film project?*

SEMBÈNE: I'm going to make a film on the Senegalese big businessman, on the birth of the black bourgeoisie.

CINEASTE: *Briefly, Why?*

SEMBÈNE: Because we're witnessing the birth of an aborted child and some of these circumstances are very dangerous—too dangerous because they are being manipulated from the outside, from Europe, and I want to show how they're being manipulated, and why the people must kill them.

Ousmane Sembène Interviewed in Munich

MARIE KADOUR/1972

OUSMANE SEMBÈNE was chosen, with nine other filmmakers (three Asians, six Europeans), to create a documentary, in color, on the Olympic games of Munich. Financed by a German corporation, the film will come out in the first quarter of 1973. Ousmane Sembène is currently finishing the editing of his sequences devoted to the African participation at Munich. With his specific mixture of dry and frank humor, Ousmane Sembène—in his turtleneck and faded jeans, with his short pipe, which he is tapping nervously—agreed to answer some questions posed by Marie Kadour.

MK: *We have become accustomed to your didactic form of cinema, a militant approach. Do you want to make a simple documentary on the Games?*
OS: This is a remittance work, demanded by those we are calling the providers. But nevertheless nobody forced me to treat a certain theme. I particularly considered the opportunity as one to realize the brotherhood, friendship of the Africans: those of the North and South, but also of the United States. Besides the athletic events, I have filmed the reunions, as those men have had in common a rupture of several centuries from the traditional cultures of their home countries. For all of them, this rupture was caused by the white man.

From *Afrique-Asie* (1972). Translated from the French by Annett Busch. Reprinted by permission of *Afrique-Asie*.

MK: *How much time have you spent on this film?*
OS: I shot hundreds and hundreds of meters. The other filmmakers did too, since the production had the means. Therefore I could do several films. The European version will have ten minutes about the African athletes. But it's possible that the next version intended for Africa will contain a sequence of thirty minutes.

MK: *The film has no title yet?*
OS: No, and this became really dramatic to the point that the production company was proposing $1,000 to the filmmaker who could find a good title.

MK: *In 1971, on the occasion of the Africa Cup, French filmmakers were asked to cover the event. Now, for this competition, taking place in Europe, it's you, an African filmmaker, who was asked. How do you explain this contradiction? Nobody is prophet on his own continent?*
OS: Well, some governments have real inferiority issues. They don't dare to trust us. Illiterate in film and culturally half-witted, they prefer to call upon foreigners. . . . This will also happen at the next Games taking place in Lagos, I'm willing to bet. It is again the myth that what is on the plate of the white neighbor is better than our soup. Personally, that doesn't offend me. After all, we have the governments we deserve.

MK: *Currently, the big question posed by the bourgeois press is if the Games are a political demonstration or not. What do you think?*
OS: For me, the Olympic Games have been political since the Greeks. And even more in Germany. In 1936 in Berlin, Hitler refused to shake hands with the black athlete Jesse Owens. From the start Munich had a political purpose: to make the world forget the scabrous episode of Nazism. Politics are everywhere. In front of the movie camera, but also behind it. I'll give you an example: When the Rhodesian matter came up, I pointed out from the beginning that if the African athletes withdrew themselves, I would equally withdraw myself from shooting. At that moment, one of the European filmmakers, Zeffirelli, let us know that if Rhodesia were obliged to leave, he would also give up his participation. And that's what he did. Doubtless, I wouldn't have been good company for him.

MK: *Was it possible for you to film the reactions to the Rhodesian matter, notably among the Africans?*
OS: I was with my team at the sportsfield the day the blacks refused to share it with the Rhodesians. But instead of filming this scene I preferred to stop shooting in solidarity, while the Rhodesians were not leaving the stadium.

MK: *Like all social activities, sports also conceals an ideology. Wouldn't the presence of black athletes among the Rhodesian delegation be an illustration of a recuperation made in the name of sport?*
OS: Yes, class collaborators are everywhere. I think that's the case for the black Rhodesians who are trying to get out of a miserable condition. But for what price! They are even not authorized to train on the same field as the whites. For the Black Americans, the problem is completely different. First, they are a minority in the United States. Then, for a certain historical period—that is also current—these brothers didn't have any chance other than sports—or jazz—to reclaim their equality, their power. And then they were able to transform this kind of "collaboration" into a political act. For example at the Olympic games in Mexico City, the gesture of the Black Panther, the black upraised fist, and, in Munich, the affront against the American hymn, which is, for them, still the hymn of the oppressors.

MK: *Besides, the black athletes occupy such an important place within the American delegation that their absence would be recognized as a catastrophe.*
OS: Agreed, but look, I don't want to say, as do certain racists, that blacks are physiologically more capable than whites. First, I wanted to film the javelin and archery competitions. According to the ethnologists, we are unbeatable in these disciplines. First disappointment: no blacks registered. Good. So I jumped to the kayak competitions where two Ivorians were participating. They were great—beautiful, muscular, perfect for a shop window in the Champs Elysées or a mine in South Africa. But on the water, nothing. They were terrible. So much for the advocates of the sporting negro.

MK: *It's above all a question of training?*
OS: Yes, an intensive daily workout such as the one that engages the Kenyan Keino; but also the circumstances of life, well-maintained stadiums (for sport, not for prestige), and finally a sports policy. When there is no economic policy, there can't be one for sports. That's what hurts our land.

MK: *What do you think about Coubertin's phrase: "It's the taking part that counts"?*
OS: I don't agree at all. The essential thing is to win, and not to "negrify" the Games to give the whites a good conscience. I saw African countries sending two athletes and twelve trainers, the latter were paid 50 francs CFA per day while the athletes didn't receive a penny.

MK: *But the battle for medals also represents a nationalist and chauvinistic aspect, no?*
OS: Don't underestimate the importance of a medal, even a bronze, for a young state. It's a way to affirming oneself to the world. Unfortunately, that's also serving to justify more contestable systems. Look at Idi Amin, who gave Ugandan nationality to his Asian winners while expelling their families. Europe is racist. Why do you want it that we are better?

MK: *And the Palestinian matter . . . ?*
OS: This is such a delicate and painful problem . . . . Above all it's necessary to reestablish the truth: the Palestinians haven't taken on the Jews, as they want us to believe, but the Israelis against whom they are at war. After this affair, we, us other blacks, need to be on our guard. We knew that Munich would release racial confrontations.

MK: *We've ended up far from cinema and your film. It will be out soon. Well before* Emitai*?*
OS: Ah yes, we are not a priority in Europe (which is normal) nor on our own screens (which is not normal at all). *Emitai* has met with a

systematic obstruction. This film, which has been screened in all the European countries and in Cuba, is still unavailable in France and Black Africa (except Senegal). But I continue to fight for its release, not only for film buffs but in the big distribution circuits, those that reach the people. And *Emitai* interests me much more than any commissioned film.

Ousmane Sembène: An Interview

GERALD PEARY AND
PATRICK McGILLIGAN/1972

Ousmane Sembène is a slight but sturdy Senegalese, a charming and provocative conversationalist, a committed revolutionary. He is also a Third World film-maker of major force and accomplishment, whose international reputation as Africa's most important director is based remarkably on a total output of only five films, though he was previously well known as a novelist.

As a leading spokesman of sub-Sahara's black artistry, Sembène has travelled the world personally, projecting his films and spreading his basic message of pride and confidence in the heritage and culture of Africa's native peoples.

On such occasions in America and on the Continent, the films of Sembène have been heralded. In Africa, however, these volatile works usually are banned, typically through pressure brought by the French government, which maintains a vigilant watch over its former colonies. Only Sembène's first full-length feature, *Mandabi*, has been widely distributed outside of Senegal.

The forty-nine-year-old Sembène was born at Ziguinchor in the rural southern region of Senegal, where the action of *Emitai*, his latest film, takes place. Unlike other European-educated African film-makers and writers, Sembène had little formal schooling—only three years of vocational training beyond the primary grades.

From *Film Quarterly* (Spring 1973). Reprinted by permission of Gerald Peary and Patrick McGilligan.

Sembène's life paralleled the story of French recruitment of unwilling African natives told in *Emitai*: he fought in the French army during World War II as a forced enlistee. He remained afterward for a time in France, employed as a dockworker and union organizer in Marseilles while training himself to be a writer.

Sembène has published five novels and a collection of short stories, a body of work so impressive as to place him at the forefront of African writers. His most famous novel, *Les Bouts de Bois de Dieu* (translated in America as *God's Bits of Wood*) documents in semifictional form the historic Dakar-Niger railroad strike of October 1947, a major step toward Senegalese independence from the French. His last novel, *Le Mandat* (1966), was the basis for his celebrated film, *Mandabi*.

Sembène trained briefly in the Soviet Union before turning his talents to film in the early sixties. But to try to detect Russian influence on his work, or indeed any influences, is mostly futile, for Sembène is very much his own creator. He is one of those rare talents who make film production seem an absolutely natural act.

Nevertheless, one might view *Mandabi* as no less than an African *Bicycle Thief*, with the same universal power and appeal. It relates a similar story of a simple, uneducated man in the city (a non-actor, as in the DeSica film) who is reduced to hopelessness in his circular confrontation with the bureaucracy, and brought to despair when stolen from by a younger generation made corrupt by a society which has lost its human values.

Emitai, Sembène's latest work, trades the slightly abstract social consciousness of *Mandabi* for a direct, historically oriented attack on French colonial practices in the African rural areas. In its use of a provincial setting, in its almost surreal treatment of tribal rites, in its absurdly comical caricatures of the fascistic oppressors, and in its utilization of a mass hero, *Emitai* also offers a parallel to Rocha's *Antonio das Mortes*, a film from another neocolonialized country, Brazil.

Sembène toured the United States late in the fall of 1972, in order to raise funds for his next film project. He stopped in Madison, Wisconsin, for a day, exhibited *Emitai*, and spoke at length to student groups at the University. Visibly exhausted from his tour, he nevertheless answered a continuous stream of questions with seemingly endless patience, a task made doubly difficult by the fact that he speaks only halting English.

Luckily, the questions were skillfully translated into French for Sembène's benefit, then the answers back again into English by his superb American interpreter, Carrie Moore.

The following interview is an edited version of Ousmane Sembène's day at Madison.

Q: *Originally you were a highly successful acclaimed novelist. Why did you make the switch of film-making?*

A: I've just finished another book but I think it is of limited importance. First, 80 percent of Africans are illiterate. Only 20 percent of the populace possibly can read it. But further, my books indispose the bourgeoisie, so I am hardly read at home.

My movies have more followers than the political parties and the Catholic and Moslem religions combined. Every night I can fill up a movie theater. The people will come whether they share my ideas or not. I tell you, in Africa, especially in Senegal, even a blind person will go to the cinema and pay for an extra seat for a young person to sit and explain the film to him. He will feel what's going on.

Personally, I prefer to read because I learned from reading. But I think that cinema is culturally much more important, and for us in Africa it is an absolute necessity. There is one thing you can't take away from the African masses and that is having *seen* something.

Q: *But are the films by native black Africans being seen at home?*

A: In West Africa, distribution remains in the hands of two French companies that have been there since colonial times. Because of the active push of our native film-makers, such as our group in Senegal, they are forced to distribute our films, though they do so very slowly. Of the twenty films we have made in Senegal, five have been distributed. It is a continuous fight, for we don't think we can resolve the problems of cinema independent of the other problems of African society.

Neocolonialism is passed on culturally, through the cinema. And that's why African cinema is being controlled from Paris, London, Lisbon, Rome, and even America. And that's why we see almost exclusively the worst French, American, and Italian films. Cinema from the beginning has worked to destroy the native African culture and the myths of our heroes. A lot of films have been made about Africa, but they are stories of

European and American invaders with Africa serving as a decor. Instead of being taught our ancestry, the only thing we know is Tarzan. And when we do look on our past, there are many among us who are not flattered, who perceive Africa with a certain alienation learned from the cinema. Movies have infused a European style of walking, a European style of doing. Even African gangsters are inspired by the cinema.

African society is in a state of degeneracy, reflected also in our imitative art. But fortunately, unknown even to many Africans themselves, African art has continued, even as the black bourgeoisie had aped European and American models. In African cities is produced what we call "airport art," whittled wood that has been blackened; true art remains in the villages and rural communities, preserved in the ceremony and religion. It is from believing in this communal art that we can be saved from the internal destruction.

Q: *What are the particular circumstances in making films in Senegal?*
A: We produce films in a country where there is only one political party, that of Senghor. If you are not within the party, you are against it. Thus we have lots of problems, and they will continue while Senghor is in control. For instance, his government has just vetoed distribution of the film of a young director, the story of a black American who discovers Senegal. The film began with cinéma vérité style, but soon became oriented and plotted out to focus on our problems, as it should be. When the government saw the change, it vetoed the film.

We are approximately twenty film-makers in Senegal. Last year we made four long films. They were of unequal value, but we produced them through our own means.

Financing is our most complex problem. We go all over the world giving talks, carrying our machines and tape recorders, projecting our movies, trying to find distribution. When we secure a little bit of money and have paid our debts, we can begin a new film. The sources of the money vary. You can find a very small group of people who have money which they might lend you in exchange for participating in the filming. Perhaps you can locate a friend who has credit at the bank. But most of us make only one film every two years.

The editing of *Emitai* was financed with laboratory credit. But the laboratories that know us are in France, where we have to go for our montage and technical work. That's very expensive. We're not against France, but we'd prefer to stay at home. *Emitai* was shot on money I received on a commission from an American church for making a film called *Tauw*. We do not refuse any money, even from a church.

Our films are shot in 35 mm for the city theaters, then presented in 16 mm in the rural areas where there is no 35 mm. It is difficult to find 16 mm projectors in the cities, a problem created intentionally by those in charge of distribution. We began by making our films in 16 mm—much more economical. But the distributors would refuse to project the films in the cities because of the 16 mm, so we had to adapt ourselves to their game.

On paper, we could have our own distribution company. But we think that isn't the solution. Why create a parallel market, spend a lot of money, then be beaten down? What exists already should be nationalized.

Q: *Are your films distributed throughout Africa?*

A: The only film I've made that has been shown all through Africa is *Mandabi*, because every other country claims that what happens in the movie occurs only in Senegal. And I say it isn't true. *Emitai* has been banned everywhere in Africa except in Senegal, where it was allowed only after a year of protests.

We tried to show *Emitai* in Guadeloupe, but the ambassador from France interceded. The film had one night of exhibition in Upper Volta but never again. When I was invited by the government and students of the Ivory Coast to show it, *Emitai* was first screened the night before by a censor board of eight Africans and two Frenchmen. The eight were in agreement but the two Frenchmen went to the French ambassador who went to see the head of the government. I was told that it wasn't an "opportune time" to show this film. They were all very polite, so I didn't say anything. I took my film and left.

Q: *Has* Emitai *been seen in France?*

A: Every time I want to show this film, the date falls on "a day of mourning for de Gaulle." De Gaulle dies every day for my film.

Q: *Who were the actors in* Mandabi*?*

A: They weren't professionals. The old man who plays the main role, we found working near the airport. He had never acted before. I had a team of colleagues and together we looked around the city and country for actors. We didn't pay a lot, but we did pay, so it was very painful to choose. There was always the influence of my parents, my friends, and even the mistresses of my friends, and we had to struggle against all of that. You laugh, but I assure you it was very difficult.

Once the police telephoned me and soon this fellow arrived who was their representative. I was a little disturbed. But he had just come to tell us that he had a friend who wanted us to put his mistress in the film. I was forced to accept or else it would have cost me. It is concessions like this one which makes work difficult.

Q: *How did you rehearse* Mandabi?

A: We rehearsed for one month in a room very much like this lecture hall. *Mandabi* was the first film completely in the Senegalese language and I wanted the actors to speak the language accurately. There was no text, so the actors had to know what they were going to say, and say it at the right moment. Cinema is very arbitrary, yet there is a limited time and during it the actors must state what needs to be stated. People often reproach Senegalese film-makers for slowness, so we must be aware that cinema is not only the image but it is a question of punctuation.

Q: *Could you talk about the role of music in* Mandabi?

A: Contrary to what many people around the world think, that Africa only spends its time dancing, our music sometimes has served a significantly more important political purpose. During the colonial period, all of the information that was diffused among the people was passed on by music at the large central gathering places, such as the water fountains or wells in the city. The musical refrain was dispersed like a serpent that bites its tail.

I composed the music for *Mandabi*, and tried to make it of maximum importance. After the film was presented in Dakar, people sang the theme song for a while. But the song was "vetoed" from the radio, which belongs to the government and is sacred. (Since the *coup d'etat*, the radio station is guarded even more than the government.) So things changed. All you needed was a new sound and it chased away the old one.

Another factor: we who make films in Senegal are looking for music that is particularly suitable for our type of film. I think it is here where

African cinema still suffers certain difficulties. We are undergoing Afro-American music and Cuban music. I'm not saying that's bad, but I would prefer that we would be able to create an African music.

Q: *Are you satisfied with your conclusion to* Mandabi*?*
A: I don't think I really have to like the ending. It's only up to me to give the situation. The ending is linked to the evolution of the Senegalese society, thus it is as ambiguous. As the postman says, either we will have to bring about certain changes or we will remain corrupt. I don't know. Do you like the ending?

Q: *What we wonder is this: do you believe it is the duty of the political artist to go beyond presenting a picture of corruption—to offer a vision of the future, of what could be?*
A: The role of the artist is not to say what is good, but to be able to denounce. He must feel the heartbeat of society and be able to create the image society gives to him. He can orient society, he can say it is exaggerating, going overboard, but the power to decide escapes every artist.

I live in a capitalist society and I can't go any further than the people. Those for change are only a handful, a minority, and we don't have that Don Quixote attitude that we can transform society. One work cannot instigate change. I don't think that in history there has been a single revolutionary work that has brought the people to create a revolution. It's not after having read Marx or Lenin that you go out and make a revolution. It's not after reading Marcuse in America. All the works are just a point of reference in history. And that's all. Before the end of an act of creation, society usually has already surpassed it.

All that an artist can do is bring the people to the point of having an idea of the thing, an idea in their heads that they share, and that helps. People have killed and died for an idea.

If I understand your criticism, then I'm happy. I had no belief that after people saw *Mandabi*, they would go out and make a revolution. But people liked the film and talked about it, though my government didn't. They wanted to censor the movie at the point where it said that "Honesty is a crime in Senegal."

People discussed *Mandabi* in the post office or in the market and decided they were not going to pay out their money like the person in my movie.

They reported those trying to victimize them, which led to many arrests. But when they denounced the crooks, they would say it was not the person but the government which was corrupt. And they would say they were going to change the country.

I know my own limits. But through nothing more than just supplying these people with ideas, I am participating in their awareness.

Q: *Do you find that people in America find similar associations with* Mandabi*?*

A: Initially, the film was not destined for other people than Africans, but we can see that certain films, whether made in Africa or in America, can give us something and teach us, and that a contact is possible from people to people. There is an old film that I like a lot, *The Grapes of Wrath*, which dates from a moment of crisis in America. But the present-day peasants in Africa are at that level. So, you see there are works that create communication.

Q: *Do you find similar communication and inspiration in the cinéma vérité of the Frenchman, Jean Rouch?*

A: Inspired by Rouch? He applied his methods a few years ago to the French problem, but didn't go far and didn't bring a revolution to the French cinema. I think the New Wave of Godard and Truffaut has contributed something. But *cinéma vérité* in the fashion of Rouch is not really *cinéma vérité* nor is it his invention. The methods date from the Russian socialist films of Dziga-Vertov.

Q: *Would you comment on your own experiences as a student of film-making in Russia?*

A: I don't talk about my Russian experiences in America just as I didn't talk of my American experiences in Russia. Every country has its methods and every system of education tries to perpetuate what it represents. Their teaching is socialist or communist just as teaching in America is linked to the establishment. You can take it or leave it. And since I was ignorant, I was forced to take what was given to me, and afterwards I used it as I thought I should.

Q: *Why did you make* Emitai, "God of Thunder," *a political film addressed particularly to the peasantry?*

A: In African countries, the peasants are even more exploited than the workers. They see that the workers are favored and earn their pittance each month. Therefore, the element of discontent is much more advanced among the peasants than with the workers. This fact doesn't give the peasantry the conscience of revolutionaries, but it can lead to movements of revolt which bear positive results.

There are many peasants who live fragmented in a closed economy, producing enough to eat without commercial relationship to the government. But there are other peasants involved in commercial activities who are beginning to understand economic exchange. Last year there were rumors of discontent among the peasants. To tear apart this discontent, Senghor distributed three billion francs to the peasants. You see, you can have hope in the peasant, but you can't base your revolutionary movement around them. But we're not discouraged. The peasantry is a force on which we can depend.

Q: *What is the historical background of* Emitai*?*
A: I came myself from this rural region and these true events of the Diolla people inspired me to present an image of French conduct in my home territory during my early manhood. During the last World War, those of my age, eighteen, were forced to join the French army. Without knowing why, we were hired for the liberation of Europe. Then when we returned home, the colonialists began to kill us, whether we were in Senegal, the Ivory Coast, Algeria, or Madagascar. Those of us who had returned from the French war involvement in Vietnam in 1946 came back to struggle against the French. We were not the same as the black soldiers at home from French-speaking Africa who participated in colonialism instead of demonstrating against it. Now, ten years after independence, it is these same ex-soldiers who are bringing about *coups d'etat.*

Q: *Aren't the women the true heroes of* Emitai*, as they also were in your revolutionary novel, called in America* God's Bits of Wood*?*
A: As *Emitai* shows, when the French wanted our rice, the women refused but the men accepted the orders. Women have played a very important part in our history. They have been guardians of our traditions and culture even when certain of the men were alienated during the

colonial period. The little that we do know of our history we owe to our women, our grandmothers.

The African women are more liberated than elsewhere. In certain African countries, it is the women who control the market economy. There are villages where all authority rests with the women. And whether African men like it or not, they can't do anything without the women's consent, whether it be marriage, divorce, or baptism.

Q: *What were the circumstances in filming* Emitai*?*

A: The Diollas are a small minority with a native language about to disappear. For two years, I learned and practiced it. Then I set out to make contact with the Chief of the Sacred Forest. In order to be able to speak to him, I needed to bring a gift offering. He preferred alcohol but I myself drank it up along the way. When I arrived and was hungry, the chief ate without inviting me. That hurt me. Afterwards he said, "You know well that to speak to the king you have to bring something. Since you didn't bring anything, I couldn't invite you."

The people in the movie are not actors, but people from the village. I had a limited time to tell my story, so I couldn't permit them to do only what they wanted. We would rehearse beginning fifteen minutes before the filming, but all the movements were free. I brought red bonnets for the young people to wear who played soldiers. They refused at first because such bonnets are reserved for the chief.

The chief is not chief by birth, incidentally, but initiated after receiving an education and training. No elected person holds advantage over another. There have been moments when the Diollas elected leaders who then left during the night. That's the reality.

Q: *Were you aware of evolving in your choice of a hero from the individual in* Mandabi *to the collective hero of* Emitai*?*

A: I'm not the one who's evolving. It's the subject which imposes the movement. This story happened to be a collective story. I wanted to show action of a well-disciplined ethnic group in which everyone saw himself only as an integral part of the whole.

Q: *Have the Diolla people seen the film?*

A: Before premiering the film for the Senegalese government, I went back to the village to project it. I remained three nights. All of the villagers from the whole area came and, because they have no cinema, their reaction was that of children looking at themselves in a mirror for the first time. After the first showing, the old men withdrew into the sacred forest to discuss the film. When I wanted to leave, they said, "Wait until tomorrow." They came back the second evening, then returned to the rain forest.

The third evening there was a debate. The old men were happy to hear that there was a beautiful language for them, but they weren't happy with the presentation of the gods. Though these forces obviously did not manifest themselves when the French arrived, the gods still were sacred and helped the old men maintain authority.

The young people accused the old of cowardice for not resisting at the end of the war. The women, of course, agreed, but were very proud of their own role.

Q: *And the reaction in the cities?*

A: Many asked me why I wanted to make a film about the Diollas. You have to know that the majority of maids in Senegal are Diollas to give you an idea of the superiority felt by others in relation to them. (The African bourgeois have two or three maids. It's not very expensive.) To see *Emitai*, the maids left the children. They invited each other from neighborhood to neighborhood to see the film. Finally, the majority Wolofs went to see the film and realized that the history of Senegal and of the resistance was not just the history of the majority of Wolofs. The Diollas are a part of Senegal. And so are the other ethnic groups. And when the Senegalese government finally decreed that they were going to teach Wolof, they were in a hurry to add Diolla. I don't know if that is because of the film, but that's what happened.

Q: *Your films obviously are influential political instruments in Senegal. Could films made in the United States have the same effect?*

A: Alone, no. With the people, yes. There are those who stay secluded and say that artists are creating important works and everything is going to change. Nothing will change. You can put all the revolutionary works on the television, but if you don't go down into the streets, nothing will change. That is my opinion.

African Cinema Is Not a Cinema of Folklore

SIRADIOU DIALLO/1973

JEUNE AFRIQUE: *With six short films and three feature films in ten years, you have become a celebrity of African cinema. But you are still a misunderstood celebrity. Are you an adventurer, a rebel artist, or simply an iconoclast?*
SEMBÈNE OUSMANE: It is hard to say what I am. They can say what they want about me. It doesn't bother me. I exist, I'm here, and I can't be rubbed off. Dead or alive, I exist and I will exist. As for my personal life, the course of my life or my way of expressing myself is something else and I shan't discuss it.

JEUNE AFRIQUE: *But at times your oeuvre gives the impression of some sourness. Are you bitter?*
SEMBÈNE OUSMANE: Bitter? What for? That's the question. It goes without saying that I am impatient for a socialist revolution, but from there to saying that I am bitter, no. I still think that the future belongs to us. I have all my time. I am eternity . . . like all men. I understand that some people don't like my way of expressing myself and explaining things. Besides, I live in Africa, I prefer to live in Africa, and want to be buried in Africa. I will say what I have to say, and show how Africans live . . .

JEUNE AFRIQUE: *The west readily imagines you in a separate, if not eccentric, living environment, one of luxury and distant from the people. But really, what is your ideal life?*

From *Jeune Afrique*, no. 27 (January 1973). Translated from the French by Arianna Bove. Reprinted by permission of *Jeune Afrique*.

SEMBÈNE OUSMANE: To share the joy in life of the whole world. I know that I have more advantages than a Senegalese peasant or worker. But I live the African way with my family. I think that being an artist does not prevent one from living like others and leading a life similar to that of the people who live in this country or in the continent. We have the same problems: at the moment, as for everyone else, the problem is rice. I need to find 300 Kg of rice every month to support different family members. This also enables me to express the preoccupations of the people, of the average Senegalese.

JEUNE AFRIQUE: *However, you are different from your colleagues. Otherwise why would you resign from the Association of Senegalese filmmakers?*
SEMBÈNE OUSMANE: I resigned, that's true. The reason is political, as for all my other actions too. Someone wanted to manipulate filmmakers. You might like or not like what an artist does, but the artist is not a sheep that bleats like all the others. An artist expresses the concerns of his own people and times. More than a simple witness, I intend to be and to remain a partisan artist. In being disliked by this or that, I am just sticking to my "red" line.

JEUNE AFRIQUE: *So you are dissatisfied!*
SEMBÈNE OUSMANE: Yes, because Africa is going through the most painful period of her history. After the slave trade and colonization we are living at a time of neocolonialism. Sure, the socioeconomic structures have changed. But in the mentality, nothing is different at all.

JEUNE AFRIQUE: *More than a rebel, you are desperate . . .*
SEMBÈNE OUSMANE: No. I'm neither a rebel nor am I desperate. I am certain that everything is going to be swept away one day. And I'd rather that day was very close. I am not desperate; I am a realist in so far as I stick to reality. In my work I could portray revolutionaries holding all the power and reorganizing society the way I wish it to be. I could show ordinary people being content and on a full stomach . . . but I don't want to make this kind of cinema, it would be the opposite of reality, so it would be false. You see, I don't invent anything. Go down the streets of Dakar and you will find there the people portrayed in my works.

JEUNE AFRIQUE: *Why did you leave writing to work in cinema?*
SEMBÈNE OUSMANE: I haven't given up writing. Next year, Presence Africaine is publishing a new novel called *Khalaa ou l'œuf*. Khalaa is the man who is impotent; l'œuf is the thing, the machine, the trick . . . So, I am still writing, novels, in particular. Having said that, what led me to try my hand at cinema is that in books I express myself in French. But 80 percent of my people don't speak French, and, out of the 20 percent who speak the language of Molière, very few take the time to read. That's what it's like in Africa. I've ascertained it. Some are so incapable of reading reports that they contact technical assistance. Thus I have no choice but to note that literature doesn't go very far. However, people go to the cinema more than they read because it is accessible to everyone. So I thought it would be wise to turn towards cinema. I am sure to reach the mass with this form of expression. For me, the cinema is the best evening school. It not only enables me to do more and to go further than literature, but it also lets people speak in their own language—Wolof in this case. I don't want to make films with Africans speaking French, the way it would be spoken at the Académie, the Assemblée nationale or in the courts.

JEUNE AFRIQUE: *So far you haven't produced films showing the fate of low waged workers, whilst you recently confided to me that one of your plans was to devote a film to Senegalese businessmen. Where does this project stand?*
SEMBÈNE OUSMANE: I only make films on what I like. It is true that I never did anything on wage laborers but cinema is a difficult affair. Already, *Le Mandat* and *Emitaï* earned me a lot of problems. If I was to tackle the concrete reality of a of workers, it would be even more despairing. Wouldn't I run the danger of facing a ban? It isn't self-censorship, but I do think about it. The problem of labor is a dramatic one. I made a film on unemployment for the BIT (Geneva) recently. I filmed scenes that take place everyday in front of the labor offices here in Dakar. When the film was released the BIT was so satisfied with the result that they commissioned me a second one. But when I returned to the labor office, they slammed the door in my face and said that I hadn't shown the truth. But that was the reality: I showed a workman and a glasses salesman. . . . People who pretend to be selling something, to be employed in order to not be the unemployed. Since there isn't any work

to offer them, they are said to be idle. But they have a sense of dignity, so they must be employed. And this is what they didn't want me to show.

JEUNE AFRIQUE: *You also produce a journal in the Wolof language,* Kaddu. *What is its audience?*
SEMBÈNE OUSMANE: It's been more than three centuries since France arrived here, but only 15 to 20 percent of the people can speak French. Therefore one can reach much of the population by publishing in Wolof. *Kaddu* is a precious cultural tool that enables us to assume our own personality.

JEUNE AFRIQUE: *You mean "authenticity" . . .*
SEMBÈNE OUSMANE: I see what you are alluding to, but we weren't waiting for General Mobutu to embark on the path of authenticity. After all, before us many others contemplated returning Wolof to the place it deserves in the cultural life of our country. During Faidherbe's times, a Frenchman called Jean Dars wanted to teach the Senegalese people how to read and write in Wolof. He was expelled . . .

JEUNE AFRIQUE: *Do you really think that your fellow countrymen would be ready to give up French in favor of Wolof as the language of modern culture?*
SEMBÈNE OUSMANE: We know for sure that it is possible to teach Wolof because 80 percent of the people from here speak the language. We could train mathematicians, doctors, and whatever we want. We have a weekly music radio program in Wolof. You must listen to it. The abbot N'Diaye explains the bible in Wolof, it's formidable. . . . It is really sad for us to listen to our leaders address the peasants as they would address academics or, even, French peasants. I find it truly deplorable. We don't have a single anthology of literature, from the Greeks to our days, translated in Wolof. The Manifesto of the Communist Party is translated in Wolof. We have the Koran in Wolof. And we have issues of *Kaddu* dedicated to mathematics . . .

JEUNE AFRIQUE: *Let's go back to cinema. In developed countries cinema is increasingly becoming just a means of distraction. What role would you assign to African cinema?*

SEMBÈNE OUSMANE: The majority of African filmmakers approach cinema in terms of education and training. We cannot afford to make cinema like the west. We are many years behind and not only do we have to train men but we also need to merge ethnicities that over the years have coexisted without knowing one another. This makes our responsibility very burdensome. I must confess, I am very scared of the power of the image I use. Before using any image, I must measure and imagine the impact and force that it can have on spectators. I stop myself from showing idiosyncrasies that if need be could be interpreted otherwise. If all filmmakers followed this reasoning our cinema could be useful. However, our responsibility towards the public is great, especially given that for a long time Africa was the victim of sociologists and ethnologists. Without knowing African culture, they showed real images but together with unfounded commentaries. They didn't know the meaning of dance or music. But they fit anything they wanted on them. The Europeans receiving this, on seeing the image and listening to the commentary inevitably formed a wrong idea of Africa and Africans. African filmmakers will make good cinema only if they acknowledge these problems and judge this duality of image and word. Besides, it must be said that African cinema is not going to be authentically African for as long as there is no well-defined cultural politics.

JEUNE AFRIQUE: *Are you concerned because Europeans reveal an ugly side of our society or because of their misinterpretation of our culture?*

SEMBÈNE OUSMANE: I am not bothered by what Europeans show, though we recently protested against an Italian filmmaker who screened some hideous things. Not that they don't happen, but such editing makes you think that we are living in the epoch of the worst of barbarisms. According to this filmmaker Africa is still in the Stone Age. I think these procedures are completely unacceptable. Europeans always have their vision of Africa. Thus so-called "Africanist" European filmmakers think that all it takes is to place a camera here, let it swallow all kinds of images, and then say: Africa is like this and here is what Africans are like. But we Africans must express *our culture*, our concerns. We must look after our authenticity, not be afraid of showing what is ugly and refuse to pander to people. Our duty is to show how we are, and saying what we can change here or there . . .

JEUNE AFRIQUE: *At least, the Senegalese state helps you as it helps your colleagues.*
SEMBÈNE OUSMANE: Sure, the state helps me but it is difficult to appreciate. We have cameramen paid by the state. Still, we use a local station and technicians. Great! But there are seven million potential spectators in Senegal. Let's suppose that a ticket for the local cinema was 100 Francs CFA. You see what that comes to. Now, the state retains up to 30 percent of the 100 Francs as tax. Where does the money go? Into which budget? The state could have afforded a support fund for the cinema, as it did for the roads. But it doesn't do that. So, considering the situation, we would say that the state doesn't help us at all, or, at least, that it doesn't give us anything at all. We have the courage to say that. We think that the state retains, and this is true, up to 100 percent of each ticket sold. With this money it build stadiums. But why doesn't it use it to develop cinema? Why wouldn't it create an independent fund for the production of films?

JEUNE AFRIQUE: *The state grants subsidies to some filmmakers, doesn't it?*
SEMBÈNE OUSMANE: It provides subsidies and gives a bit of money. But giving us four or five million doesn't do the cinema any favors. We don't ask for the state to help, we demand that it drafts a policy and tells us: "You have a budget, and this budget is managed by X or Z." When the government gives a filmmaker one or two million, it doesn't expect a return. What it should do is follow the example of the Centre national du cinéma français, where the government advances a sum that is later deducted from the revenues, because let's not forget that at the same time as being an art, cinema is also an industry. And the government here confuses the industrial with the cultural element.

JEUNE AFRIQUE: *Don't you think that your problems can find a solution with the Société africaine du cinema?*
SEMBÈNE OUSMANE: It is still too early to say what this initiative is going to result in, but it is founded on two contradictory choices: one emphasizing the search for maximum profit, the other tied to prestige. Which one will carry it off? That's the question.

JEUNE AFRIQUE: *You learned your craft with great masters. What do you owe them?*

SEMBÈNE OUSMANE: It's true; I learned how to make films in the Soviet Union. I didn't have a choice. To get training, I initially turned to people in France, notably Jean Rouch. I had written to America, Canada, etc. and was rejected everywhere without being given a chance. Then I got in touch with George Sadoul and Louis Daquin. They suggested the Soviet Union. I spent a year there (1961–1962). It must be said, before I went there I had my ideas and my ideology. I'd been a unionist since 1950. I was very happy that it was eventually the Soviet Union that offered me a scholarship.

JEUNE AFRIQUE: *You did the French military service . . .*
SEMBÈNE OUSMANE: Yes.

JEUNE AFRIQUE: *Were you an instrument of colonial power there?*
SEMBÈNE OUSMANE: Yes.

JEUNE AFRIQUE: *How did you come to your current position?*
SEMBÈNE OUSMANE: It's logical. At the time, I was like everyone else, proud to defend France. It was believed that France was our only country. Every time a French soldier was killed, you would say: "He died for France." Every time a Negro toppled: "He died for the homeland." One day, one was from the coast of Italy. Then . . . "Shit! What's the difference between the homeland and France?" and from then on, things changed. Much happened after the war: the Thiaroye events, the tough rail workers' strike, etc. All of this was important in raising a man's awareness.

JEUNE AFRIQUE: *Do you get a pension?*
SEMBÈNE OUSMANE: What pension?

JEUNE AFRIQUE: *From the French army.*
SEMBÈNE OUSMANE: No, and I don't want one.

JEUNE AFRIQUE: *For an old soldier, you are very exceptional. Generally old soldiers show great loyalty to France . . .*
SEMBÈNE OUSMANE: I am not an exception as an old soldier. It could be a generational question. Besides, after the war, there was the RDA, and Gabriel d'Arboussier, the Doudou Gueye, the journal *Réveil*, and

everything else. This probably made things easier. When we came back after the war, we became aware of racism. Still, there were the issues of French language, of slaveholders, of the assimilated, the natives, and the indigenous.

JEUNE AFRIQUE: *Aren't you a bit racist after all? At least in your works?*
SEMBÈNE OUSMANE: We are all racist.

JEUNE AFRIQUE: *And yet?*
SEMBÈNE OUSMANE: Nothing . . .

JEUNE AFRIQUE: *On the wall of your apartment there are pictures of Samory, Che Guevara, Lumumba, Angela Davis, Lenin, etc. Does that mean that you identify yourself with these figures? Do you see them as exemplary or as mirrors?*
SEMBÈNE OUSMANE: It depends. I see Samory as the greatest of all of them. I think Che Guevara contributed something to my generation. Lumumba, let's not talk about him. As for Lenin, whether we like it or not, he is and will be, after Marx, one of the greatest thinkers of humanity. They have the right to figure in this gallery of the dead because they all gave me something. That's all.

JEUNE AFRIQUE: *At what stage is your film on Samory?*
SEMBÈNE OUSMANE: If it were up to me, I'd say that you could see it within six months or a year. The project had started off well, but political hitches delayed it. To say it all, there were incidents between the states responsible for making the film. These are the states of OERS [Senegal River States: Mauritania, Senegal, Guinea]. You know about the political argument. Besides, I would rather wait for the dispute to pass, so as to avoid raising problems or being cornered. I'm still waiting.

JEUNE AFRIQUE: *Do you think you will make this film one day?*
SEMBÈNE OUSMANE: If I were to die without having made it, you are allowed to write that Sembène died dissatisfied. If I made a film on Samory, afterwards I would leave cinema straight away . . .

JEUNE AFRIQUE: *Like many others who say, before every work, that it will be their last.*

SEMBÈNE OUSMANE: I said it and repeat it: if I make Samory, I'll leave cinema behind me. Personally, I have no ambition in life. This is my drama: I want to be like everyone else, like my wife, like the members of other families. My goal is not to make films. I made *Emitai* when I wanted to make *Samory*. Actually, I was asked to make *Ba Bemba* in Mali. But if anyone gave me the green light to make *Samory* I would leave my family and everything, go back to Guinea and start working. Afterwards, I'd leave cinema because *Samory* would be the great oeuvre of my life. I like and admire the man and everything he did! No head of state measures up to Samory and I doubt any ever will.

JEUNE AFRIQUE: *What about your film on Lat Dior?*
SEMBÈNE OUSMANE: When I talked about *Samory*, people suddenly jumped at the chance of doing Lat Dior. I was given a screenplay. It was shameful. When you compare Lat Dior, a great Senegalese resistance fighter, to an unreasonable, irresponsible, inconsistent type, it is disgraceful! Sure, unlike Samory, who unified the Mandinka, Lat Dior never managed to unify the Wolof ethnic groups. He had his limitations, but I couldn't possibly agree with the way he had been presented in the script, so I refused the offer. It seems that Blaise made the film, but I have no idea where they are at in this respect. You know, Hermentier, who deals with this business, isn't a filmmaker; he is an adventurer but the European way . . . five or six Senegalese men wrote about Lat Dior. It would suffice to bring them together to have them produce a text on Lat Dior. Then a filmmaker can cut it, and the film is made. It's not more complicated than that . . . Hermentier came to see me and I said no.

JEUNE AFRIQUE: *Do you think that African cinema has a future? Can it be other than a pale copy of European or Anglo-Saxon cinema?*
SEMBÈNE OUSMANE: African cinema is not a cinema of folklore. We navigate very difficult waters but, honestly, respect to African filmmakers! We try to express ourselves in African with our difficulties and means.

JEUNE AFRIQUE: *So, where is African cinema heading?*
SEMBÈNE OUSMANE: But this is what we are in the process of finding out. In Africa, cinema is made more by images than expression or gestures. And the gestures are more important than the spoken words. The only

way for us to have a framework is to find our own way. Obviously, we encounter many financial difficulties because we don't have much money. Note that we could have money if films were allowed to circulate in Africa, and we could recuperate just a fraction of taxes on what goes to Europe. African cinema risks getting caught into commercial cinema; all the more so given that there are well-intentioned people who are looking for directors to show "the buttocks of Fatou." That pays!

JEUNE AFRIQUE: *When you make your next film, will you refer it to foreigners?*

SEMBÈNE OUSMANE: We conceived and made *Emitai* by ourselves, with our own means. Producers are a bit like editors. Different people ask for certain things. When I wanted to make *Le Mandat*, I was told "Great! You can have the money, but you must show some ass." I refused. Why would I show the rear end of a good-looking woman? I'd rather have it in my own room. So we had financial problems. They would have frozen our revenues. We had to go to court to get our money back. Afterwards, the film was blocked. Since then we have been trying somehow or other to produce our own films. I only make films every two years. I am preparing the next one for 1973. The title will be *Khalaa*.

JEUNE AFRIQUE: *You received many awards. You were chosen to be part of the jury at the Cannes Festival, etc. Don't you worry that you'll end up being taken down the slippery slope and turned into the "hot shot" to be recuperated by the Establishment and finally become the "good Negro" of cinema?*

SEMBÈNE OUSMANE: Look at me carefully! Do I look like the adoptable type? Had I chosen to live in Europe, I might have been bound to fall on the wrong side. We have been aware of the problems of the use that is made of me since the new Brazilian cinema. You could see some Brazilian and other directors in European houses. They would go back once a year, or not at all. Whereas in our case, if we want to work, we must live in Africa all the time. When one of my films went through London or elsewhere, it is the film that is used, but as long as I live in Africa, it is difficult for me to separate from my people. There is something else. When I finished *Emitai*, the first thing I did was demand that it first be shown in Africa. But it wasn't possible. You need to show the film to the European press in order to get the authorization.

JEUNE AFRIQUE: *You said that Africa is going through difficult times. How do you see the future?*

SEMBÈNE OUSMANE: I stay optimistic, regardless. I think that tomorrow's Africa will be a very pleasant place to live in. It's a shame that you can't be born twice. I could have taken a break and come back to see. But the period of transformation we are currently going through is the richest for a creative person. The thing that I hope for above all is that the Vietnam war ends. I can no more forget Rhodesia, Angola, Mozambique, South Guinea, or the Palestinians. Behind all of it one finds American power. I think that Africa can change many things in all of these conflicts. It would be enough to not keep silent.

Interview with Ousmane Sembène

MICHAEL DEMBROW AND KLAUS TROLLER/1975

DEMBROW/TROLLER: *How does the process of creation occur for you?*

SEMBÈNE: It is very difficult to explain the question of creation, in that I myself don't believe in what one might call a formal manner of inspiration. I think that if I must create something I pose questions somehow or other at my level—why this subject and not another, why I should do this and not something else, what is the objective, what aspect of human beings do I want to reveal, in a general setting. If it is a personal film, I concern myself further with knowing if the problem I'm raising would interest everyone, and how to go about making it of interest to others.

And there, I think that for me it is at that moment that the work of investigating the very level of human beings, of the nature of this subject with individuals, with other subjects, begins. I don't know if I'm making myself understood; creation is never detached from the social context of the man himself.

DEMBROW/TROLLER: *You've said that you personally aren't interested in making "direct cinema." What is the difference between your films and "direct cinema"?*

SEMBÈNE: I'm not sure what's meant here by cinema direct, or cinema vérité. As for Jean Rouch, he says, "I place my camera in the street, the

From Michael Dembrow's website, http://spot.pcc.edu/~mdembrow/Sembene_interview.htm. Transcribed by Kiki Dembrow. Translated by Michael Dembrow. Reprinted by permission of Michael Dembrow.

subject enters, and that's it." I don't think that's true at the level of cinema. One is obliged to select, to point out, to edit, to collate, to make a collage from beginning to end, and one must make a segregation of images, because if you place your camera at the corner of the street, everyone is going to pass by, but if you project that in front of people, there's nothing new there. One sees the street, one sees the automobiles, one sees the people—perhaps they stop to speak, but that means nothing. Jean Rouch and Edgar Morin do that, I've seen it. Perhaps it's right, but I don't believe so, because they're taking up these ideas again from Vertov—Vertov the Russian who in 1917 after the revolution spoke of cinema direct in trains and other things. Perhaps in his context, that was one thing.

But in the context of Africa, I think that a kind of cinema can be created, but the director is obliged to select and to sort out, so that there's a head and a tail to what one is narrating. And I think that at this time direct cinema has no chance for life. The people who go to the theater or to the cinema or what not, they want, I think, to be told a story—I don't know whether that's good or bad. At any rate, they want to have a subject. It depends on how you regard them. At least if it were an underground cinema, a parallel cinema, it would have a chance to live. It touches perhaps the cinephiles, those who love cinema, who think they're satiated with narratives, and who seek another form of truth-masturbation, saying, "That, that's very good!"

You see, I think cinema vérité is like the product of a bad painter who buys an empty frame and who goes among flowers and there hangs the frame, saying, "I have a very pretty picture," ignoring all there is around, that's that. Someone who buys a frame, who goes in a very pretty garden and who frames the flowers and says, "Here's a pretty picture. Here."

DEMBROW/TROLLER: *You've said that at the moment you begin, you ask yourself questions such as, "Is this relevant or not," but where do these questions come from? What is there before that?*

SEMBÈNE: Everything is there! For example, at the moment I'm working on a scenario. It will soon be six months that I've been working on it, every morning, even here [in Bloomington, Indiana]. It's difficult for me to say, it's an aspect that escapes me perhaps, why this must come first. I think that when things are collected there's a mathematical law which escapes us all. But I think it is a mathematical law. And in matters of cinema it is very technical and rigid. Because I only have a certain amount of time in which to tell a story, which can recount fifty years or twenty years of a person's life. I must tell the story of that life in an hour and a half. Therefore I've got to choose. From the moments, the actions, the looks which enfold the entire past or the period of which I can depict so little in the film. It's a different thing with literature. In a literary work you can say, "Fifty years later," one knows then that it's fifty years later. But as for the cinema, you can put in a written title, but it interrupts the story. The film has to move forward. The filmmaker has to select. But this selection process, I think a director has difficulty explaining it in a truly technical, formulaic manner.

DEMBROW/TROLLER: *But where do you find your stories?*
SEMBÈNE: How do I find my ideas? Ah, that's another story! Perhaps . . . I have many ideas in my head, because I see things around me, and every event deserves to be recounted, it seems. But aside from that, it's usually a little bit of news, a speck of an event. I see something, I tell myself, "Wait, that's got to be told." I don't know whether or not you were at the showing of my film last night. [The film was *Borom Sarret*, 1963.] The story of that baby, I'd like to write a book about that.

The story hit me so hard that I was obligated to it from that moment on. I had to reenact the events myself, in my own mind, the tragedy of the bus, to know at what hour the story takes place, to imagine how many people are there, where they come from. You see, from this moment on, I dig, dig, dig, dig, until I find the end of my story. And I think that in my case, this is the hardest time. Because I also have to try to see why this, and why that. I write the same things over four or five times. I ask myself if I'm satisfied. Then I reformulate the questions, and I believe it's there that the mathematical side of creation enters. I remain convinced that there is a very emotional side, but there is also an important intellectual element. Yet this mathematical element escapes even the author.

DEMBROW/TROLLER: *When you're developing your ideas, do you begin by establishing individual images, or is it the continuity of the story which interests you?*

SEMBÈNE: I think it's the continuity of the story which interests me. I don't know what's going to follow. There are times when there are people obsessing me, figures whom I didn't expect to find. You see, these people are pressing themselves on me.

For example, if I take the case of that baby, it's the individuals I see, these characters pressing, jostling one another in front of me—there's this father and son whom I don't know. I must therefore invent a father and a son. Good, I have to go to the hospital, more or less, to see what occurred previously. Perhaps a vision of one of the deaths there is going to spring to my mind. As soon as I begin to set them on an itinerary, to locate them, other ideas and characters have already begun to appear, characters who speak to me. To me. At that time I make a note of these people, I mark them as X, Y, Z, but advancing the story all the while.

DEMBROW/TROLLER: *You've said that for several films you've prepared note cards on which the shooting script is broken down to individual scenes. For which films did you do this?*

SEMBÈNE: I did it for *Borom Sarret*, *Black Girl*, and another film, *Niaye*. *Niaye* is the story of incest in a village. It was easier for me to work that way because I was working in the bush and all that. I had my knapsack. And on each card was written a character or a scene of the film. Because I'm always pressed for time when I film. When I'm filming a room, I have to film the entire scene at the same time. Perhaps even later scenes, i.e., the room as it must appear ten or twenty years after the initial scene. Therefore, I have all these cards with the characters, their dress, their dialogue, the appearance of the room, set out as much as possible. Barring accidents, I cannot modify them.

But now, in my room here, in Bloomington, I'm working on an event which took place in Africa during the last century. Good. Here I can think what I like, and that's what I do. I write it down and all that. But when the time comes for me to be out there, what I thought in Bloomington is perhaps no longer true, and doesn't jibe with, say, the lay of the land where I'm filming. But as I have all my little pieces of paper, I know what improvisation is not going to work. Because I'm in a real setting, I have to scratch things out, add others. What I've altered becomes something new. It sometimes happens that by chance, I'd already been thinking along those lines, but I'd fashioned it in a way that didn't correspond to reality.

For example, I'm at a wine merchant's, one who sells wine to the natives at the beginning of the century. He had huge jugs and he had amphorae. Good. I like his shop and, imagining myself the merchant as I prepare my script, I hang as many guns or whatever as I like all over the place. But when I go to make the story, in reality, perhaps the real shop on location has no rifles hanging. You see, for me, an image is charged with something, it should correspond to an action that must come from somewhere—if the merchant doesn't hang his rifles, if he places them on a table, then I have to change the whole scene that treats those rifles. To align it with these rifles that are on a table or wherever. And that's why the cards are utilized, because already they are serving as a memory pad.

DEMBROW/TROLLER: *You mean at the moment you arrive on location it becomes necessary to change certain things to accord with the physical reality that you find?*

SEMBÈNE: Yes, it's I, not the actors. Their phrases are the same, their acting is the same, it's the things around them which change. For example, let's say this room is, I don't know, before television. You try to shoot in this room around the TV. Bah! You have to take out the TV or at least find something to mask it with. You see . . . it's always the little things and so on which can encourage creation or make it grind to a halt.

But still I doubt that one can actually teach the creative process. You can teach methods in a technical manner—that was true for me. In Moscow there is a school for cinema, a school for literature, and so on. Good, there were many Africans with me who went to these schools. But I took a shortcut. I didn't stay five years, and I didn't take any courses in theory. But I would be present at all the filming, even if it was snowing. For me, that's how you learn technique, and I think it's most important. When the directors had time, I'd ask them questions: "Why this?" Good, I'd write it down. "Why that?" I'd write it down. And afterwards, when he had the time, he'd say, "This fits with this or that; look in the scenario." Good, I'd write it down, tell him, "OK, I've got it." I think that often in filmmaking schools—I'm speaking of schools where films are made, not just studied, there are so many theories on the creative process that the students pay too much attention to theory and don't think about all these problems.

DEMBROW/TROLLER: *Can you give us an example of where you've had to improvise on location?*

SEMBÈNE: Often. There are many, many examples. I spoke earlier of that child with the gun. [Sembène is speaking of a scene in *Emitai* where the woman and children of a village which had refused to give up its corn to the French are forced to sit in the town square. At one point during the shooting of this scene, a child surprised everyone by suddenly leaving her place, wandering over to where the "French soldiers" were standing guard, and picking up one of their rifles, which had been stacked nearby. This unexpected element works extremely well in the film.] And the same thing occurs in my last film also. I place the actor in a framework and leave possibilities open.

Because sometimes everything looks fine on paper and as long as it's on paper, it's fine. But on location, when we're shooting, we need transitional elements, and it's often the actors who give them to me. An actor might say, "Wait, what if this is done?" I look, I say OK, I see the cameraman and say to him, "Wait, we've got to do this. It's not my idea, it's his." Then he looks, says OK. We change the placement of the camera, do what the actor suggested, and we continue with our work. It doesn't cost us anything and it makes him happy. All it takes perhaps to make him feel good is this little gesture of improvisation.

For example, in my last film [*Xala*] I had once again as my leading actor the man from *Mandabi*. He had a pair of glasses which I'd never seen him with. These glasses could be taken apart, and when we weren't shooting he would take them apart piece by piece and then put them back together. Then when we were shooting he did the same thing. I said OK, we've got to film it, so we filmed it and he was happy. And I myself hadn't foreseen this action.

There are many such instances with women in my films, and it's often with women that I find myself doing the most improvisation. I usually give them more freedom than I give the guys. Because the women usually are playing themselves, their own roles, and on paper I'm very limited by the fact that I don't know them very well. They modify the scenario accordingly. And that also, I think, that brings something to the act of creation.

Particularly in Africa, where we shoot outdoors in direct sunlight. It's not the same in a studio, because in a studio there are a number of steps which must be taken. With studio lighting you're limited, since the zone of illumination extends only three meters before and three meters behind the subject, so he can't move more than six meters. Whereas I have over a hundred meters at my disposal. I place my camera in such a position that I leave the subject time and space to move around.

DEMBROW/TROLLER: *How do you choose the roles that you yourself play in your films?*

SEMBÈNE: Myself? No, you see, these are tricks, there are times when actors who've promised to come—because often certain actors aren't paid, they just promise me they'll come—but they don't show up. Then I say, "OK, I can do it, I think I can do it." Though I don't plan to play a part at the beginning. Except in April a friend of mine asked me to play the leading role in his film, but that's different: it was he who asked me. But I never intend to do it in my own films. I haven't chosen to play a part in my next film, but I have to be ready in case of an absence.

DEMBROW/TROLLER: *You mean the choice of playing a soldier in* Emitai *was purely the result of an accident? [There is a satiric sequence in* Emitai *in which the picture of Marshal Petain in the local army headquarters is replaced by one of General De Gaulle. A Senegalese native soldier, played by Sembène, finds this "changing of the guards from the "fascist" to the "republican" rather incomprehensible, and he makes some humorous comments regarding it. Sembène was himself a soldier in the French colonial army in Senegal during this period.]*

SEMBÈNE: It was by accident. We had an actor who was supposed to do it, but unfortunately he couldn't come. Because this man who was supposed to act in *Emitai* is the village clerk, and is therefore a member of the town council, an elected position. The day we were supposed to film him there was a meeting of the town council. OK, what were we going to do? Because I'm limited for time by the sunlight, and I can't allow myself to stop shooting every time somebody doesn't show up. You know that when they're in session these council meetings can last four or five days. So I couldn't wait—I did it. The same for *Mandabi* and so on.

When someone's missing, you've got to take their place. It often happens in our films. You don't know it, but everyone in my crew appears in the films, even the cameraman at times. It happens that we're missing a character, so everyone says, "Hold it, the cameraman's got to do it." I take over the camera, he does it, and we continue. So that in each film there are always one or two guys from our crew who appear in it; but it's never planned that way a priori.

DEMBROW/TROLLER: *In* Mandabi *you played . . .*
SEMBÈNE: The scribe, yes.

DEMBROW/TROLLER: *And I've read that in reality you do sometimes serve as scribe in your village. Is this the same thing?*
SEMBÈNE: Yes, but that's, no, you see, in the village they're perhaps illiterate. In French. And there are times when things have to be written. That's neighborliness. You help out, it's not an obligation. I do it a lot, but I think it's the laws of being a good neighbor that are responsible. Because I am a neighbor in the village, and they know I am lettered in French, naturally they come to see me. I can't say no to my neighbor, for in exchange I receive a good deal of recompense. It's a village of fishermen, and sometimes they give me fish, sometimes they give me lobsters, sometimes they give me vegetables, and so on. It's not payment, it's returning a service—so by this act we're more or less joined in this solidarity.

DEMBROW/TROLLER: *You see, I have the impression that for you it's all very simple when you explain your choice of roles. We've been taught to make theoretical statements. So we asked ourselves if it perhaps wasn't by accident that it should be the scribe here, or the soldier in the other case—because the day before you had told us of the changeover from Petain to DeGaulle, when you were in the army. So for us there was a particular significance in that.*
SEMBÈNE: Yes, of course. I lived that story myself, but in the film I didn't plan to play the role. I think that in the schools . . . you see, schools are a good thing, I've always wanted there to be schools. But the relationship between the theoretical teaching and the actual work with

cinema, particularly, I think is very hard. Very hard, whether it be in Africa, in America, or elsewhere. The cinema is too hard because its existence rests on money. There is its industrial aspect to consider. The producers don't want to lose money, so they don't allow certain improvisations. They really want something tidy, so they can count on the returns. In the case of Africa, we have an advantage, I think, in that we can do pretty much what we want, since most African directors up to now have been their own scriptwriters. It's they themselves who write their scripts. You see, it's still very rare in many countries today for the director to both write and direct. They are real creators. In the evolution of our cinema there is nevertheless a new method: scripts created by two filmmakers—a director and a writer. That's a good thing, but still, on location it's another story—it's the director alone who is in fact the owner of the film.

DEMBROW/TROLLER: *The other day you said that, for you, there is a medley of film techniques that you could learn in Europe, but your narrative methods are perhaps the contribution of African storytellers.*
SEMBÈNE: Yes, storytellers . . . yes, that's perhaps why the African cinema is slower. It's slower, admitted. Often, the people who are making films in Africa, the majority never attended the great European schools. For a long time they remained very attached to their culture, in which stories are told. We say that they are storytellers. The story is clear and simple. At first glance you say good, that's really clear, but when you dig, you find philosophy. You find that there is something within that simplicity.

DEMBROW/TROLLER: *This story you're talking about, did you find it in the "fait divers" ("human interest") section of a newspaper?*
SEMBÈNE: No, no, no. Some people told us that story. Because these people went to see *Borom Sarret.* They discussed the story of this boy. Good, OK, this is after 1963, but people didn't want to believe that in Africa a person could go all by himself to bury his child. But when they saw this happen, they ran to tell me about it.

Interview with Ousmane Sembène

NOUREDDINE GHALI/1976

GHALI: *Did the village where the action takes place in* Emitai *really exist?*
SEMBÈNE: It is a Senegalese village which was destroyed by the colonial army, but which still exists. We keep these villages like relics of our history. I was relatively young in 1942, not yet in the army, when the Diola massacre took place. Later, while making a film and being concerned somewhat with history and the heroism of everyday life, I thought a start might be made on something more contemporary.

It is true that people are always talking about the great African resistance fighters, but often people do not know what they were really like and how certain countries and certain tribes resisted. The independence movement was not born like that; it was born in different contexts. If this movement was born from what is called the ideology of "negritude," I am unaware of it, because I was living with my people, in the same conditions as my people.

I have tried to demonstrate that if the negritude movement brought something to birth, it was still the act of a minority, but that the people had already engaged in the struggle to be free, you see. The story of *Emitai* takes place then in a Diola village, next to Guinea-Bissau. The same tribe lives in the south of Senegal and the west of Guinea-Bissau.

While the film was being shot, some extras came from Guinea-Bissau, and the fighters and the resistance people of the time helped us a lot.

From *Film and Politics in the Third World,* edited by John D. H. Downing (New York: Praeger, 1987). Translated by John D. H. Downing. First published in *Cinéma* 76, #208 (April 1976).

At the film's premiere in Casamance, President Cabral came to see the film with some fighters; as people were leaving, they all came to tell us that the film had been made for them, and not just for other people, because it was the same struggle.

I say this, because when certain intellectuals in Europe think about the liberation of Africa, they ignore internal resistance. For the struggle against neo-colonialism, it is possible to reactualize all these scattered and little-known battles.

GHALI: *Amilcar Cabral is present in* Xala, *in a photograph in the bedroom of El Hadj Abdou Kader Beye's daughter.*
SEMBÈNE: Yes, the struggle in *Emitai* was an anti-colonial struggle, but had nothing to do with a class struggle. *Xala* is a kind of allegory, or more precisely a fable, more accessible to my people, on several levels of understanding. Between *Emitai* and *Xala,* we see the two phases of a struggle: to begin with, the first violent struggle against colonialism, then, with *Xala*, the beginning of class struggle in Africa.

GHALI: *This class struggle seems to have several aspects in* Xala. *Amongst others, the role of language: Wolof is mostly spoken by the poorer classes, and French is used by El Hadj and his like as a sign of superiority . . .*
SEMBÈNE: I think this is still the complex many of our rulers have. Perhaps you will forgive me for being a little didactic, for I feel the need to explain the work inasmuch as I want it to make a political contribution. In the Francophone countries south of the Sahara, we have a bourgeoisie whose official language is nothing but French. They only feel significant when they express themselves in French. They merely copy the West and western bourgeois culture.

Whereas, in the West itself, there is a tendency to deny the value of this bourgeois culture, the African bourgeoisie's only reference point is the West. Dakar, Abidjan, Libreville, or Yaounde are simply the capitals of French provinces. They are just the peripheries of neo-colonialism, whence their danger. But when these types find themselves face to face with the people, they are often illiterate in the country's national language—they are alienated to such an extent, for inside themselves they are colonized. They are always the first to say people's mentalities have to be decolonized, but it is actually their mentality which has to be.

For example, when El Hadj, in an upsurge of rebelliousness, wanted to speak in his own language during the debate, he was told French was the official language and he accepted that . . . Whereas his daughter, rightly or wrongly, brings a synthesis together and sets out to express herself only in her own language. In her room she has photos of heroes like Cabral, perhaps because it was in fashion, but she feels solidarity with them.

The people's only form of self-expression is in the national language: Wolof. But our African bourgeoisie currently has no ambition other than to be a copy of the western bourgeoisie; you have to see its manner of holding receptions, its etiquette; you have to listen to its speeches—it speaks to the peasants in French. In a country with 80 percent illiteracy, its speeches, which are supposed to talk about their problems, go right over their heads.

The most serious matter is that when these bourgeois committed this flagrant error, they drew an entire people after them. For Black Africa's traditional culture no longer responds to and can no longer cope with urban development and its architectural structures. For this bourgeoisie only consults with European architects who come to hand out European models, without taking account of the way of life, the meaning of the family, the meaning of the civilization of Africa. The homes are designed for a single couple, whereas in African societies the dwellings are much more spread out, and much more ventilated. They build houses for us in order that we can then buy air-conditioning . . .

We know all these little signs that are in the film, the air-conditioner and other things, and we observe that they alienate the individual. And all these businessmen are only sub-contractors. Financially, they do not have the resources of the major industries, and they cannot do so because we are no longer in the period when industry was born. We are in a period of monopolies, trusts, multinational corporations.

GHALI: *The main character's job seems to have been chosen with great care: he is simply an intermediary who takes with the left hand and gives with the right . . .*

SEMBÈNE: He gets commodities and simply distributes them. He is a sub-contractor. It is not he who goes to buy in quantity, it is not he who has ships at his command, it is not he who gives loans to the bank. He gets his subsidies from what people are happy to leave him. For us, it was a question of showing that when types like him become embittered, they always come back to rediscover the masses . . . When they are set up at the apex of society, they say the beggars have to be run in because these people are, they say, human refuse. But when they themselves fall, they borrow the vocabulary of revolution. It is very symbolic and very true at the same time. You find the same thing in a good number of African and Asian countries; as soon as a leading bourgeois is let down by his own kind, he returns to the ordinary folk and tries after a fashion to purge his past . . .

Xala was shown at the Bombay festival last January and the Indians told me that the film's content applies to Indian society. They have all these beggars and bourgeois, and they had to have a film get to them from Senegal to allow them to identify with something on their doorstep.

The pickpocket who steals from the peasant in the film symbolizes the man who becomes a businessman, and instantly finds himself at the apex of society. It's a poor man who becomes rich. Maybe it's all still full of contradictions, but in the development of our society, that's how things are. There are people like sharks waiting to live off dead bodies. We call them carrion-crows . . . The problem is important, but it is hard to explain how it operates. You can only try to give clues to people who go to see the film—and this film was very successful in Senegal, despite the cuts.

GHALI: *Apparently these cuts were ten in number. To be sure, the print distributed in France is complete. Can you let us know some of the censored scenes, and do you know the reasons?*

SEMBÈNE: I don't know. Because this problem is located beyond censorship. It is the Inquisition. At the very beginning of the film, there is the removal of Marie Antoinette's bust. I don't see how this could offend anyone, but it was taken out because it's important all the same not to offend our French cousins.

There is also the scene where the businessmen open their brief-cases and find bank-bills. That offended a lot of people. They also cut all the scenes where the police chief, a European, appeared before the Chamber of Commerce. It happens that our Interior Minister is a Senegalese with white skin; he was French, and now is a naturalized Senegalese.

I don't ask the reasons for the cuts, and I don't ask for justifications. I know the people I am confronting will use the weapons of censorship to keep me silent. They also cut the scene where the beggar, in answering El Hadj's wife who wanted to call Babylon, says prisoners are happier than workers and peasants because they are fed, after a fashion, housed, and sometimes given medical attention.

The film continues to run in Senegal with these ten amputations, and people go to see it and fill in the cuts for themselves. I have also distributed flyers which indicated the scenes which got cut, so people can get a sense for what is missing.

GHALI: *The UGC has signed contracts to get films to Senegal. Isn't* Xala's *situation some sort of counterpart to this?*

SEMBÈNE: We have a reciprocity contract with the UGC. In this framework, two years ago we produced five feature films the UGC was supposed to distribute.

The UGC saw *Xala* as a test-case. If the film takes off, it will continue. If not, it will only distribute Senegalese films in driblets. Currently we are deep in negotiations to alter the structure of our relations with the UGC, and Senegalese cinema is starting a second phase. We have more or less got the creation of an assistance fund which would be derived from taxes levied on films the UGC distributes in Senegal. Only the law still has to be passed. That can happen quickly, or drag on. But all the same, we have problems with the UGC.

GHALI: *But would this assistance fund be enough to resolve the problems of Senegalese cinema in whole, or in part?*

SEMBÈNE: We have no illusions. The problems of Senegalese cinema are bound up with a cultural policy still to be defined by Senegal. We also know that film problems cannot be resolved in ignorance of the other aspects of the social life of a country, and we realize the limits of our collaboration with the UGC.

For ten years, we have been explaining the situation of Senegalese film-makers to our people. Two years ago, the Senegalese government bought back all the theaters and created a mixed-capital company in which the UGC had 20 percent of the capital. But the UGC, very gluttonous despite this 20 percent, wanted to swallow up everything and absorb cinema entirely. It was on these grounds that the film-makers alerted the public authorities, who put a total stop to theater sales to the UGC. This is the current phase of our negotiations.

We are aware of the fact that *Xala* constitutes a kind of guarantee, but we cannot reject that. It will be a test to see how the UGC will operate. A test of collaboration, I won't say of a frank and honest kind, but in our mutual interest. Nonetheless, we know the solution for our cinema will be for all the theaters to be taken over, and the African states will get to that point one day. We will do like Algeria, and we will control production, distribution, and management, in short all cinema from A to Z. Up to now, and even though it has only 20 percent of the capital, the UGC imposes its own programming. Now we want to decide by ourselves what films to distribute in our country.

GHALI: *El Hadj, the main character, has two wives who seem to belong to two poles: the first is traditional and the other is Europeanized.*

SEMBÈNE: He got the first wife before becoming a somebody. Along with his economic and social development, he takes a second who corresponds, so to speak, to a second historical phase. The third, his daughter's age but without her mind, is only there for his self-esteem. She is submissive (unlike his daughter), and only appears once or twice: she is of the "Be beautiful and shut up" variety.

Polygamy, especially in the bourgeois or urban setting, means the wife is only some flesh for whom a commodity value is paid. It is these bourgeois and their wives, by the way, who had this supposedly brilliant idea to open the doors for International Women's Year. Not working women, but a stratum of privileged women to whom the christian religion has given no satisfaction and who talk on the subject of men's and women's equality. But there is, undoubtedly, an undeniable problem: polygamy, against which we struggle. There is a problem, but the problem is clear because the woman's inferior status is visible. We do not, however, find any solution in the Western concept of the family, for that model only produces a deterioration in human beings. In reality, the problem should not be posed in terms of sexes but in terms of classes.

GHALI: *You are a writer and film-maker at one and the same time, which gives you a place apart in Senegalese cinema. Does the fact of being a writer help you in creating a thematic and a style?*

SEMBÈNE: There is a kind of interaction. For me, the cinema begins with literature. But when I write, I wish the final product to be cinematic. I seek for words to become images, and for images to become words, so that one might read a film and see a book. But what led me to the cinema is that it goes further than the book, further than poetry, further than theater. When I brought out *Xala*, each evening I had a least three hundred people all the time in the audience, with whom I used to debate in small groups from time to time.

Film simply serves us as a canvas on which to reflect together with each other. What is important is that the cinema becomes eye, mirror, and awareness. The film-maker is the one who looks at and observes his people, to excerpt actions and situations which he chews over before giving them back to his people. Often the worker or the peasant don't have the time to pause on the details of their lives: they live them and do not have the time to tie them down. The film-maker, though, can link one detail to another to put a story together. There is no longer a traditional story-teller in our days, and I think the film-maker can replace him.

But in my writing I have to remain in the background in order to advance ideas so we can progress further. I reflect on issues, and I want to bring back to my people their own situation so that they can recognize themselves in it, and ask questions. For the Third World film-maker, it is not a question of coming to overwhelm the people, because technical prowess is very easy, and after all, cinema, when you know it, is a very simple thing. It is a question of allowing the people to summon up their own history, to identify themselves with it. People must listen to what is in the film, and they must talk about it. This is why the language used plays a very important role: that is why I use the national language, Wolof, which is the language of the people.

GHALI: *One gets the impression that certain scenes are profoundly symbolic. When El Hadj is obliged to strip at the end of the film, it seems that it is the character's shady dealings which are actually unveiled and stripped bare . . .*

SEMBÈNE: All the same, you have to know that for me, this scene is an appeal to revolt. If those people had had guns, they would have killed this fellow. Colonialism only survives with us through the mediation of this bourgeoisie.

We know for example that a good part of the African heads of state support Savimbi and Holden in the war in Angola, who, as is known, are tied in with South Africa. We see what kind of heads of state they are who support Unitá, and the masses or the workers of those countries will have no respite until they can spit on their own bourgeoisie or shoot it.

GHALI: *There are many songs in the film's soundtrack which have not been subtitled. What do they say?*

SEMBÈNE: It's a sort of popular song that I wrote myself in Wolof. In one sense, it calls to revolt, to the struggle against injustice, against the powers-that-be, against the leaders of today who, if we do not get rid of them, will tomorrow be trees which are going to overrun the place and have to be cut down. The songs are tied in with the deeds and gestures that I have written. They did not come from folklore. I had thought at the start to have them translated, but in the end I gave up the idea because it is unnecessary for a European public.

It is the allegory of a kind of lizard, a lizard who is a bad leader. When he walks in front and you behind, he kills you while saying you want to murder him. When you walk as tall as he does, he kills you while saying: "You want to be my equal." When you walk in front of him he kills you while saying: "You want to profit from my good luck." The song says we have to think very seriously indeed about these leaders who resemble this animal and get rid of them. It ends something like this: "Glory to the people, to the people's rule, to the people's government, which will not be government by a single individual!" I also wrote the song in *The Money Order*.

GHALI: *There are many observations on people's lives, on the lives of the beggars who, by the end of the film, come to form a compact mass capable of action . . .*

SEMBÈNE: Yes, they had been deported but they came back. This is the community which one day must come to clean up the cities of the bourgeoisie. These beggars are unwell, but they are citizens in every sense. In many states south of the Sahara, the worker is very unhappy. He does not live; all he does is to survive. In a certain fashion, the peasant is in a still more wretched condition than the worker. I remain convinced that, even sick or crippled, the people will get rid of their bourgeoisies, because it is both essential and inevitable.

GHALI: *Let us return to* Emitai. *Did the public respond to these problems of war, of Pétain and Gaullism?*
SEMBÈNE: Yes, but apart from Senegal, the film is banned in all the other francophone states because the French embassy does not agree with it, France does not agree with it. Outside of Sékou Touré's Guinea, the film has not been seen anywhere.

For us, who were then the colonized, Pétain and De Gaulle were the same thing, even if young people today know there is a difference between them. The story of the soldiers killed in Senegal is De Gaulle; the story of Algeria in 1945 is De Gaulle; the story of Madagascar is De Gaulle: why do people want De Gaulle presented as a hero or a superhero?

GHALI: *The French themselves have realized he was far from being a hero . . .*
SEMBÈNE: Where I come from, he was a colonialist and he behaved as such. For the soldiers sent on the mission to requisition the rice, it is the same army. There is one of the Diola who says: "We are here to bring them the rice, they are here to kill and pacify. De Gaulle or Pétain, it's the same thing!" I think that is the film's attraction, and it is that which has caused the film such a mass of problems.

GHALI: *The film also recounts the relationship of the Diola community with the gods.*
SEMBÈNE: They always wanted to mystify us. We were always hung up on this notion of gods, on negritude, and a lot of other stuff. And throughout this period, we were colonized . . .

The gods never prevented colonialism from establishing itself; they strengthened us for inner resistance but not for an armed resistance. When the enemy is right there, he has to be fought with weapons. The Vietnamese for example did not wait for Buddha to free them . . . The gods are a subsidiary, but inessential element.

During the struggle for Guinea-Bissau's liberation, Cabral wrote a very good book on this theory of cultures. We are from the same region, and we have a multiplicity of tribes. Their traditions were respected, but they were told: "We must take up arms to struggle against the Portuguese."

What I wanted to show in *Emitai* was that the gods could no longer respond to the people's needs, and the first elder, the king who died, could no longer really accept the advice to hold off from action. The French came, they took their children to make war against them, they took their rice. We have to die with dignity, weapon in hand; that is what I wanted to show. The problem is to struggle, even in everyday life. The important thing was to show a culture which people are unaware of, at a moment in our present-day struggle. Now people know Emitai (god of thunder), the village of Effok where it happened, and that is part of our national heritage.

The time-period has to be specified: at that period France was occupied by the Nazis; the Germans behaved in the way we know about in Oradour. We can cite eighteen cities or countries where the French army did the same thing: Senegal, Grand-Bassam, Casamance, Dimboko, Abidjan, Sétif, Madagascar . . . For me, the problem over whether it's De Gaulle or Pétain, is a problem of which horse's ass you are talking about.

Sembène Ousmane in Kinshasa

PIERRE HAFFNER/1977

SEMBÈNE OUSMANE gave this interview at the Intercontinental Hotel in Kinshasa on November 13, 1977. Sembène had stayed in Kin-la-belle (the capital of Zaire was still called that at the time) from October 30 and was going to leave on the following day. He presented all of his cinematographic work up to *Ceddo*—which actually celebrated its premiere in the continent—and talked with students, senior officials, writers, filmmakers, priests, and ordinary people from the Popular Movement of the Revolution; at every opportunity, he opened up with extraordinary and generous honesty. For me, the most difficult thing was to arrange this talk: despite our complicity for the previous fifteen days and our fifteen walks through the "cité" kinois (which is what the popular districts are known as), Sembène pretended to have resolved once and for all to avoid answering these questionnaires with his incurable and often tiring curiosity . . . It would be inappropriate to pride myself with overcoming the resistance of a friend, so I simply want to share with the reader the privilege of having constrained for this long the man who dedicates all of the power of his love and work to the transformation of this "bitch that is Africa" (in *L'Harmattan*).

PH: *When coming to Zaire, you appear as a pilgrim filmmaker. Is it a personal mission or the coincidence of an invitation?*
OS: For me, after all, it is about the development of African cinema and its embedding. African cinema is in a position to sustain itself on

---

From *Recherche, Padagogie et Culture*, no. 37 (1978). Translated from the French by Anna Rimpl and Annett Busch. Reprinted by permission by Claude Haffner.

its own resources and public. More than what I do, it's about going to meet filmmakers, trying to raise their awareness. I did that in the Ivory Coast, Togo, Bénin, Mali, and Niger; I talked to the authorities, to create competitions: if one country can do it, others can too. Independently from that, I am trying to discuss with filmmakers about our limits and possibilities. The most important thing for me is to talk to them, because we have to make sure that our cinema can develop when it has its own circulation here—I see Europe as being a support, but that is not there where our public is.

PH: *Have you had this mission at heart for a long time?*
OS: Since I began making cinema. [When] I started in Senegal, there was the Association of Senegalese Cinema, which allowed me to create Fepaci with Tahar Cheriaa. We had meetings in Dakar and Naples, where we had been invited, and at every occasion I would use the opportunity to get together and lay down our problems . . . Meeting in Europe is indispensable, but we should generate these calls and possibilities of encounters here.

PH: *Zaire seems to have a particular importance for you?*
OS: First I left here, when I was forty years old, to start making cinema, initially in this city . . . I have been here during the time of Lumumba. I had the idea to make films because of these events, because of the things I saw and experienced, which literature couldn't represent . . . The public, the great African public does not have access to literature yet, and even if it did, the world of images, the magic of images, the oral civilization itself are such that cinema is the intuitive replacement of the palaver tree for us . . .

PH: *The Congolese experience was initially of political importance to you. So does cinema and making movies come from a political need?*
OS: For us, cinema is always a revolution; it has to be an object of revolution . . . The revolution, before being carried out at the practical level, must go through our mentalities. "Urbanity" only allows for the social circulation of things, so it is necessary that it first happens in the head . . .

PH: *But did the street of Léopoldville also make you want to make films?*
OS: Léopoldville, the Congo river . . . I do not analyze myself, but many things struck me: I saw Kisangani, Mbandaka, and all that, and thought that only cinema could express them. You have to note that everything is full of contradictions. I left here, but I never made films on this subject and on what I had seen . . .

PH: *The river is very present in* Emitai *. . .*
OS: This is not enough, it might have been one day, but . . . In any case, what is important now is not how I approached cinema at the time. What interests me today is whether there is African cinema that is more dynamic than my own.

PH: *Is that why you returned?*
OS: Zaire is the great absentee from African cinema, yet something important is going on here, and I am not even talking about the social or political organization. Zaire is almost a continent, four times the size of France, and it can therefore survive as a country and become a leader in attracting cinematography. For instance, there could be Carthage, Ouagadougou, and perhaps Kinshasa . . . It depends on the authorities; perhaps it would be a good thing.

PH: *You think more of Kinshasa than Brazzaville?*
OS: No! It doesn't matter which country does it; they just need to welcome us and we go there! Some situations are open. I was invited to Zaire, and if I had been in Brazzaville I would have told them the same thing.

PH: *Does the African premiere of* Ceddo *in Kinshasa represent something special?*
OS: One must take risks! The only problem is that here is the first place in Africa were *Ceddo* came, but no Zairian distributor wanted it, neither this film, nor any other! You have to be realistic; it had its role in events!

PH: *Did you have any contacts with Zairian distributors?*
OS: There are no Zairian distributors; I did not see any. There are only cinemas where the Belgians operate a sub-distribution . . . Little did I

know that Zaire is the richest sub-Saharan country, apparently with over a hundred fifty theatres, and that Kinshasa has more than fifty cinemas! What I saw is that these theatres are very badly maintained, and kept in the same conditions of the colonial times; there has been no improvement.

PH: *You are leaving. What are you going to take away as the most precious thing of this city?*
OS: I bought many objects! But I could always come back in five or ten years. I am not disappointed! I met filmmakers, writers, painters, theatre people; we spoke about African culture and whether at this delicate moment there still is production or creativity. I hope I have been able to initiate or awake something, to create desires. Zairian culture needs to be stimulated and I only offered a push in the right direction! One must lead by example so that people can get on with it themselves!

PH: *What about your personal impression?*
OS: My personal impression is that it is a large country with an enormous potential that is yet to be used . . . They lack, I think, something like a locomotive. Creation, this work, is an individual problem; it is not a problem of regime, and it is true that you need money, but you also need convinced and determined men.

PH: *What advice would you give to these individuals, young filmmakers for example?*
OS: First they have to put together their individualities in a group and have a single objective: to want to make cinema. Cinema is the result of collective work. One has an idea, my idea is good, and from then on you find yourself with three or four others and start modestly trying.

PH: *Is there an organization of filmmakers in Zaire?*
OS: Yes, which at some point had difficulty to breathe like a puffing engine. Perhaps the motor was badly run? But there we have just pushed it up the top of the mountain. Let us hope that it will start descending!

PH: *A parenthesis, you sometimes mentioned a film on Simon Kimbangu.*
OS: I do not want to make a "Simon Kimbangu" [film], but I think that the man revolutionized something. Perhaps there were people like

him in other countries, perhaps he has followers in Senegal, but nobody suffered like him. In Bénin, the Ivory Coast, and Cameroon, people left the Catholic or Protestant church to create their own church; the revolt took place inside the Church.

PH: *Does the theme of revolt and suffering attract you?*
OS: Suffering is not a pleasure. I do not particularly like martyrs, but I like the lucidity of this average man who was able to create something and fight for his dignity and respect. We need to recall the situation in which the native of that time found himself, his intellectual and cultural level, and his limits: he had no freedom and was imprisoned in his own place . . . At the time it was easier to attack the colonists than the Church, which was really the good conscience of the colonial system: one could attack colonialism, and even request indulgence from the Church; but to attack the Church, one would still have to have faith in one's actions! Today, a man like Simon Kimbangu, who was the grandfather and father of so many revolutionaries and militants, interests us very much.

PH: *Let's jump to another subject. Were you marked by any childhood memory? The slap of a teacher?*
OS: I do not think so. Really, I'm not looking for childhood memories; I think we have to move on. Perhaps later in life I might try . . . I had a happy childhood like everyone else. My father was a man of the church, I suppose he was a good man.

PH: *What dissuaded you from religion?*
OS: I do not know, really, you know, at the moment. I try not to analyze the why of these things; perhaps I could return to religion tomorrow. Man is a God to me—what's good and bad here is man. Right now this is where I am, and the present is what matters to me.

PH: *When you realized that there was a need to make cinema, Congo was certainly not the only factor, was it?*
OS: I wrote many poems to portray the events of Lumumba, for example, but who gave a shit? Who did I write for? Writing in French, sure, but I was not satisfied. Literature can only touch a few people, but cinema goes further. People go to cinema all the time.

PH: *In* Voltaique *and* The Docker *the characters go to the cinema.*
OS: But I always go to the cinema! I spent almost half of my childhood at the cinema. People from my generation know it. Even in Casamance I went to the cinema and until now, when I go there with my generation, we laugh because I used to show off about never paying, I sneaked in, which was called "to burn the cinema". . .

PH: *Did your father agree?*
OS: You know, my father was special; he was a funny man.

PH: *Talking about cinematographic creation, which procedure do you follow?*
OS: I have an idea, something that inspires me, and I work on the point, deepen it, and expand it, to create a different reality.

PH: *There are also visual motifs in your work—for example the tree, the baobab, or the cheese maker—which recur with certain insistency.*
OS: I like trees! But we need punctuation, we look for metaphors, we couldn't refer to bell towers like a Western country, or to railways that come by to punctuate the hour . . . There is a way to punctuate the day, and I search for a punctuation, which can determine and signify . . .

PH: *To locate and authenticate.*
OS: Not to authenticate, but to locate, perhaps, that's it . . . When the camera revolves around the tree in *Mandat,* one day has gone by; in *Emitai* people are under the tree, that is time going by infinitely . . . The story unfolds, I think, within twenty-four hours, but the tree there signifies the infinite time of the dialogues.

PH: *Most of your films are strictly set in time and space.*
OS: First, that allows to save money. I have to think about how to make a cinema whilst economizing on time, work, and money . . . Changing decorations, costumes, or seasons takes the means! For example, where we saw the harvest in *Emitai,* it took me two years. I had to film one year the women's harvests with my actresses, and then we could film the rest within the following year, because at the time I filmed *Emitai* the harvest in the rice plantations needed to be finished; otherwise we

wouldn't have had anybody, everyone would have been on the fields . . . The problem then was to support my actresses for one year; it was necessary to maintain them financially, not to discourage them . . .

PH: *I suppose that you really care about the idea of team spirit.*
OS: We always went with Cartisan and Ibrahim Barro, it took twenty-four hours in Zinguinchor and back to Dakar. Sometimes they would leave me in Zinguinchor, I get on well with them . . .

PH: *Are they the pillars of your team?*
OS: Yes, with Vieyra, since *Borom Sarret.*

PH: *How does it work?*
OS: There is everything, because these men are not sheep!

PH: *Do you have to face problems that are specifically African?*
OS: Many, it is not just about being able to fix the camera when you are one or two thousand kilometres away from the capital, where you have nothing anyway apart from a connection in Europe where you could quickly repair the camera! There is no electricity where you shoot, so it is necessary to create some, to invent some . . . The sun! People say that there is enough of it, but the sun is tiring! And it needs to be said, the black is the most "blanched,"—with the sun it blackens even more, so it is necessary "to bleach" the face to find its features . . . But we also keep our secrets!

PH: *Do you follow the working plan?*
OS: I modify it a lot; sometimes I even rearrange the order of the shooting according to the possibilities. The problem of the screenplay is easy, I am in a room or an office and dream of all I want as the decor, and without knowing it, I do studio work while shooting "the cinema in an open sky." This is a chapter of my book. What I have seen in my "laboratory" is no longer at the level I am. I could dream, idealize a decoration, a feature, or a landscape, but when I am there, I have to acknowledge that the condition of the place has changed. I have to use it wisely, and the terrain is the infantry, which I use as a weapon.

PH: *Is an enormous discipline necessary?*
OS: I write the screenplay, find the location, and can modify it at once, before shooting, but while changing I need to inform the others.

PH: *The shooting seems to be very hard.*
OS: You pass out, but we love this work!

PH: *You often speak of the need to have a great cinematographic culture.*
OS: For me it is a question of aesthetics, it is necessary to take the short cut of history . . . Some cars are, so they say, tropicalized or adapted to African countries, but the principle of the engine is the same, and so it is with the camera and great filming. It relies on the sensitivity of a public who loves the big cinema and contributed something to us. To ignore it would mean to escape, so I say: we can only gain from knowing the classics of world cinema!

PH: *But here the public does not know the classics.*
OS: It is still too early; filmmakers have to know them first. When we will have enough film clubs and libraries, the enthusiasts will know of them. The French know them because of people like Moussinac, Sadoul, or Langlois; cinema does not only evolve through the people who make films, but also through the intellectuals who act in-between the public and cinema.

PH: *Is criticism essential?*
OS: Criticism yes, but there are the others . . . Langlois was not a critic. He did enormous things, all of us know it. He did a lot for us from the beginning. I no longer remember the dates, but he organized one week of African cinema in the Cinemateque . . . Then we had meetings with him in Florence, Naples, at the UNESCO. He did a lot for the Cinemateque in Algiers, in Carthage . . . The only thing I did not agree with is that he always wanted to honor me!

PH: *Did you know Melville?*
OS: Ah yes, Jean-Pierre! He was a funny guy, a recluse. It is a pity that French cinema did not understand or entirely appreciate him, and he had to make his films against winds and tides . . .

PH: *Have you met him at a festival?*
OS: When somebody fascinates me with his work and I know he has something to teach me, I ask to see him. Likewise in literature, why not? When I have difficulties and what I want to do is . . . When I wanted to make cinema, I went to see Sadoul and Daquin . . . Daquin gave me an appointment at seven o'clock in the morning; I had coffee at his place. He told me what he had to say and I was satisfied.

PH: *Did other filmmakers teach you anything?*
OS: There was one, an old man whom I had the fortune to meet very old, Charlie Chaplin; he told me that everyone could do this job, but that it is very demanding. I think that was in London, after the story with McCarthy, well before I got into cinema. I was over there for a trade-union conference; I was still far from cinema . . . He was the only guy who you couldn't see in bars, nightclubs, or at receptions. He told me one had to stay at home and work, and I got the same response by Roger Martin du Gard when he was in Marseilles at *Cahiers du Sud* (*Books of the South*).

PH: *I have the impression that the loners fascinate you.*
OS: But the work of creation, a significant reflection on given subjects, requires this loneliness. One should not even answer the journalists.

PH: *Roger Martin du Gard, Chaplin, Melville: are they roughly part of the same family?*
OS: I do not know. I needed to know them, after I knew Senghor, Birago Diop, Césaire, Ousmane Socé Diop, Frantz Fanon, Richard Wright . . . I was new and I had to learn everything from each of them. It really does not bother me to learn from others. I always told myself that it is through contact with others that I would be formed. The people who taught me are all different . . . In Moscow I met other writers and filmmakers, in America, the same thing, the Japanese too, and Kurosawa was in Munich, and so on . . .

PH: *In* Ceddo *one might think of a Japanese influence.*
OS: Maybe, maybe . . . But the influence by others, when it is good, I like it! You know, it is very difficult to reinvent things. It is necessary

to know, and it is necessary to go through this training period, as the others will teach you little by little.

PH: *I suppose that you believe that filmmakers have an intense relationship towards literature or writers.*

OS: I saw many young people who want to make films and really believe in cinema—it is not a reproach—but my concern is that sometimes they are very weak in literature. There is a problem with culture in general, and first with their own culture, which they have ignored to an extent that they have not been brought up in a purely African culture, but neither in an European one. These young people are in a state of redemption (I dare not say "unrootedness"). If they want to close the loop and return to something, a synthesis, they need knowledge broader than others . . . A deeper knowledge of these two cultures allows them to end the tearing apart.

PH: *And the writer can contribute to . . .*

OS: Yes, both, both. The man of letters often has a lyric knowledge of literature, he is familiar with words, and he often has better observational qualities than some of our filmmakers. The filmmaker knows the techniques well, but he is not able to write a screenplay.

PH: *Would writers dramatize and visualize more than filmmakers?*

OS: At the moment, yes. How many filmmakers, in France, in Europe, are the authors of their screenplay? Their first work is often a story that they carry about inside and manage to bring to the screens, but when it comes to their second and third one, they realize that they had already said it all in the first work! But they know all the techniques.

PH: *Do filmmakers have ultimately not enough relations with their entourage?*

OS: They are poorer than writers and less spoiled . . . Writers are often professors. They have a job, whilst most filmmakers are not really paid; they do not have an income.

PH: *In Zaire are all filmmakers civil servants?*

OS: Zaire is a special case. They had television before they had cinema. As soon as the Zairians had finished their studies to make cinema, to take responsibilities in a production, television drew them in, and from there on it was difficult. With television one becomes a fly in a cobweb. There is a contradiction between the State and creativity, because the State has a fixed idea of what has to be television, not *the* television but *their* television . . . Once inside, it is difficult to get rid of it!

PH: *Do you think that here filmmakers cannot use television as a tool of expression? Could the State also intervene in cinema?*
OS: Television is the most political box and everyone keeps an eye on it.

PH: *Should filmmakers turn their backs to the State?*
OS: I do not know! I do not have to tell African filmmakers what to do. I have no recipe, and my dream is for there to be great African films, that can be [then] distributed . . . The topics, the subjects, the working methods, and the production don't really bother me at this stage. The essential thing is for African films to get priority in the African continent, and for our screens to be decolonized!

PH: *Would you really watch films on certain great African personalities, even very reactionary ones?*
OS: Yes, there are contradictions . . . If Mobutu wants to make a film he will do it. He has the means, he has the technicians, and, as it often is in cases like that, they are European mercenaries, the art intellectuals who come to make the film. It is always the mercenaries of certain men of culture, a self-elected left, who sometimes have the impertinence to say, "If I do not make it, a Black will do it"! We know them—I do not want to cite names—and we understood that in this field solidarity does not count for much . . . It is up to us Africans to battle on our grounds. When you see these people in Europe, they describe themselves as leftist and want to be even more revolutionary in the salons, but when it comes to Africa they behave like the last louts . . . The film mercenaries are numerous, they often come from the left, even the French left!

PH: *You are angry . . .*
OS: No, I just say that when we Africans are asked to make films, they—Mobutu or Senghor or Eyadema and the others—will find filmmakers to make films. That does not bother me; I would like to see these films . . .

PH: *A mercenary who does a film on Mobutu, using Zairian actors and technicians, could . . .*
OS: Don't find any justifications! We talk about a film on Mobutu, I say, "Why not us?" We have our own experiences with filmmakers who described themselves as leftists. I shall not mention any name, I am not talking about anybody but us, we know whom this is about, and he, he will know when he reads it, that's his business.

PH: *What do you currently think of a man like Rouch?*
OS: Nothing!

PH: *You returned to literature. You are writing* The Last of the Empire. *What is it?*
OS: You'll have to wait.

PH: *You also said that you were in Zaire for volume 3 of* Harmattan.
OS: Yes, I am looking for elements, but I do not want to talk about my projects. These things are personal to me. I do not have to discuss . . .

PH: *You talked about loneliness, which is necessary for relevant thought. What are your other needs as a creator?*
OS: Nothing. My family, that's all.

PH: *You sometimes say that the theatre is your family.*
OS: That is my African family—elastic, everything there is my theatre—but I have my individual family, my small family, and they do not derange me. I am there; I am in my family. I am ultimately not isolated. I can come and go whenever I want. I feel that I am associated to people whom I need and who I know need me . . .

PH: *Do you have manias as a writer?*
OS: No, I have a large Waterman. It goes back to all that and is a pleasure to hold. It takes time to change the feather when it breaks; when I change the feather, I have difficulties adapting to the new feather!

PH: *Let us return to cinema!*
OS: Is it not finished yet?

PH: *No! You often insist on the question of identification, which leads to a cinema of heroes. Isn't there a danger? The heroes, don't they usually alienate spectators?*
OS: Which heroes? Pecos, Django? That is foreign cinema, which alienates us. The ability to identify yourself with someone, precisely, is creating our own heroes: many people want to be Django, and this is a complex identification . . . Why does an African spectator want to identify with Django? That is the problem, it is all there. We are wondering precisely what to do to leave him behind and restore his own heroes, which he doesn't know. Cinema that he is used to seeing does not show him in his context. So I think that is where our cinema has a role to play.

PH: *Do you believe that spectators want heroes other than those in karate films or Italian westerns?*
OS: If I agree on this reading, well! We just have to let the fight for independence and economy happen. I say, Europe has stopped bringing us something on a moral and spiritual level . . . What remains is obviously the technique.

PH: *And a certain number of evils . . .*
OS: Yes, perhaps some words.

PH: *I wanted to say accidents . . .*
OS: But we would have the accidents even without a car! Although, I don't want to say that all our evils come from Europe. There has also been African feudalism, which was stopped at a certain moment but was displaced and was doubled by the Senegalese tirraleurs, the colonial army, the civil servants who demeaned themselves to become a privileged class, the auxiliaries of the colonial system . . . We have our evils! For me . . . But it would be necessary to read my book; these are all the problems I covered there.

PH: *When will we read your book on cinema?*
OS: I hope that Présence Africain will publish it the next year.

PH: *So who would the positive hero of African cinema be?*
OS: I do not know, it is up to the public to . . .

PH: *A girl like Dior in* Ceddo, *isn't she likely to risk comforting spirits that are weaker than hers? When she kills, the spectator does not need to go so far . . .*
OS: It is very difficult . . . I do not think so, I do not think so . . . The weak spectator, but the other, the powerful spectator . . . That can provoke reactions in many senses . . . The cinema that was given to us did not provide any solution to social problems. Cinema cannot solve anything alone . . . You write about cinema and think that African cinema has to go further than others, but really, you are deluded and you delude us!

PH: *You are a soldier among other things.*
OS: I would not say that we are soldiers; we are creators; that is all. The creators and the French cinema have gone far since the Bastille, and France is always in search of what no one will really come to tell us: this is African cinema, this is how it should be.

PH: *But the social function that the European cinema lacked, the passage from oral history to cinema that you often talk about, will it possibly allow it?*
OS: I do not know; it is difficult for me . . . Everything is possible in Africa, but I am not a dreamer. I do not confuse bladders for lanterns.

PH: *In your films you are looking for new symbols, or symbolic situations. Do you think that the spectator is ready to read them?*
OS: If they are explained to him, yes. The same goes for French cinema, all the cinemas in the world. The critics, everyone who writes and reflects on cinema, beginning with Africa. For two days, we have seen the press here talk about cinema . . . Finally, to summarize in one sentence all of the problems that bother me, I demand that governments have a policy on culture, within which we would have the cinema and work on it. From there on things would happen. All the rest interests me less and less—I do not say that by pedantry . . . Certain questions from journalists are always losing me . . .

PH: *In what sense?*
OS: Always asking if I think African cinema should be like this or that . . . It is difficult to say how it should be; we all have our demands on how African cinema needs to be. That is not enough. It is also necessary for filmmakers to argue with their people and determine

a well-defined cultural policy, and within this framework we can then handle cinema. No relation with Godard's cinema!

PH: *But it could happen as it happened with television, which is part of a policy . . .*
OS: Everything is part of the risk. It is not because Godard made films that May was something . . . You should ask Rouch, Enrico, we were all together in May '68. I witnessed assemblies in the street of Vaugirard, but I have never heard as many stupid things as in these meeting. It was worse than under the palaver tree! Politically! It was about the role of filmmakers in society . . . They knew their profession really well. They worked well, but the pretension they wanted to give to cinema by forgetting the social aspect, by forgetting others, was absurd.

PH: *Why is a militant cinema, for example, difficult to support?*
OS: I leave the effort to judge to the French!

PH: *I will not talk about Samory . . .*
OS: Don't talk about Samory! We will leave and you'll close your shop!

PH: *I still have three or four . . .*
OS: Three questions and then it is finished, but don't let us go back to Samory. Let us only talk about my stay. There are things I do not want to speak about; I want to write them!

PH: *A summary of the Senegal experiment could be useful for us . . .*
OS: We do not want for Senegalese cinema to become a myth.

PH: *You had fights?*
OS: Yes, we always fight, but there are ups and downs . . . Now we think we are in the bottom of the wave, compared to what we did four years ago.

PH: *What did you do?*
OS: It was the first time we produced five full-feature films, and since *Xala* we only produced *Ceddo*, so I was the only producer, well! What caused this interruption? We are still searching.

PH: *Have these films been depreciated in Senegal?*
OS: Some have. Others, but not all, were a flop; we are looking to improve our work.

PH: *You did very important work on the distribution.*
OS: Yes, this is a pleasant experience, but it is not enough for us, though our distribution has to be nationalized 100 percent.

PH: *It is said that the UGC . . .*
OS: In the two first years, the UGC represented a great power. They controlled the theatre halls and the distribution. They established certain things, but there have been changes. There is now a general president-director who is in Dakar.

PH: *A French man?*
OS: No, no, no! There are no more French; we threw them all out of the door! And I hope that it will not be a bad thing . . . Currently we control the cinema ourselves, and the domain of culture. We made a huge leap; films can now circulate freely, and if they are not censured the public is there.

PH: *You work a lot with the tax.*
OS: Yes, tax can help us, and also government aid funds . . . But we are still not satisfied. We hope that the next meeting with the filmmakers will allow us to say what we have done and what we still have to try to do.

PH: *So, since the distribution belongs to you, you only made one or two full-feature films?*
OS: Yes, there are internal problems, problems with possibilities, political problems. For example the national production and distribution company, whose president was Korka Sow, who established the basis of these films, was dissolved by the government . . .

PH: *It is recent then, and for what political reasons?*
OS: Yes, it is very recent. It is difficult to say why, because they did not consult us. But our concern is to see our problems from inside; we will see and we will hand the results of our research to the press. We will reflect . . .

PH: *Do you have a very tight meeting schedule?*
OS: We do not have any rules. We are as free as artists can claim to be, and we are only responsible for our tools and what we make of our work.

PH: *Do you have a journal of cinema?*
OS: No.

PH: *Is cinema a topic in* Kaddu?
OS: Yes, criticisms. It is the public who writes them, in Wolof. It is about African films . . .

PH: *A film like* The Mandat, *how many copies exist in countries other than in Senegal?*
OS: Ah—I do not count that. You have to ask the lab; I do not know. The film was everywhere—in the Soviet Union, Eastern European countries, Cuba . . .

PH: *Did you cover your expenses even without Senegal?*
OS: Yes, same thing with *Xala*. *Emitai* had many difficulties; it was an unwanted child, but it now begins to exist for Africa. We will see what it will give.

PH: *I do not dare to ask more!*
OS: You are nice!

PH: *A last question with one word for an answer: where is Africa going?*
OS: *[Sembène is already on his way to take a shower and says very emphatically:]* Towards Scientific Socialism!

Interview with Ousmane Sembène

ROLF RICHTER/1978

WE HAD THE CHANCE to meet and talk to Ousmane Sembène in Moscow, as we attended the press conference for of his movie *Ceddo* and were permitted to read the director's notes on it. We provided this information for the film und television industry.

RR: *First of all, we were interested in finding out why an African author decided to become a director.*

OS: Film helps us to understand reality the way it is. I want to talk to my people and speak to everyone, regardless of the color of their skin, via my films. Since the majority of Africans are illiterate, I need film to reach the majority of the population. It would be impossible to do that with literature at the moment. Films are not the privilege of the elite. Therefore, it is the most important form of art that we have in Africa at the moment. It is a political form of art, which addresses the people.

RR: *What is the situation of African cinema at the moment, in your opinion?*

OS: The process which we might term "the birth of African cinema" has not yet been completed. We have come closer to that objective, but there are still many obstacles to master. At the moment there still is no African cinema, but there are cinematographies of African people, which are more or less developed. Each has its own form and issues. This does not mean, however, that African filmmakers avoid the issues, which

---

From *Film und Fernsehen*, vol. 6, no. 2 (1978). Translated from the German by Gabi Schneider. Reprinted by permission of Erika Richter.

move the world—the fight for peace and disarmament. That is also true for the problem of neocolonialism, which concerns the whole of Africa. Nevertheless, we emphasize presently the particular national problems of each ethnic community. In Africa there is a multitude of ethnic communities, and each speaks its own language, has its own traditions and customs. Each wants to have a cinematic style of its own and uses it to help define itself. Before cinema came to Africa, the ethnic communities were separate from each other. Films helped them to get to know each other. I don't know any African filmmaker or cinematographer who dares approach the problems that concern the whole continent at the moment. A particular obstacle for any director who would want to do so would be the linguistic differences that still exist in Africa. In order to be able to speak to the whole continent, the filmmakers have to create their own language with images that are understandable to the masses. Thus they would have to use symbols and values that emerge from cultures of all the different ethnic communities that existed for this language.

At the moment we are in the process of changing the style of African films. This process will be a slow and careful approach—no revolution and certainly not a technical one. We want to create a film style in accordance with the current stages of development in the African society. That way our problem is a political one. We are not interested in individual problems, but in questioning the whole population. First and foremost, we are interested in starting a political dialogue with the audience. That is how our films differ from the European films—the French ones for example.

RR: *How does the audience in Africa react to the films? What impact do they have?*

OS: The common people understand difficult issues, too, because it is about their problems and therefore not as difficult as it might look at first sight. Rhythms, objects, the actors' gestures are familiar and meaningful to them and thus an important utility. It is impossible to understand African cinema in its variety and complexity without studying the history and culture of the African people. You have to know which myths, symbols, and metaphors the African filmmakers use as their repertoire. Sometimes a director makes a film in a language which is spoken by approximately a million people. However, he addresses the film to an audience of two hundred million. He wants to tell the other ethnic communities too what problems he, as a representative of his people, is facing and what happiness and morals symbolize in his opinion. He also wants to be understood. That is why it is our task to create a standardized language of images. So far, we have not really thought about all this. Since we have now learned the basic knowledge of filming, we have to start to seek the fundamentals of that new culture. That is why I do not object anymore to the term "African cinema" as diligently as I used to do. The onset is taking place at the moment, and it is not because the government encourages it but is due to the work of filmmakers.

I would like to add a comment on the reception of African films in Africa: when African films are shown in Africa, the cinemas are full. I know many people who can describe every single scene of my films. The visual experience is very strong. Europeans, whose knowledge of Africa is only limited, often think that our films are not typically African but they do not seem to understand them. This is not a bad sign. It just means that as long as they do not understand these films, they do not understand Africa.

RR: *African films are not freely shown in Africa.* Ceddo, *for instance, has not yet been shown in Senegalese theatres. Is this due to economic or political censorship?*

OS: Both. There is economic and political censorship. If African filmmakers are scared, they begin to censor their own films. If they are not scared, it is possible to go to extremes. However, it is up to the filmmakers to make use of this right. It is they who show the problems to the people.

As far as economics are concerned, if you have come up with an issue that is good enough for a film, you begin to think about money. That is where it begins to get difficult. You order the material and the technology you need for filming from France, you shoot your film, and then you go back to France to finish the film there. In Africa there is no film industry or processing laboratories. Apart from that, we are directors and set designers simultaneously and have to edit our own films. That is why they express our individuality, our way of perceiving the world, and all of our demands and hopes to a great extent.

As soon as the film is finished, we return to Africa. Thereafter the films have to be distributed, which is a problem again. The production and the distribution are two things that are so terribly difficult here. You have to get the money first, and then you have to organize the marketing. To create a film is not difficult. I have so many ideas that I could make a film every year, but I do not have the money to do so. In order to shoot *Ceddo*, I had to mortgage my wife's house and had to borrow money from friends and even from my children.

I love cinema, the power it has. That is why you have to make a lot of sacrifices. Eventually the film is made. It exists and has become a political film. However thereafter censorship interferes and forbids the film from being shown. When I go back to Senegal, I will have to begin to fight for *Ceddo*, and the right to portray the film. We have to find solutions for these problems in Africa. Certainly sometime in the future it will be possible to run African films in Africa too. It is important that progressive countries buy our films, even if it still is difficult for African films to find their way to the audience in Europe. It is important to get in contact with this audience. It is not only important that the films are viewed, but they should also provoke discussions.

RR: *You are interested both in historical and contemporary subjects. Is this linking of the past and the present your agenda?*

OS: Yes, it is my agenda. History is of great relevance to the present. The children learn history in school, but from our point of view today, the history taught in schools has to be corrected and revised. Africans have to study each event in history very closely. Africans call upon their friends to understand this endeavor. You cannot create something new without considering the past. After all, there is hardly a continent which has had to endure that many atrocities in the last centuries. Each people has to go their own way of liberation, and for Africa this means that the past has to be taken into account too.

RR: *What role does the influence of France and other western European countries play?*

OS: Europe is frustrated by Christian culture. It has ceased to be a model for Africa. For a long time we believed that Europe with its laws and taboos was an exemplary society. However, this society is frustrated now and to get rid of this frustration it claims that this is an expression of freedom. There are many unemployed people and many prostitutes in the bourgeois world. This is also a moral problem. You would say to a woman that she prostitutes herself, sells her body—this is true to an even greater extent for the worker, who is subject to the worst form of prostitution: he has to sell his workforce. This is why directors do not follow these idealistic social norms anymore.

Many Africans feel inferior because they think that you have to have a Greek nose in order to be beautiful. However, one can be beautiful with a flat nose as well. Europe is not a model for me anymore.

[Ousmane Sembène commented on the problems pertaining to the presentation of violence and sexuality in films.]

OS: Violence is part of our lives. It does not exist alone. In Europe it exists in the form of violence carried out by individuals who do so in order to survive. Films show men who break laws and isolate themselves from society. They are not interested in the community, but how they, as individuals, can survive. Contemporary Europe reminds me of a basket full of crabs. Each of these crabs wants to survive. Imagine how they crawl over each other, tread on each other because they are all trying to get on top, climb out, and then survive.

In Africa people have to fight too in order to survive, but human dignity is always a priority. This fight is different. Let's talk about sexuality, also. It is not necessary to show the sexual act—the presentation of the act is of no importance to the story of film. One can portray beautiful naked women and men, without the act of coitus, since that is no proof of creativity. We know how children are made. The image of a penetrating penis has nothing to do with art. That is what dignity is all about.

RR: *Where and how do you study the art of filmmaking? Where do you look for inspiration?*

OS: The director most important to me is Sergei Eisenstein. His legacy is very important today. I am teaching young filmmakers in Senegal. They were trained in France, Italy, or in the U.S.A. but they only learned how to master the technique of filming there. They had no idea about how to use montage as a means of expression. The aesthetics of filmmaking remained a mystery to them. I gave them Eisenstein's essays about montage, and the world of cinematic art and thereafter great opportunities came their way. I have not mentioned montage by chance. The rhythm montage is of great importance to Africans. It encourages us to use it in order to express our great sensitivity to rhythm. The actor's gestures, too, are of great importance to us. The African cinema in the years to come will be far less superficial than it is today. The heroes of our films will have to speak less but with greater impact. We will learn that, too, from Eisenstein.

At the moment we are in a period of transition. Our most important objective at the moment is to establish a high cinematic culture in Africa. That is why we study the experience of filmmakers in the Soviet Union and progressive filmmakers from all over the world.

RR: *What is the situation for films like in Senegal? How many films are shot there per year?*

OS: Six films per year. That is not a small number, if you consider how low our budgets are. However, we do not give up irrespective of the number of obstacles.

It is important for us to realize how great our audience's knowledge and interest is in politics. The filmmaker must not fall short of his audience's expectations and interests. The Senegalese cinema is closely linked to its audience, and they determine the subject of the film as well as the means of expression used. The cinema is like a tunnel, whereby the director and the audience move towards each other. That is why, when we project our films, they are often followed by discussions. In this manner the audience takes part in making our films. It cannot take place differently because we have to deal with the people's vital questions, we have to create a problem, and we have to broaden the people's awareness. If art does not address the vital changes taking place at the moment and the explosive problems of today's society, art will become self-satisfied, careless, and sooner or later it will degenerate into commerce.

Interview with Ousmane Sembène

ULRICH GREGOR/1978

S: I have the distinct impression that the Catholic Church, whose origins are every bit as foreign as those of Islam, is achieving the very thing which the Islamic religion brought about: an effect of syncretism. In black Africa Islam established a kind of syncretism between paganism and the religion itself. The Catholic religion, represented by white missionaries, had a monopoly before independence. Now we have black bishops who preach to the sound of tam-tams and in their own language. They close their eyes to many things which religious purists would have condemned earlier on.

Q: *In your film the Catholic priest is shown as slightly less violent than the Imam.*

S: You cannot have two enemies at the same time. Even as it is, the Catholics in Senegal don't like the film. I don't think it's desirable to have the Church and Islam as opponents of the film at the same time.

Q: *How are religious faiths distributed in Senegal?*

S: About 70 percent of the population is Moslem, 15 percent are Catholics, the remainder are animists.

Q: *Do you think that the ancient African religions—fetishism for instance—are less totalitarian and violent?*

S: It is imprecise to talk about religion in this case; it is more a question of types of faith. Fetishism for example: these forms of faith enable a

---

From *Framework*, no. 7/8 (1978). Reprinted by permission by Ulrich Gregor.

social community to survive. It is not a question of the essence of what one believes or does not believe. There were very free religions. Africa cannot return to the past, going on living in this way. But through these forms of belief a feeling of brotherhood has nevertheless been handed down—a sense of solidarity, of social organization, which is still of great value today. Here Africa must make a very difficult decision. The civilisation of the Christian West must also be examined to see what it has produced upon which one could build further. The concept of democracy for example. The forms of life of our fathers and grandfathers are of no further use to our sons. We must produce a synthesis of the two—but how? I don't know that either. It is very difficult. We did not want to attack anyone in the film—but rather to reveal, in relation to a particular epoch, as against what is usually said: of course the West is responsible for much, but there is another kind of responsibility on the part of blacks themselves, their involvement in the slave trade, cooperation with the colonialists on the part of tribal leaders.

Q: *You show that in the film, you lay the responsibility to a large extent on the Imam and his machinations.*
S: No, the Imam does not talk to the Europeans, he doesn't like Europeans, that sort of coexistance never existed. I'm thinking of the entourage of the king, the prince, for instance. Because the king had accepted the presence of the whites.

Q: *We see two whites in the film. What is their function?*
S: One is a priest, the other a slave trader.

Q: *Was there no revolt against the slave trade?*
S: At one time slaves in Africa were a kind of currency. One group of Africans sold the other. That is hard and painful for us, but that's how it was. I believe today that Africans must get beyond the question of colour, they must recognise the problems which confront the whole world, as human beings like other human beings. If others undervalue us, that has no further significance for us. Africa must get beyond deriving everything from the European view. Africa must consider itself, recognise its problems, and attempt to resolve them.

Q: *When is the action of your film set, in the eighteenth or nineteenth century?*
S: I can't give a date. These events occurred in the eighteenth and nineteenth century and are still occurring.

Q: *Is there no fixed location either? And the language of the film?*
S: Wolof is spoken in the film, but it could take place in any part of Africa, at any time. At this very moment we are witnessing a war for areas of influence, a war of such vehemence that we must protest against it. It is a struggle for supporters. In many African countries, the state power depends on the power of the Imams, the Moslems, and there are religious communities in Africa, particularly in Senegal. where the Imam has much more power than the MP or the minister.

Q: *Is the population of this village all descended from one tribe? The features of the Imam seem to distinguish him from the rest.*
S: When Islam came across the Sahara into the countries of black Africa, its first representatives had lighter skin. But they married the daughters of kings, brought up their children. Islam very rapidly penetrated the social structure as I show in my film while the Catholic Church remained more on the surface.

Q: *The film often gives the impression of a stage play, particularly in the rich argumentative dialogue between the characters.*
S: Before we had a national assembly, that's how our public life was. You could address yourself directly to the king, talk to him, via some intermediary. Such a person has a loud voice, it explains everything but does not betray. With the spread of the Imams this ancient custom, of being able to address oneself directly to the king, was abolished. Perhaps that may seem a form of theatre. In African rural civilisation, however, people really did speak to their monarch in that way. Everything was dealt with in public; there were no decisions taken on the quiet. There were chosen speakers for individual groups, they were called spokesmen. In Senegal there were also spokesmen for the slaves.

Q: *Could you say something of the role of women in the film? It is after all the princess who has the courage to murder the Imam.*

S: Perhaps that is our modern spirit. Often in Africa it is only the men who speak, but one forgets the role, interest of women. I think the princess is the incarnation of modern Africa. She kills the Imam and for several reasons it is her right to do so: as a princess because he had killed her father and because the men had certainly talked a lot but have done nothing. There can be no development in Africa if women are left out of the account. In a modern Africa women can take part in production, education, but they are still refused the right of speech.

Q: *What are the prospects for the film's distribution in Africa?*
S: For the present it has been banned in Senegal.

Q: *You are both director and producer in this film.*
S: I prefer it that way; every time one makes a film of someone else's production one feels dissatisfied. *Xala* was produced by the national production company. But that wasn't very serious; there an attempt was made, but it ended up a fiasco. For the simple reason that there is no cultural policy in our country. You could organize a production, of course, it's not the fault of the director Corca Sow. Poor Corca did as much as he could. But behind him there's the administration. And, like it or not, a production company is dependent on the capitalist system. For *Ceddo* I got credit of 20 million from the government bank in Senegal.

Q: *How does censorship function in Senegal?*
S: There the censor and the inquisition. By the latter I mean the Politbüro, the politically responsible body which views films. And then there's the normal censor. They are officials whose job it is to judge a film. But they don't decide, they merely present their report to the prime minister. In the case of my film, however, it wasn't the censors but the politically responsible group who were decisive—from the Party and the government.

We can't understand the government's uneasiness. Officially Senegal is a secular state, even if the power of the Imam is very great. Here we're caught in a contradiction. The other Arab states in Africa have already made it quite clear that they can't show the film. The representatives of these countries are shocked by it. And they are often people who make out to be progressive. They cannot agree with the way in which Islam is portrayed in the film. However much assistance may be given to Africa by the Arab countries, Africans are quite clear among themselves that Islam is an imposed religion.

Q: *Is there any chance that the ban on the film may be lifted?*
S: Those responsible consider the film antireligious. So they are not even looking for a solution.

Q: *Your film* Xala *had difficulties too.*
S: That was the bourgeoisie. In Senegal eleven sequences had to be cut.

Q: *Apart from the problem of censorship, can your films be seen by the population anyway? What's the situation of the infrastructure of cinemas and distributors?*
S: My films aren't shown since the cinemas are controlled by the national distribution company. No progress has been made here at all. We've got the structures, it was nationalized, but things are the same as ever, and the conditions imposed on the African cinema are actually more difficult since nationalisation than they were before. The control exercised by the bourgeoisie over film is even stronger than in colonial times.

Q: *The African bourgeoisie takes no interest in the circulation of your films then?*
S: No, no. Perhaps they do want to support a certain kind of African cinema. But a cinema asking questions, raising problems—that they do not want. If I had made a film against Catholicism or an anticommunist film perhaps it would have been shown. But if I make a film about our own problems which is supposed to bring the viewer into an awareness of them, then they're against it. The African audience isn't even to be made to notice certain problems.

Q: *What will be the consequences of showing your film in Europe? Will it make an impression in Africa?*
S: There lies the weakness of African regimes allied with France. If you're in France everything you say gets reported in Africa. If you've got an article in *Le Monde* then the whole of the francophone Africa reads it, even the president of the Republic. If something appears in the German

press, then someone at the embassy cuts it out and sends it to the Ministry of Foreign Affairs. That can have a positive effect too. At the moment there are the Festivals of our allies. At present the European festivals are doing more for African film than the African governments.

Q: *Could at least your earlier films be shown in Senegal?*
S: *Emitai* is forbidden in all African countries. Only now, after the Paris opening, will the film perhaps come out in Africa. If the French have brought it out, then in Africa they'll close their eyes. If the film is on in Paris, Berlin, Moscow, or London and the press reviews it, that's good. It's part of the struggle for freedom of expression; even if we made some other kind of film, they wouldn't even take that—folklore or tourism films may be pretty but they don't contribute to the development of the cinema. Festivals like the Berlin 'Forum' try after all to contribute to the development of cinema in its progressive forms and content. And the African cinema can also learn from these experiments and experiences.

Q: *The film's music is very interesting.*
S: Actually it's not music. Manu Dibango recorded it in three days and nights specially for the film. With bottles . . . it's not music connected with dance—that would be the African criterion for music—, it's much more noises, rhythms, repeated. A harmony had to be established between sounds and rhythms. It wasn't supposed to be music in any sense resembling African, European, or American music. We were looking for music which would not, in any traditional sense, make the film more attractive. Africans have got used to the idea that African films always have to have traditional music. But we're trying to provide through the music a route to a world problematic, a sense of the world. The music should not be limited to Africa.

Q: *How many films per year are now produced in Senegal?*
S: Three or four years ago five were produced for the first time. They were the first in the history of film. But since then there has only been one more: mine. It has to do with the organization of our state—a capitalist state trying to be socialist. Senegalese film depends on the French company U.G.C. They provide the films—American, French, Italian. Everything goes via Paris. Compared with five years ago the

African film has also gone down numerically. Fewer and fewer films have been made over the last three years.

Q: *For what reasons?*

S: They are political. One should no longer think of Africa simply in terms of its colour—but like any other country. An African national leader can be just as fascist as any other.

In the Name of Tolerance: A Meeting with Ousmane Sembène

JOSIE FANON/1979

THE LAST FILM BY OUSMANE SEMBÈNE, *Ceddo,* has recently been screened for the first time in the movie theaters of Paris. The Senegalese have been waiting for the release for more than three years. *Ceddo* has been a victim of a de facto interdiction, the object of a bad linguistic quarrel provoked by the government of President Senghor; the film is therefore not accessible to those to whom the filmmaker had emphatically devoted it to. However, based on the tempered and controversial reactions to it, one can predict that the film will evoke such passionate responses between the Africans who have seen it in Paris that it will be finally distributed also in Senegal.

In *Ceddo,* a historical movie, history has been mistreated to some degree, Sembène Ousmane sacrificing it to symbolism and allegory, shortening several historic eras to one single anecdote. Are we in the sixteenth or seventeenth century? That's the first objection historians will necessarily make. Moreover, as the film deals with the penetration of Islamic religion in West Africa, one should have the right to ask the filmmaker: which interpretation of the role of the Islam do you want to give? A historical subject, of course, but also a current one. Sembène Ousmane talks to *Demain l'Afrique* about all of these issues and addresses first the motives behind the interdiction of the film.

From *Demain l'Afrique,* no. 32 (1979). Translated from the French by Annett Busch. Reprinted by permission of Olivier Fanon.

OUSMANE SEMBÈNE: The film is not really forbidden. It was subjected to the commission of cinematic control that made two recommendations: first, I had to declare that the film was not about current events; second, I had to change the spelling of the title, which meant replacing the two letter 'd's of Ceddo by one, following the issuing of a presidential decree. The commission of control declared itself overtaken by this matter. I protested because I consider that the highest authority, my government, is not empowered to give me counsel. The person that signed this decree as well as its counselors are illiterate in the matter.

JOSIE FANON: *You have therefore sacrificed the broadcasting of your film in Senegal to a question of orthography?*
OUSMANE SEMBÈNE: That's part of our internal problems. Actually, that could resemble a Byzantine quarrel but for us it's a matter of cultural nationalism. The ban, or in any case the intention of banning the film, refers to a language that is not taught, that has not the right to be quoted in Senegal. To prevent the broadcasting of a film under this pretext is an abuse of power. At the time I wrote an open letter to the President Senghor, and in the Senegalese press there was a big debate about the role of national languages. The University of Dakar published the first Senegalese dictionary and conceded to me on the question of the two 'd's. Nevertheless the film hasn't been screened.

JOSIE FANON: *One can therefore surmise that the film bothered the authorities. In what way?*
OUSMANE SEMBÈNE: I have no reason to believe that this film will raise the masses but it will possibly provoke some thinking on the current situation. It questions the problem of spiritual and temporal power. If one knows Senegal, one understands that nobody can come into power without the agreement of the religious leaders. To become minister or delegate, to gain a constituency, one addresses oneself to the religious brotherhoods, the marabouts. The fact that the head of state is a Catholic doesn't change anything. He is obliged to take them into account.

JOSIE FANON: *What is the meaning of the word "Ceddo"?*
OUSMANE SEMBÈNE: Those who are called to this day the Ceddo are not an ethnic group. It's a Pulaar word that designates in one way or

another those who resist slavery. That means those who "conserve the tradition." The Ceddo are "the people of refusal." One finds the spirit of the Ceddo just as much among Muslims as Catholics.

JOSIE FANON: *Your film itself seemed to me exactly that: a refusal, a rejection of Islam, a description of the negative aspects of the penetration of Islam into West Africa. Do you not think that* Ceddo *risks being interpreted in this way, in particular in the Muslim African countries?*
OUSMANE SEMBÈNE: That would suggest that the film has not been understood or that I have poorly expressed myself. It's not about Islam in essence but the use that has been made of it in the face of an ignorant mass. If I had wanted to do a critique of Islam, I would have focused on the verses of the Koran. I don't ever do that. We need the courage to look things in the face. At the moment we see the leaders of African states playing with religion. We must have the courage, in a secularist state, to assign limits to the spiritual leaders. My deepest fear is that we should fall into the hands of a right wing power that would use religion.

JOSIE FANON: *On two occasions a character in the movie declares that no faith is worth the life of a man.*
OUSMANE SEMBÈNE: I said and repeat it: No faith is worth the life of a man. Neither Allah nor God is worth the life of a man. For me, all religions are on the right.

JOSIE FANON: *The character of the Catholic priest in* Ceddo, *seems to be privileged compared to the imam. This could mean you prefer the Catholic religion to Islam. Was this your intention?*
OUSMANE SEMBÈNE: This is a subjective, superficial vision, a wrong vision of the character of the Catholic priest. I didn't make a film on the Catholic religion. This is not my problem and not the problem of Senegal or West Africa. In the film the priest is there alongside the arms dealers. I wanted to show the existence of three forces: Islam, the Catholic religion, and the merchants. Two religions, of these Islam having penetrated the furthest. Besides, in *Ceddo*, the death of the imam doesn't mark the end of the Islam. On the contrary, the priest has a vision of a black church, but his dream won't come true. We assist with the death of the Catholic religion and the rise of Islam. Once again, the Catholic

religion isn't our problem. And Islam as a religion isn't in charge, the last image of the film, when Princess Dior, after the murder of the imam, passes in the midst of the disciples, indicates quite obviously the continuity of this religion. What's at issue is the abuse of Islam in West Africa at a given period.

JOSIE FANON: *What does Princess Dior Yacine represent? At the end of the film, when she kills the imam, she symbolizes the popular revolt but in other moments she appeared to be a passive character.*
OUSMANE SEMBÈNE: No, this is not a passive person. She is the reflection of her education; she is confident of her rank, her role, but she was able to change along the way. It is necessary to avoid falling into the error of believing that people cannot change. The character of Princess Dior is also a wink at modern times. The liberation of Africa won't be made without women. But that does not mean the participation of women during the revolution amounts to firing a shot and then returning to the kitchen. The last scene of the film also shows that whichever system and power comes to be, women will remain.

JOSIE FANON: *Out of the seven films in your cinematographic oeuvre,* Ceddo *seems be something different. Does it correspond to new research?*
OUSMANE SEMBÈNE: I very much like what I did in this film. Without being pretentious, I would say that the writing corresponds to what I wanted to do: to strip Africa of all these structures one is always surrounded by, the plants, the bananas, the mangos. Trying, if it's possible, to show the heart of man, the kernel with its contradictions, so that the film could be used as an element of reflection, or an introduction to thinking about ourselves, what we've done, what we want to do. Reflection and not gratuitous criticism, because we are responsible for the past, for the good as well as for the bad things. We are also responsible for the neocolonial presence in our country. The arms dealers are still the same. Formerly, our land was occupied but at least we kept our traditions. Today, they still exploit us economically but they also colonize us even in our homes on a cultural level, with television, cinema, the western press. And we accept it.

JOSIE FANON: *How you do see yourself politically in Senegal?*
OUSMANE SEMBÈNE: My pretension is to be a Marxist.

JOSIE FANON: *Do you think that the broadcasting of the film in France will help to annul its ban in Senegal?*
OUSMANE SEMBÈNE: The risk is worth the trouble to me.

JOSIE FANON: *Do you have other film projects? Or participation in festivals?*
OUSMANE SEMBÈNE: I'm dreaming of other films. As for festivals, I rarely leave Senegal. I came to Paris for a few days to promote *Ceddo* but normally I hardly move. I have just finished a novel, *Le Dernier de l'Empire*, which retraces the events of the birth of the Senegalese bourgeoisie. It will be published next year.

JOSIE FANON: *Which publisher?*
OUSMANE SEMBÈNE: In Paris, Presse de la Cité.

JOSIE FANON: *What's your opinion on African cinema?*
OUSMANE SEMBÈNE: Courageous men do it. Crazy men. You have to be crazy to make films in Africa, especially in the current context. All African films pose the problems of African societies. That means they have an elevated political conscience. You see, what's missing in Africa is not dialogue and tolerance. We speak of Arab-African dialog, for example. Africans have to start talking to each other. I prefer to speak of a dialogue of African cultures. This is also a project on the theme of "Islam and black culture" being studied in association with Unesco in Paris. Islamic scholars from Egypt, Maghreb, and black Africa will be invited.

Samori: The Last Grand Oeuvre of Sembène Ousmane

ALIOUNE TOURÉ DIA/1986

BINGO: *When can we see the first scenes of your film about Almamy Samori Touré?*

SEMBÈNE OUSMANE: Next year, we hope, depending on funds that begin to come in. Considering the ambition and the scale of film, we solicited contributions from all of the states, knowing that the states of West Africa were part of the Malinké territory. We have Gabon, where historically many things concerning Almamy happened (his exile). I contacted President Bongo to ask if we could shoot in Gabon. He gave his agreement. We also have promises from Cameroun and Congo. And I have to admit that it is thanks to the support of President Abdou Diouf that the film can be realized. It was President Abdou Diouf himself who wrote to the heads of state.

BINGO: *Where are you with the preparations?*

SEMBÈNE OUSMANE: We made some progress with photographs and video. Currently we are quarreling about the decoration. First I designed it on paper. In this kind of cinema, the architecture of the film has to be made. We got permission to shoot in the triangle of Guinea-Senegal-Mali. This is more or less the same landscape. We have an area of 50 km where we can install all we need and shoot the gunfire. We couldn't do it downtown because there is no studio. We also found some locations up

---

From *Bingo* (1986). Translated from the French by Arianna Bove.

there in Casamance (Senegal), where we began our work with installations and made some contacts with the inhabitants. Now we have to solve the question of catering for thousands of actors and observers.

BINGO: *Isn't it an adventure?*
SEMBÈNE OUSMANE: Sure, it is a great adventure. You can't shoot this film in only one town. History has more than one century.

BINGO: *When did you begin your preparations?*
SEMBÈNE OUSMANE: I began my research on Samori in 1962, so up till now, twenty-four years.

BINGO: *Why precisely Samori?*
SEMBÈNE OUSMANE: This is very difficult to say. These fragments of the life of Samori accompanied my whole life, without my being aware of it. I was raised by the Soce and Bambara. I think the first time I heard about Samori was in songs. Thereafter, as children in Dakar, we played games of Samori. Now, with our independence, there is some foundation for research programs on our history and our past. And there are symbolic characters we have to get to know and to analyze. I found myself more attracted to Samori. And the more I learned about the man, his time and companions, the more I got fascinated.

BINGO: *By Almamy?*
SEMBÈNE OUSMANE: By Almamy and his companions. We say Almamy, but one man by himself does not make history. I got to know Yves Person, the author of a thesis on Samori. We worked together because we did the same research on the same character. He taught me a lot. I was his only interlocator concerning unresolved questions. When you begin to study Samori more deeply, you will be fascinated by his courage, what he accomplished. He understood how to capture the attention of the sleeping intelligentsia, and to weld them together.

BINGO: *Yves Person, the French historian, did a remarkable thesis about Samori of almost 3,000 pages. He underscores the fact that the empire of Samori was not built to confront the whites but to answer to a crisis of the Malinké world, which was only partially and indirectly due to the influence of Europe. Do you share this opinion?*

SEMBÈNE OUSMANE: Yes. Samori came up at a crucial moment, at the end of slavery. It was inhuman. His mother was a slave. It's true, he didn't build his kingdom at this time. In 1880 he clashed with the colonial power. What people don't see is that the fall of the French Third Republic of Jules Ferry is due to Samori.

BINGO: *How was that?*

SEMBÈNE OUSMANE: At a certain moment, the Sudan campaign became a problem for France. The fight was so hard that the French soldiers weren't able to leave Senegal (Dakar and Saint Louis). They could not go to Sudan. The French admiral minister for the Colonies was ready to give up Sudan, because the French National Assembly and the president of the Republic refused to approbate a budget for Sudan. This is one reason. The resistance of Samori, the creation of the Samori Empire, is another one. With his experience and his men, he knew how to create a state, by treating them as equals. Maintaining resistance against the colonizers is another thing. The Samori Empire wasn't made to face colonialism.

BINGO: *What are your reasons for bringing Samori Touré to the screen?*

SEMBÈNE OUSMANE: I think we weren't taught our history. We hardly know anything about it. At some point cinema can be a kind of evening school. To show how these people lived, how they could resist and how they died, we can learn something there. The objective is that everybody can know these men, who, under very hard conditions, managed to do something extraordinary. We are doing something here that goes beyond our imagination. Everybody has to know his past. This is also an objective and a motive for satisfaction.

BINGO: *What audience do you have in mind?*

SEMBÈNE OUSMANE: Three types of spectators will see the film. First, all of the Malinké will identify with it. It is the sum of their whole history. And there are now those who follow and who are more or less satellites of the Mandinke groups. And those who nationalistically recognize that something was done by these men. Now, everybody thinks what he wants. This is also another problem, the concern about the unity of these men, the unity of the area, the unity of their common fight. How they spoiled the unity of this fight. We talk about unity nowadays. But what keeps Senegal, Guinea, and Mali from unifying with each other? We often forget that Samori and Ahmadou Tall were in contact; the son of Oumar Foutiyou Tall Samori also had contact with Habidou Tall, his second son, and also with Ba Bemba to create a united front. It is also forgotten that Alboury Ndiaye (Sénegal) left to establish a united front. Why didn't all these men, at a certain moment, know how to unite? The film will try to find an answer.

BINGO: *Almamy Samori Touré was often presented as a wild and sanguinary merchant of slaves, a cruel chief of war and sadist who exploited the conquered populations. What version is right according to you?*

OUSMANE SEMBÈNE: Most men from Faidherbe to Monteil were confronted with Samori. And never did they repeat such untrue things. They were their own historians. They themselves glamorized their own patriotism. And to justify their search for capital to fight Samori, for them it was necessary to depict him as barbaric. You have to contextualize him in his era. For example, in front of certain French forts, stakes with dead heads were arranged to frighten the Blacks. Nobody speaks about it. Now, to deny that at a certain moment Samori practiced the sale of people would be quite false. But you should know when and under what circumstances. When Samori created his first Faamaya Kingdom he abolished slavery. In 1892–93, he made more than 2000 km in the forest with his people, prosecuted by all the armies (French, English, German), and when he returned to Dijmini (in what is now the Ivory Coast) he realized that the only value of money was slavery. In this moment he behaved like an Attila. Samori displayed the characteristics of four types of men: Pierre le Grand, Charlemagne, Napoleon, and Attila. This is the image I can give. We do not make an apologia.

BINGO: *Do you accept the expression "pitiless realist" for Samori?*

OUSMANE SEMBÈNE: In the regimes at that time, the king had to merge the power of life and death. We heard about Samori killing his son. It is true. He killed his son Karamogho. It was him who introduced the French into the fields. Professor Joseph Ki-Zerbo pointed out: "When a Roman General (César) executes his son to benefit the nation, it's seen as patriotic heroism. When Samori did the same, they shout cruelty. Karamogho was ready to desert with a whole battalion. We can prove it now.

BINGO: *With all these death's-heads aligned at the entry of the French forts, won't the set design be grim?*
OUSMANE SEMBÈNE: We weren't searching for the macabre side of film. Our intention is the quintessence of this history. It is so easy to show blood in cinema. This is not our business.

BINGO: *Did Almamy Samori Touré also fight for religion?*
OUSMANE SEMBÈNE: There was a period when he fought for religion. Thereafter, he renounced, and then he converted again at the age of fifty at the court of the religious (Tidjanya and Quadrya at the time). It was a question of having temporal and spiritual power at the same time. He created a theocratic power, which was fatal for him. By the time he was between twenty and thirty years old, he had mixed up his society completely. But at the age of fifty, he introduced the "Sharia"; the worm had entered the fruit from the inside. He had not given up Islamization, but he showed himself more flexible under the pressure of an internal revolt, which lasted eighteen months.

BINGO: *This Islamist episode of your hero doesn't disturb you?*
OUSMANE SEMBÈNE: No. The man is fascinating. How a guy who started from nothing, a simple Dioula, a small merchant, could become Samori?

BINGO: *Is there, do you think, something common between Sekou Touré and the emperor of Wassoulou concerning their methods of control?*
OUSMANE SEMBÈNE: It was said that Samori was the grandfather of Sékou. Why is it important for us to know who is the son or the grandson of Samori! Essentially, it is that powerful men refer to the image of Samori. Indeed, Sekou Touré did copy a lot from Samori: the division of the Guinean Republic just like the Samori kingdom, the obligation of the ministers to live in the provinces, and this same kind of direct democracy. There are many similarities on an individual level between the two men.

BINGO: *You had good relations with Ahmed Sékou Touré?*
OUSMANE SEMBÈNE: Yes, as with all the African head of states. But nobody can say: "I gave money to Ousmane Sembène." This is all I'm interested in.

BINGO: *Honestly, has Sékou Touré promised you something for your film about Samori?*
OUSMANE SEMBÈNE: No. I never asked for money. When Sékou was there, I simply asked him to support the project as an interstate project and not as an Ousmane Sembène Ousmane project. With that in mind, the Senegalese state spent 600 million francs CFA for the film. The other states will give what they can. Their decision to participate is quite clear.

BINGO: *The new regime of Guinea is also engaged?*
OUSMANE SEMBÈNE: Completely. They even gave technicians to my disposition.

BINGO: *Which actor did you choose to play the role of Almamy Samori Touré?*
OUSMANE SEMBÈNE: I already have Sidiki Bakaba in the role of Morifindiang Diabaté who was the elder, the friend, the witness, the companion of deportation, and the alter ego of Samori. It is a very difficult role. For the role of Samori, we have many young auditioning actors: a Senegalese, two Guineans, a Malian, a man from the Ivory Coast. Who will be Samori among these young comedians? We will try out all of them. There is also Myriam Makeba, who portrays the mother of Samori. That problem is resolved.

BINGO: *In which language will the actors express themselves?*
OUSMANE SEMBÈNE: The scenario is in French. But Professor Djibril Tamsir Niane translated the text into Malinké. There will be only one Malinké version, but some versions will be subtitled in English and French.

BINGO: *Does that mean that there is already a market of distribution?*
OUSMANE SEMBÈNE: Yes. French, English, and German television already agreed to program the film. The cinema version will last six hours, three two-hour episodes. For television, our ambition is to make a series

of twenty episodes. There will also be an international version of three hours for European televisions.

BINGO: *Don't you fear Western criticism because of the image you will give of Samori?*

OUSMANE SEMBÈNE: Personally, for a long time now the West has ceased to be my crucial reference. It is true that the West dominates culture and the market. That is a result of our weaknesses. But my jury is not the West.

BINGO: *It is certainly a major film, with characters from various African countries, but also from European countries. Which actors do you have in mind?*

OUSMANE SEMBÈNE: Obviously, Samori had contacts with the French, the English, and the Germans. He had a staff worthy of what we would today call a Ministry for Foreign Affairs. As for English actors, Peter Ustinov gave his agreement in principle. This is very helpful. His participation is not paid. He comes to work for one week only with one appearance of a little more than ten minutes. We will also have young actors. There will be fifty-five French actors, twelve English actors, five German actors, and thousands and thousands of African actors, including the all the extras.

BINGO: *You are used to working with amateurs, who don't have much experience. Will it be the same in this film?*

OUSMANE SEMBÈNE: The majority will be amateurs. It is slower, more difficult. But that gives me more satisfaction. The amateur is not an animal. When he understands the subject, he transmits what the director wants him to. And he has also his opinion to give. Professionals usually come only to repeat their dialogues and then go away. But the most difficult role I committed to Sidiki Bakaba. He plays the alter ego of Samori. Any actor can play a king. But to play a court jester, only Sidiki, with all his experience can do it. It is him who tells the story of the film.

BINGO: *You are a filmmaker deeply connected to the problems of history. Why such a passion for the past and the African traditions?*

OUSMANE SEMBÈNE: It's important to know the past. The past is nothing more than a reflection of the present or the future. The past interests me. But not only past. It has a great richness. The past of men like Samori has something identical to our time. In African history there are periods that we can't perfectly grasp today. There is the beginning of slavery, the installation of French rule, the assimilation, and in between all these times, there was the war of 1914–1918, the war of 1939–1945. At each period, an external event knocks against the wall of Africa. Africa cracks, changes. For me, without being a historian, I try to analyze these aftereffects. The period of Samori is rich because it was the end of slavery.

BINGO: *Some already see connections between your film and Alex Haley's* Roots. *What do you think?*

OUSMANE SEMBÈNE: My film should be a kind of evening school, a history lesson for the present. I hope that it also will exist in videocassettes, that it can be seen and serve the public for reflection. It is not a film that will revolutionize.

BINGO: *In the age of 63, isn't it crazy to throw all your economies and your money into one film?*

OUSMANE SEMBÈNE: What else can I expect from life? Besides, after Samori I will retire from cinema. I am returning to literature. I have two collections of short stories, *Nivone* and *Taw,* waiting to be published. I will give the maximum to this film; afterwards, I will be able to rest. In terms of money, I will have the same problems of any father of a Senegalese family at my age. That's all.

I Am Tired, My Desire Is to Leave

MEISSA DIOP/1988

THE EVENT HAS BEEN EAGERLY awaited for over ten years—since 1977, when Ousmane Sembène finalized the shooting of *Ceddo*. A long time torch carrier for Senegalese and even African cinema, the man is certainly no longer the monument that he once was. The emergence of other directors and films with a more contemporary and different take on African life has affected his popularity and so has the criticism from a new generation film critics from which he has not been spared. Their opinions are reflected in the answer given by a man of culture to the question of who is the best Senegalese cineaste: "Sembène, unfortunately . . ."

At a gala evening on December 22, in anticipation of the screening of *Camp of Thiaroye*, a film for which the polemics surrounding its production sufficed for publicity, Sembène speaks about it, as well as about Senegalese and African cinema and about his projects.

MD: *Your film* Camp of Thiaroye *will finally be screened in Dakar on December 22. However, its history has been marked by controversy? What happened? What is your account?*

OS: My account is summarized with this: there was the history of a scenario, *Thiaroye 44*, which was presented to the SNPC by Ben Diogene Bèye. This was before I was called to the presidency of the Council of Administration of this country. At that moment something changed at

From *Wal Fadjri*, no. 141 (1988). Translated from the French by Anna Rimpl.

the head of SNPC: Mbengue was nominated as the general director instead of Johnson Traoré. For this film, still a preliminary project, he spent more than 30 million Francs, although the shooting had not even started. When the new team came, elements of the film were unsatisfactory. Not to me but to the others. It was then decided either to reexamine the film or to rewrite the scenario. Based on this decision, I was asked to write a scenario with Thierno Faty Sow; we presented it; we found cooperation partners and realized *Camp of Thiaroye*.

MD: *That's all?*
OS: In my opinion, yes. Everything else is only blah, blah, chattering. And if I did not tell you the truth, I should be condemned for slandering.

MD: *Wouldn't it have been fairer to revise the work together with Ben Diogoye Bèye?*
OS: I did the work that was entrusted to me in collaboration with Thierno Faty Sow, whom I had chosen as partner. This choice was for me a question of confidence, of familiarity. In any group there are affinities between individuals. That's all.

MD: *What is it that doesn't exist between Ben Diogoye and you?*
OS: The work of creation is related to sensations, which attach me to one individual rather than to another. It is neither a mark of hostility, nor a rejection, to others for whom I do not have these feelings. For example, while shooting, I never want to see a family member in the surroundings. And my family knows that. However, I live with my children. It is in my nature. Perhaps it's excessive but such is my sensitivity.

MD: *Your own son, however, played in* Xala.
OS: Yes. He had asked me before whether he could take part at the game. I accepted, but his appearance only consists of crossing a street. He did not open his mouth once, thus passing in the group of famous unknowns, those whom one calls the "observers' zero." Moreover, it was necessary to know one another well, my son and me, to make this presence normal.

MD: *You declared that you made* Camp of Thiaroye *initially for the Africans, but we are among the last to see it. First, the film has been screened on other continents: Europe, America.*

OS: The Africans were not the last to see *Camp of Thiaroye*. The Festival of Cannes needed to watch it, to see whether it could be selected or not. Afterwards it wasn't retained. We returned at once to Senegal, but it was the turbid time of the postelectoral events. We had wanted to secure the organization of a gala evening chaired by President Abdou Diouf. However, a fully booked calendar made it impossible for the Head of the State to accommodate us. We thus have, Thierno Faty and me, asked for the event to be postponed. As you see, it is neither Abdou Diouf nor the government who required this. The delay in showing *Camp of Thiaroye* in Senegal is ascribable to us, the directors.

MD: *So, it is you who bound the premier of your film to the availability of the officials. Thus you are responsible for the delay?*

OS: You did not understand. I repeat. I said that after the editing of the film and its passage in Cannes, we, the directors, asked for one gala evening. That was in June, July, August, September 1988. We got the agreement in principle of President Diouf who had, however, a full schedule. At this point we asked for a new release date. Thus we did not bind, nor issue conditions. We simply formulated a request. Before that even the censor had agreed and there was no problem on this side.

MD: *Do you think that your film was rejected in Cannes because it was too hard on French colonialism?*

OS: That I cannot answer. But I can say that my collaborator and I were never pressured in any way. The artistic tool is nowadays a weapon. In this case it is not so much the work of one producer over another that is important; it is rather a question of making films that crystalize or raise questions that help people gain better understanding in order to solve their problems.

MD: *Algerian journalists whose country was associated with the production of the film considered it regrettable that such an interesting theme was treated with little consequence. In other words, the film lacked sensitivity.*

OS: If what you say is true and I believe it is—it is because the Algerians wanted me to make it with more rigor. My answer was that they are not Ousmane Sembène and that I am not Algerian; that they are not Thierno Faty Sow and he is not Algerian. This is important.

MD: *Other critics mentioned that you seem to be a caricature and a Manichean at the same time. They noticed the influence of Soviet cinema.*
OS: In the French press I read a lot of those things. In other European countries it is completely the opposite. I think we have to understand, when we evoke memories of a not very glorious past for some, that it is completely normal that interested people find something to say about it again, are touched by it. In the history of humanity, there never has been good colonization. Any colonization is bad, whatever its nature or spirit may be. Any form of bondage has to be rejected and any person who considers otherwise is a stranger for me who could abuse power and should be combated. We are currently at a crucial turning point of our cinema, one where some European nations are producing films on their own history to recover a good conscience. I do not make any difference when it is the question of an occupation.

MD: *How much did* Camp of Thiaroye *finally cost?*
OS: Ask the production company. Today, as the film is finished, it is easy for the SNPC to evaluate the costs. Nevertheless, I tell you that it will be shown in England, in Italy, in Germany, and elsewhere. We are promoting the film in these countries. After its screening in Dakar, we will spread it to other African states who are willing to buy it.

MD: *How far are you with* Samory, *your superproduction?*
OS: It was in good shape before *Camp of Thiaroye*. This last film came quite simply as an interlude. I have other projects, but before continuing these, I want to finish *Samory*.

MD: *When do you think you can finalize it?*
OS: For me it's necessary to have started. And I hope doing it next year.

MD: *How long do you think the shooting will take?*
OS: I do not have a meeting with history.

MD: *Will* Samory *be the swansong of the cineaste Sembène Ousmane?*
OS: I confirm what you seem to doubt. I am tired and my desire is to leave. *Samory* required twenty years of personal research thanks to my own capital.

MD: *You retire at a moment when Senegalese cinema stumbles. However, in the seventies, Black African film was dominated by Senegal. Today the predominance has moved towards Burkinian and Ivorian cineastes. What is happening? Why?*
OS: We were starting cinema under precarious conditions, very difficult. We were a group of individuals with different options, but our common ground was our affinity with cinema. We realized our power in this autonomous community nevertheless united. This companionship, belief, and affection helped Senegalese artists advance. We wanted to demonstrate that it was the anticolonial engagement which motivated our work. True or false? We succeeded because we set up an association of cineastes. Later, through work, we could create the federation of cineastes. Thereafter, there were other newcomers, a new wave and the Senegalese state invested its money . . .

MD: *This wouldn't be the case any more?*
OS: No, it is not a question of money. What I wanted to make you understand, in regard to artistic creation, is that it's difficult to say why there was an opening at a certain moment and why, at another time, things are falling apart. With regards to cinema, sure, the problem is related to money, to an industry. Nevertheless, you don't reach the public only by having money. I speak, of course, about the cinema of the Third World, because it is the most political one, demonstrating the concerns of the people there. We are not inevitably politicians but films approached by such a cineaste have a political substrate. They asked the same questions as the average African asked about his future. Then we witnessed the sudden appearance of a new group where each one put forward his own problems; and it was necessary to respect the opinions of each and everyone.

MD: *As you retire, do you have in mind to prepare a changeover? Clarence Delgado, he seems to be your next in line—what kind of relation do you have to him?*

OS: I've been involved with many African cineastes, not only the Senegalese. Clarence Delgado has been working with me since he finished school, like so many others. He is going his own way to make his first film.

MD: *That would be* Niiwam, *one of your written works. This will be the first time that you've let somebody else adapt one of your writings.*
OS: He asked me for it; he is my collaborator. I could not refuse. I am retiring indeed but I will make scenarios for the cineastes, those who ask me.

MD: *A man from the Ivory Coast and a Congolese have already done so, haven't they?*
OS: Yes. For me, cinema is a permanent engagement, every day. Today I thank those who taught me this art. It is my turn to give. But do you realize that cinema in Africa has its limits? You do not have any material and you have to reinvent all with your collaborators. When you have your schedule, you are on the plate; each day you immobilize millions. A delay of one hour is enough to lose a million. You cannot have what you need, but you work with the raw material. What obstructs the African cinema is that we work with new matter. This work requires a lot of investment and less noise. Once the film is finished, it does not belong to you any more.

MD: Camp of Thiaroye *will be out at a moment when Senegalese cinema is ignored.*
OS: You are mistaken. Wait rather until next February. The SNPC did the coproduction for five films, beneath three full-length films.

MD: *A light in a dark sky.*
OS: It is you who says that. But I think that it's necessary that the filmmakers meet to reflect and discuss the reasons for it.

The Language of Real Life

KWATE NEE OWOO / 1989

KWATE NEE OWOO: *How are you able to reproduce the language of real life working with non-professional actors?*

OUSMANE SEMBÈNE: If you are working with actors who are not professionals, and you are trying to reproduce the language of real life, you have to take special care with gestures and movement, to be careful not to destroy anything of the original atmosphere, nor destroying anything of their personality. Africans talk a lot. That doesn't mean that what they say doesn't make sense, but they do talk a lot. For instance I personally can speak/understand Wolof, Bambara, Malanke. Take for example the question of greeting. People will greet each other and go into some other matter, and in the middle of the other matter they would suddenly start greeting each other out of the blue.

The cinema is rational, therefore, you have to suppress the repetition of greetings, but if you tell non-professional actors this, they can't grasp it. The roundabout way of thinking, the ins and outs of thought, it is very difficult to get people to change them. So when you are rehearsing the actors, you have to rehearse the language, gesture, and look, to make sure that there is no dead space. I am a product of the Soviet film school and there we learnt about the Italian method, the French method, and the English method.

For instance, if you take English theatre, there is English theatre and Irish theatre, but the English theatre, was more or less nothing like Irish theatre, which keeps you awake.

From *Framework*, vol. 36 (1989), and *Framework*, vol. 49, no. 1 (Fall 2007). Reprinted by permission of *Framework*.

The spoken language belongs to a particular ethnic group. For instance, in Senegal you will have people who can speak several languages, and in that case, you may have the gestures of one language going with another language, and you have to learn to deal with that.

Also you may have people moving within the same conversation from one language to another language quite unconsciously.

Now this question of redundancy or of people repeating themselves. You'll find that if you're working with peasants, for instance, they would tend to repeat themselves, and sometimes put in a lot of unnecessary words. So in the first rehearsal, I allow them the freedom to talk until they get this thing out of their system. Then during the second rehearsal you explain to them that some of this must be lightened up or cut out.

KNO: *But in* Camp Thiaroye, *I found this repetition of lines sometimes quite refreshing actually, I mean the way in which sometimes, with a different flavor, or even with a touch of humor, a character repeats or reinforces what another character has just said.*

OS: Also you must remember that first of all we are dealing with the army, and the army is an interesting phenomenon for most of us. Most of us don't know any more about the army than the uniform. So it's interesting to show how the army functions and how these guys in the army are ordinary human beings. One would repeat what the other fellow has said, naturally, to show that one is actually participating fully in the conversation, to show that you are agreeing with him. If I was making this film in a Western style, then I would cut out all of that.

KNO: *Well, for me this is the most crucial and central and problematic area of our struggle as filmmakers or artists, to develop an African film language: the language of real life. For instance, in* Borom Sarret, *one of your earlier films, the French language is superimposed or dubbed onto Wolof language, without synchronization between gesture and movement. So that one gets the impression that the French language has been deliberately superimposed on the film in the same manner as it has historically been impossed on the Senegalese people.*

OS: Well, I started out from the same thought. What I did was to take *Borom Sarret* and another of my films to the peasants at home in Burkina Faso and various places to show them. My attitude then was that there was nothing wrong with imposing the French language on the films, because the French language is a fact of life. But on the other hand, the peasants were quick to point out to me that I was the one who was alienated because they would have preferred the film in their own language without the French.

KNO: *For me the most fascinating of all the characters in* Camp Thiaroye *was the deaf and dumb man called Pays. In him we experience the irony of everyday life; through his eyes, solitary feelings, and mutterings we become sensitized, awakening to another impending tragedy. His Gestapo helmet symbolically reminds us of his traumatic experiences in a POW concentration camp in Fascist Germany, which his colleagues thought had driven him nuts. His quick reflexive response to the barbed wire surrounding the transit camp (Thiaroye) was reminiscent of his experience of the concentration camp in war-torn Germany. To be welcomed home by barbed wire was like going from the frying pan into the fire. What was there to celebrate? His response to the barbed wire was electrifying and ominous. Why did you choose a deaf and dumb character to convey this awakening?*

OS: Yes, I agree with your observation. First of all, the dumb character's name is Pays, which means Africa. In him we see the concentrated experiences of all fellow soldiers of the way in which some of them fought and died, while preferring to escape and make merry. Do you remember the scene in which Pays first encounters the barbed wire in total disbelief and astonishment. He is assured by one of his mates who scoops some soil from the ground and rubs it on Pay's head and hands and says, "Look, Pays, look, we are home, back home to Africa, back on your own soil. Wake up, man, this isn't Germany . . . this is Senegal." Pays, of course, remains unconvinced. Pays is Africa. He has been abused and traumatized. He can't talk. He is alive, he can look and see, he can touch, and he can see the future. He is the beholder of the drama of the past, on the concentration camps of colonization, very disciplined, very alone, very solitary, but he can't express it. And in these circumstances nobody believes him. Remember in the final episode, just before they were massacred by the French colonial soldiers, he instinctively and symbolically and tragically and furiously knocks his helmet against the wooden sheds to arouse them from their stupor, but alas it is too late. So as a result of this, everybody is killed. A tiny mistake in life and your whole life is ruined.

If I Were a Woman, I'd Never Marry an African

FÍRINNE NÍ CHRÉACHÁIN/1992

OUSMANE SEMBÈNE is one of francophone Africa's greatest artists to date. Born in Senegal in 1923, he was expelled from school at fourteen and worked successively on construction sites in Dakar, in the French army in the Second World War, and as a docker in Marseilles, where he continued his education in trade union night-schools. His first novel appeared in 1956, and his great literary masterpiece, *God's Bits of Wood*, in 1960.

He had joined the Communist Party in 1950. Realizing the inadequacy of the novel in French as a vehicle for raising the consciousness of his main target audience, the Senegalese masses, at the age of forty he turned to the cinema. He took a course in film-making in Moscow in 1962. His first full-length feature film, *The Money Order* (1969), based on his book of the same title, and with separate sound-tracks in French and Wolof, had a major impact in Senegal, drawing to the cinema in Dakar people who had never watched a film in their lives. It also put African cinema on the international cultural map, paving the way for film-makers like Soulaymane Cissé (*Yeelen*) and Idrissa Ouedrago (*Yaaba*). Since then, Sembène has continued making films, and also writing, which he claims to prefer. His films have won major awards at international festivals, and his literary work has been translated into a wide variety of languages, including Arabic, Russian, and Chinese.

From *African Affairs*, vol. 91, no. 363 (1992). Reprinted by permission of *African Affairs*.

Throughout his life, Sembène has opposed French colonialism, and later the Independence régime under Senghor's Parti Socialiste. He has consistently attacked Senghor's *négritude* and African socialism from the standpoint of Communist Internationalism, and also Senghor's promotion of *La Francophonie* (the French-speaking Commonwealth), which he sees as the post-independent prolongation of the French colonial cultural policy of *assimilation*, a policy which has had more effect in Senegal, where French influence goes back four hundred years, than in the rest of francophone Africa. Sembène deplores the on-going erosion of indigenous culture in Africa, including the current American cultural invasion (mediated, ironically, by France, which supplies *Dallas* and *Dynasty* dubbed in French), and his work increasingly reflects his preoccupation with the link between Westernization and economic dependence in Africa. His novel/film *Xala* (1973) is a biting satire of the economic impotence and cultural alienation of the indigenous comprador bourgeoisie, while in the film *Ceddo* (1977), he delves into Senegalese history to depict the struggle between indigenous values and imported religions, notably Islam, which is now practiced by over 80 percent of the Senegalese.

Ceddo was banned by the Senegalese state. In a country which rarely bans artistic works, it shares this honour with Salman Rushdie's *Satanic Verses*. Although the official reason for the ban on *Ceddo* cited Sembène's failure to respect the newly decreed Wolof standard spelling in the title, few were in doubt that, as with Rushdie, the real reason was more closely related to the régime's deference to the powerful leaders of the Muslim brotherhoods in Senegal. This was particularly true under Senghor who, as Christian president of a predominantly Muslim country, relied heavily on the latters' support.

The *Ceddo* case is of interest in several respects. It raises the issue of language, over which Sembène had always opposed Senghor. The latter, while paying lip-service to the national languages, did little to encourage their development. Nowadays, thirty years after independence, in a country which recently hosted the *Francophonie* summit, the national languages are still not taught in Senegalese schools. Sembène has been among those who have consistently advocated education for the people in the people's languages. In the early seventies, he collaborated in the founding of a Wolof newspaper, *Kaddu*, which unfortunately died an early death.

Ceddo is also interesting in that it is a rare example of Senegalese state action against a radical and extremely outspoken artist. None of Sembène's other works has been banned outright. Indeed, he has received state aid for some of his films (as he has from the French government). Perhaps the height of irony, his novel, *God's Bits of Wood,* which deals with the 1947 railway strike, is now compulsory reading for all students taking the Senegalese *baccalauréat,* and is perceived by some of the latter as a major inspiration for their own virtually annual strikes for improved educational facilities.

Some credit Sembène's escape from the fate of so many radical African artists—exile and imprisonment—to an older tradition of democracy in Senegal than elsewhere in francophone Africa: Senegal had been voting representatives into the French National Assembly since 1914. Certainly, the approach of the conservative Senegalese government to radical art is similar in many ways to that of Western democracies: administer regular doses of imported soap-opera, and rely on the system to create enough obstacles indirectly to minimize impact. Rumour has it that the state decided not to ban Sembène's satire of clan politics, *The Last of the Empire (1981),* but to simply allow the neo-colonial machinery to defuse it indirectly. Written in French, published in France, and very expensive, ten years after it appeared, the novel has hardly been read by anyone in Senegal.

As an artist, Sembène is something of a workaholic. He has produced a total of six novels, four novellas, a collection of short stories, five full-length, two medium, and two short films. None of his subsequent literary works has the power of the early *God's Bits of Wood,* but as a film producer, he has gone from strength to strength: his latest film, *Camp de Thiaroye* (1988) is perhaps his best to date. Like many of his works, *Thiaroye* is based on a historic event: the French massacre outside Dakar in 1944 of African soldiers just back from serving in the French army and demanding their demobilization entitlements. Sembène, like many other radical African artists, sees the decolonization of history as a vital step in ideologically equipping the present generation to confront neo-colonialism. The film he is working on currently, *Samory,* also fits into this category. *Samory,* which examines the heroic stand against the French by Samory Touré at the end of the nineteenth century, has been a life-long ambition for Sembène, who threatens that it will be his last film, after which he will concentrate on his first love, literature.

Now almost seventy, Sembène devotes all his energy to artistic production, and maintains a very low profile socially in Dakar (unlike other major African artists, international recognition has not tempted him to live abroad). He rarely attends official functions, and relies for the most part on his films and novels to express his stand on public issues. He has never been seen in the flesh by the vast majority of Dakarois, though the media keep the country abreast of his activities, and, at least in the capital, nearly everybody, including office-cleaners and taxi-drivers, has seen his films. The young people, many of whom have great admiration for him, seeing him as one of the rare elders who has never betrayed the masses, are somewhat disconcerted that the "people's artist" is so rarely visible, and regret the lack of opportunity to consult their oracle. But Sembène's refusal to play guru is perfectly in character: too many of the African leaders whom he condemns have been all too ready to set themselves up as Fathers of the Nation, Supreme Guides, etc., and demand obeisance accordingly. Sembène, refreshingly, encourages the present generation to carry on the struggle in their own terms.

Firinne Ni Chréacháin, who was in Senegal for six months attempting to assess the Senegalese reaction to Sembène, interviewed him at the premises of his film company, Filmi Doomi Rewmi, on the eve of his departure for Casamance in southern Senegal to film the long-awaited *Samory*. (We have recently been informed that Sembène postponed the filming of *Samory*, and is currently filming *Guelewar*, a full-length feature film on Muslim-Christian conflict in Senegal).

FNC: *How do you feel about the cultural situation in Senegal and Africa generally at present?*

OS: A sort of cultural fusion is taking place in Africa. Up to 1990, there were many African cultures. There might have been a similarity in politics, but there were many cultures: Yoruba, Ibo, Hausa, Fulani, Wolof, and so on. Now a new culture is emerging. But the danger is that this new culture, which is struggling to consolidate its hold, is being transmitted through European, not African languages. While it looks solid enough, it is ready to crumble at a touch.

FNC: *You've always tried to work against French cultural hegemony. Do you consider present-day Senegal more or less "assimilated" than during the colonial period?*
OS: Senegalese, or African society (I'm talking about the francophone countries) is no longer secreting values for the next generation. Take myself, father of a family, and others like me: we are no longer typical, living examples for our children. It's the cinema, the TV, the video which are the channels for the new cultures, the new values: we, the older generation, are absent in our own families. I was born in the colonial era. I witnessed all the humiliation and self-abasement my father had to put up with in order to survive. But in the evenings, when we came home to our huts, we rediscovered our own culture. It was a refuge: we were ourselves again, we were free. Nowadays, the TV is right there inside the hut where, in the old days, the father, the mother, the aunt held sway and the grandmother told her stories and legends. Even that time is now taken away from us. So we are left with a society which is growing more and more impoverished, emptying itself of its creative substance, turning more and more to values it does not create.

FNC: *At present, is French influence not giving way to an American cultural take-over?*
OS: America is a liberal capitalist country, an imperialist country which simply wants to call all the shots. But if America is calling the shots in Senegal at present, it's because those who govern Senegal allow this to happen. So we find ourselves with a society on its knees, waiting for America to provide. Never, ever, ever, in the space of ten years, have I felt so humiliated by my society as now. They give us "gifts": a few thousand dollars worth of rice—mere chicken-feed. A society can't live on handouts. A society that has its own culture can confront all sorts of calamities and adversities with its head held high. I always say, if I were a woman, I'd never marry an African. Women should marry real men, not mentally deficient ones.

FNC: *That's very hard. Do you mean Africans in general, or just a particular class? Can the young people, for instance, be blamed for being victims of this type of hegemony?*

OS: It's not the fault of the young people: they are reflections of my own short-comings. What I find humiliating is the incompetence of those who make speeches in the name of a people whom they sell into prostitution . . .

FNC: *Don't you feel you have an important role to play with regard to the young people? They expect you to serve almost as an oracle, but they feel that you hide away, unlike the other writers. They are anxious to hear you pronounce on national issues.*

OS: But Sembène can't solve the problems by himself. And Sembène is not in power. My opinions are like those of every other citizen. I've said everything should be nationalized, beginning with my own house. You can't just say nationalize, you have to say, start with my own house. I don't hide away from people. But I can't be everywhere at once. I'm involved in literature and cinema. I've just finished the scenario of *Samory*. At the moment I'm working in order to pay the people who will be working on the film. I'm not working for myself, I'm working for the country. If I wanted to be rich, I've only to go and work in America. I get so many invitations, but I say no. I have my own country. And I've told my children, and my people, that if I die outside of Africa, bring me back, don't give out a penny of what I have left before you have paid whatever it costs to bring me back and bury me in Africa—anywhere in Africa. And preferably standing, not on my back! Let me show you the *Samory* scenario: three volumes.

FNC: *How long has this taken you?*

OS: More than twenty years—from '62—to get it to this stage.

FNC: *People tell me they couldn't get in to see your last film,* Camp de Thiaroye, *the queues were too long.*

OS: There were huge crowds. But apart from that, my government is afraid. I love my country, and if I have a racial attitude towards other peoples or races, I agree that I should be sanctioned. But the historical facts are there. Every people should have the memory of their own history. Africa has not yet acquired that historical memory, especially in the francophone countries. I try to trace things back as far as possible . . .

FNC: *I get the feelings the young people would like you to write about the present, about their own strikes, for instance.*
OS: I've written two books on contemporary history.

FNC: *That you're keeping locked in a drawer, as you told me in London in 1988. What about* The Last of the Empire? *I get the impression that most people here haven't read it.*
OS: It's not talked about in Senegal. Even the critics haven't reviewed it.

FNC: *Your novels and films have made you famous, but you've never tried theatre. Yet, it is obvious from Ngugi's experiments that theatre is also a powerful ideological weapon. What do you feel about theatre in Senegal?*
OS: *God's Bits of Wood* has been adapted for the stage. I think the colonial influence had a very negative effect on theatre in the francophone countries. We've had the William Ponty theatre, and, since 1966, the Daniel Sorano National theatre, which, by the way, needs to be rebaptized—Daniel Sorano wasn't Senegalese: that's the problem, that's the way things get done. Now it's up to the theatre people to do like the film-makers, to be independent and make theatre about everything. But I'm sure that too will come. Young people are making an effort . . .

FNC: *The young people seem to think that some of the theatre experiments in Nigeria—for instance, plays criticizing the World Bank and Structural Adjustment—couldn't be performed here.*
OS: First you have to try. There's no such thing as absolute freedom. Those in power never grant freedom of their own accord. All Governments are politically and ideologically conservative when it comes to art. Conformity has to be broken.

FNC: *So you think young people should get involved in street theatre, for example?*
OS: They should do what they want to do. When I began to make films, I was forty years of age: it's never too late for crazy ventures. Where there's a will, there's a way.

FNC: *Let's come to the question of literature in the national languages. I hear there's a lot of progress with literacy in Wolof, but that it's mainly foreign NGOs which are responsible. Isn't that somewhat ironic?*

OS: That's the quarrel I had with Senghor, when he brought in an Austrian linguist to teach us Wolof. No, listen, let's be serious, would they invite a Chinese to Oxford . . .

FNC: *to teach the English English . . .*
OS: Exactly. And this Austrian didn't even speak the language. That's what you really call colonization. I was talking to Ngugi in New England about certain Africanists who teach African literature—I said literature, mind you, not medicine—and who don't speak African languages. When an English person teaches French literature, isn't he at least expected to know French? But to come back to the national languages in Senegal, yes, there's progress, especially in the countryside.

FNC: *So you'd advise young people to write in the national languages?*
OS: They should do what they want to do.

FNC: *But they expect you . . .*
OS: But I don't have any advice for them. If what they do is good, it will get the recognition it deserves from the people.

FNC: *You don't see yourself as any kind of guide?*
OS: No, no, no. I'm caught up in the struggle, and I'm still eighteen-and-a-half. I'm the oldest, and I want to be the youngest. That's what I keep telling the young film-makers: I tell them, I'm in there competing with you all the time.

FNC: *You were with Ngugi in New England. Given the similarity in your approach to art and social change, I imagine you get along very well with him.*
OS: He's a real friend. He writes in Gikuyu. He wants to learn film-making now.

FNC: *How do you explain that fact that he has been imprisoned and is living in exile and that you have managed to escape all that?*
OS: It depends on the society. Children of the same father and mother don't necessarily have the same character. The societies are different. Anyway, Senghor banned my films for ten years . . .

FNC: *All your films?*
OS: *Ceddo*. And he cut *The Money Order*. But I stayed put. I didn't budge.

FNC: *Your films are show on Senegalese TV now. Couldn't you make a series to counter the influence of* Dallas?
OS: *Dallas* is a gift from the Americans and the government needs it to keep people quiet. Tomorrow, if I get the green light, I'm ready to postpone *Samory* for six months to do a TV series on what's happening in the country at the moment. But on one condition: that it's my ideas from start to finish.

FNC: *Some scenes were cut in* The Money Order?
OS: Now, they show it in full. *Xala* too. But it's an on-going struggle. Freedom is never won outright.

Ousmane Sembène

JAMES A. JONES/1992

OUSMANE SEMBÈNE is an internationally famous author and filmmaker from Senegal. Among his works is his second book, *Les Bouts de Bois de Dieu* (God's Bits of Wood), a novel about the 1947–1948 railroad strike in French West Africa. From other interviews and archival research, I was already aware at the time of this interview that Sembène's novel about the strike actually synthesized events from the 1938 and 1947 strikes, and manufactured the "women's march to Dakar." However, I was interested in Mr. Sembène's ideas about the significance of the 1947 strike and how people perceived different aspects of the railroad.

This interview took place in Mr. Sembène's office in Dakar. He had no warning because I just dropped in at the suggestion of Mr. Kassé of the University of Dakar. However, while I talked to his secretary, he opened his morning mail, and then invited me into his office which was papered with posters from his movies and color prints of images from the colonial period.

JONES: *Did the strike bring together people from everywhere, even in France?*
SEMBÈNE: All the rail lines—BN, CN, etc.—and independent of that, all Africans.

JONES: *I'm studying the impact of the railroad in the Middle Niger Valley, in the region where there was no railway. I realize the railroad had a commercial*

From James A. Jones's website, http://courses.wcupa.edu/jones/his311/archives/intervus/Sembene.htm. Reprinted by permission of James A. Jones.

impact, but I'm also interested in the railroad as an instrument of imperialism, as the carrier of abstract ideas like progress.

SEMBÈNE: No, not progress. Moving around, carrying merchandise, commerce were important. But don't forget that the Europeans built the railroad for their own needs, and it didn't correspond to any of the major African trade routes. It was intended to connect the interior with the ocean at a large city. Africans were used to weekly markets. In cities, they could trade all of the time. Cola, peanuts, gold, etc.

JONES: *But Africans traveled for commerce for centuries before the French arrived.*

SEMBÈNE: As far as Mecca; even as far as Mecca.

JONES: *Did the railroad really change the way that commerce operated, or just the places where it operated?*

SEMBÈNE: Both underwent modification. The most important markets were Tombouctou, Jenne, Bamako on transit, Kankan and on as far as Kong. That was the route taken by cola, gold, slaves, etc. Commerce to the coast was slight. But the demand [created by new cities] modified commercial routes.

JONES: *Okay, something else. Did everyone, even those people with no personal experience with the railway, really understand and support the strike? Did they think the strike would gain them anything? Is that how it was?*

SEMBÈNE: There were two things to the strike. There was a new political consciousness. There were strikes ever since 1880. But now the workers had a conscious notion of class. They were able to communicate with organized workers in France. Men like Senghor.

JONES: *Aimee Cesaire?*

SEMBÈNE: Not Aimee Cesaire. He was later. There was "le prince Tomajo" from Mali and Senghor of Senegal. They led the post-WWI movement in France that set the scene for the railroad [strike].

The action on the railroad was related to that of the teachers. The *cheminots* had connections with the teachers, so their ideas were not original. But the population supported the *cheminots*. For example, Thiès owed its existence as a city to the railroad.

JONES: *Like Kayes?*
SEMBÈNE: Well, Kayes already existed. The French started in Kayes to go to the Soudan. Even in 1902 or 1903, . . . I have a photo . . . [Sembène indicated a photo on his wall] Samori's sofas were put to work on the rails for the railroad.

JONES: *In the* villages de liberté*?*
SEMBÈNE: Yes, that produced a new economic structure. You also had the railroad as an agency that created an African elite that wasn't composed of soldiers or teachers. It was composed of workers. [Pause to see if I'd understood.]

JONES: *Uh-uh. [I do not sound convincing on the tape.]*
SEMBÈNE: A new type of society was created in the region along the rails.

JONES: *Permit me to speak in a Marxist fashion for a moment. The* cheminots *became elite workers. They had bigger salaries than everyone else. Did this affect their relationship with other people?*
SEMBÈNE: No, it wasn't a problem. The *cheminot* earned a salary that was more than fifteen peasants earn. But that didn't give them a consciousness of class.

JONES: *All right, but after two or three months, gas was short in Ségou. [I listed a few more hardships.] Why did the people continue to support the strike?*
SEMBÈNE: Because by then, there was a common denominator. By 1947, the idea of independence, liberty, dignity were already known. There was a confrontation between black and white.

JONES: *So people saw the strike not as a triumph by the* cheminots *for themselves, but as a triumph of blacks over the whites?*
SEMBÈNE: Okay, there was that, but there was more to it. There was a notion of class in the Marxist sense, an entire political pedagogy devoted to that. It wasn't just a dispute between whites and blacks.

JONES: *It was the workers against the* grands patrons.
SEMBÈNE: Right. Even the workers in France—the CGT—sent money to Dakar.

JONES: *Sure. The* cheminots *of the SNCF sent a letter of support as well. So by the end of WWII, it was no longer a colonial struggle . . .*
SEMBÈNE: In 1938, there was a strike in Thiès.

JONES: *I just finished Iba Der Thiam's thesis on that. You mentioned it (the strike) in your book as well.*
SEMBÈNE: Yes, that's true. All of it was involved [in creating working class consciousness].

JONES: *At the moment of independence in 1961, when the Mali Federation was formed, what was the attitude towards the railroad? Was it better then than now [1992]?*
SEMBÈNE: Definitely. It operated on schedule, the trains were clean.

JONES: *Okay. Then it's only since 1960 [that things have deteriorated].*
Now I have this idea, but I'm not sure that it's valid. Was the railroad, or the cheminots, *a force that supported the Mali Federation? I know of several forces that worked against the Federation to separate Senegal from Mali.*
SEMBÈNE: After the [1947] strike, politics modified the homogeneity of the union. Afterwards, the union was divided along political lines.

JONES: *You even had the Syndicat Libre of GNING and the Syndicat des* Cheminots *Africains.*
SEMBÈNE: Exactly. You had divisions, and they contributed to the weakness of the *cheminots* as a political force.

JONES: *Yesterday, I saw a telegram from Fily Dabo Sissoko in the archives that referred, at the time of the strike, to the Soudanese* cheminots *as elite workers, the conductors, the metal workers . . .*
SEMBÈNE: Yes. They were skilled workers.

JONES: *Right. The implication was that Soudanese* cheminots *were less interested in the strike than the Senegalese workers. Is that possible?*
SEMBÈNE: Perhaps it was possible, but in any case . . . [Pause to think] the bulk of the skilled workers were at Thiès . . .

JONES: *. . . at the Cité Ballabey?*
SEMBÈNE: . . . the "Cité Bambara," it was called. I disagree with Fily Dabo Sissoko—the bulk of the workers were in Thiès, but there was no difference in salaries between Soudanese and Senegalese. The majority of the line was in the Soudan and there were more Malians than Senegalese. There were more Malians in the cadre; they were station masters, *"chefs de convoi,"* etc. But *"mechanos"* had the same salary.

But above all that, there was a notion of unity. No one wanted their ethnic group to be the one that would betray the strike. There was a oath taken at the exit to the Cité Ballabey, next to a tree.

JONES: *. . . near the* passage a niveau *(grade crossing at the entrance to the workshops)? [Although Sembène agreed, later I learned that the oath tree was located about two hundred meters away from the grade crossing, near to the workshops.]*
SEMBÈNE: Right. All the workers were there and nobody was willing to betray their oath. At the time, their conception of group behavior was based on the idea of family in its most noble, most dedicated form, for their own independence.

JONES: *All of this was about a year after the Congress of Bamako had united the political parties.*
SEMBÈNE: Exactly. And were there *cheminots* in political parties?

JONES: *Certainly.*
SEMBÈNE: Who? [Throughout the interview to this point, I HAD answered "oui" to many of Sembène's statements, but had done little to show the extent of my research. Sembène tested me with this question.]

JONES: *Alassane Sow, for example.*
SEMBÈNE: Yes . . .

JONES: *Sarr didn't really get into politics . . .*
SEMBÈNE: Yes, he did. Later on, he got into bad politics. But Sow did a lot . . .

JONES: *After the strike, Sow changed sides and joined GNING in the Syndicat Libre.*
SEMBÈNE: Right.

JONES: *Sarr, did you know him?*
SEMBÈNE: Yes.

JONES: *What was he like?*
SEMBÈNE: During the strike, he was extraordinary. He was a man of dignity and valor, in all ways. Unfortunately, afterwards he did not appear to develop politically . . .

JONES: *He remained at the same stage as in 1947?*
SEMBÈNE: He didn't really reach 1947. He remained stationary.

JONES: *Afterwards, what did he do?*
SEMBÈNE: He became a government deputy with Mamadou Dia. He had his "adventure in Libya." For him, the group was everything, but not individuals.

JONES: *Thank you for all of this. It's been very helpful. May I ask a couple of biographical questions?*
SEMBÈNE: OK.

JONES: *You used to be a* cheminot?
SEMBÈNE: No. When I was a boy, the union headquarters was right in front of my house.

JONES: *Here in Dakar? So you heard them talking?*
SEMBÈNE: No. It was someone else's house. [Sembène appeared slightly insulted that I had accused him of eavesdropping.] But at the time [1947], there was a sense of solidarity. Since my house was across the street—I was twenty after the war—we carried water, we ran errands, thus we knew everything that went on.

JONES: *This was in which neighborhood? Near the railway station?*
SEMBÈNE: Check your facts! [laughter] You know the Rue Thiong? [sound of Jones unfolding a map while Sembène continued to speak] You see the police station. It was across the street.

JONES: *Here's the train station [pointing at the map].*
SEMBÈNE: The train station is down here. Look for the Rue Thiong at the corner of Blanchot. [Note: The Rue Blanchot is now known as the Rue Moussa Diop. The name of Rue Thiong is unchanged, and the *Gendarmerie Nationale* is still there, occupying the entire block between Rues Thiong and Sandinien, and Moussa Diop and Raffenel.]

JONES: *And you lived behind that?*
SEMBÈNE: I lived next door to it, with my grandmother. Before the union had it, the building was a maternity hospital during the 1920s. It was given to the union . . . it was a maternity hospital, but they transformed it into a union hall. The mayor gave it to the union . . .

JONES: *Just before the war . . .*
SEMBÈNE: Even before that. After the Popular Front. Across the street, there were the offices of the newspaper *l'AOF*. We lived next door. It was the place where the intellectuals congregated. We were kids and we grew up there. You should go see another guy, if you are going to Thiès—Bouta Seck, El Haji Bouta Seck. He was one of the first workers to finish at the *École d'Apprentissage* and he was assigned to work for the railroad.

JONES: *The* École d'Apprentissage *at Gorée?*
SEMBÈNE: Exactly. Pinet-Laprade.

JONES: *He's still alive?*
SEMBÈNE: Sure. I saw him a month ago.

JONES: *How do I locate him in Thiès?*
SEMBÈNE: Just go there and ask the *cheminots*.

JONES: *Okay, I'll see. There's less than two weeks to go and I've still got a lot of documents to read (in the archives).*
SEMBÈNE: The "human documents" . . .

JONES: *Are more interesting?*
SEMBÈNE: More interesting. You should go to Thiès and see the "human documents."

JONES: *Okay. Well, I know that there are regular trains to Thiès.*
SEMBÈNE: Right. Of course, they were there before [independence]. We didn't invent anything. [laughter]

JONES: *Thank you very much.*

Postscript: I took Mr Sembène's advice and went to Thiès to look for Mr. Bouta Seck. I learned that he had passed away recently, but was able to interview one of his contemporaries, Ahmadou Bouta-Guèye.

Interview with Ousmane Sembène

FRANÇOISE PFAFF/1992

THIS CASUAL INTERVIEW-TALK about this and that with Ousmane Sembène was conducted by Françoise Pfaff on July 10, 1992, during the festival of African cinema in Toronto, Canada.

FRANÇOISE PFAFF: *Yesterday evening you presented* Camp de Thiaroye. *This film was realized in 1988, twelve years after* Ceddo. *Why did you take such a long break from your cinematographic work?*
OUSMANE SEMBÈNE: Because I had to finish the script for *Samory* and I had to write. Don't forget, after all, that in 1981 I published a two-volume monograph. And also with regards to cinema I was not idle. You can't produce films all the time.

FRANÇOISE PFAFF: *Did you need this time for digestion?*
OUSMANE SEMBÈNE: Do you have to be faster than creation? Things need time to develop. I am convinced that each and every creation needs quite a long time for incubation. Of course, there are ideas which simply come to mind and force me to realize them. They could be good or bad—but I have to deal with them. And there are other concepts which come into being only very slowly. Somehow, this process is similar to the formation of stalactites, these drops of water which do not drop but accumulate steadily until, in the end, they form roots.

Previously unpublished. Translated from the French by Anna Schrade. Printed by permission of Françoise Pfaff.

FRANÇOISE PFAFF: *We were waiting for your film about* Samory *and instead you presented* Camp de Thiaroye.
OUSMANE SEMBÈNE: The film project about *Samory* moves onward. I don't have an obligation with years, nor with history, nor with anyone. I will do this film about *Samory* when I am ready to do it.

FRANÇOISE PFAFF: Camp de Thiaroye, *that's the story about a massacre of the Senegalese "tirailleurs" by French soldiers during the second World War. You coproduced this film together with Thierno Sow, although you directed all the other films alone. Can we still talk about "cinema d'auteur" in the case of* Camp de Thiaroye?
OUSMANE SEMBÈNE: Is it still a "cinema d'auteur"?

FRANÇOISE PFAFF: *Did you play the active part with regard to the decisions?*
OUSMANE SEMBÈNE: No, I wouldn't say that. What is essential for me is that we are moving forward. Someone has to take over from the first generation of African filmmakers. We have young filmmakers that are very able on a technical level, but their ignorance concerning the African cultures is frightening. It is not their fault; it is the "ecole française," the french education they have been given. They are victims of colonialism. If you don't know a culture to its roots, it is very difficult to express specific purposes or attitudes from inside of a cultural system. Sometimes I hear myself saying that some of our fellows, the new generation of Africans, are not different compared to the people of the diaspora. They live on African territory but nonetheless they ignore the African cultures. We, those who had the chance to go to school, we know that what they teach us there involves Greek or Indo-European civilizations, but not a word about African civilizations.

FRANÇOISE PFAFF: *This was certainly true during your school time but is it still today? I thought that since the independence, in the University of Cheickh Anta Diop for example, the African cultures have become an important subject.*
OUSMANE SEMBÈNE: Where? In which department?

FRANÇOISE PFAFF: *In the department of history, of sociology etc. . . .*
OUSMANE SEMBÈNE: Okay. But did the filmmakers attend courses like that?

FRANÇOISE PFAFF: *No, because lots of them are going to study cinema in Paris, at the IDHEC for example, and this is not the place where they will teach them African cultures.*
OUSMANE SEMBÈNE: Voilà! You see!

FRANÇOISE PFAFF: *Haven't they acquired certain basics about African cultures in college?*
OUSMANE SEMBÈNE: Yes, but in my opinion the classes about African history in the colleges are not very profound at present. What do they teach you? They tell you in one breath that there was slavery, colonialism, and then the fathers of the nation.

FRANÇOISE PFAFF: *So you think that the young filmmakers are not equipped with the necessary cultural baggage.*
OUSMANE SEMBÈNE: Maybe I am wrong, but I think that a European filmmaker who starts to express himself has a great knowledge of the philosophy, the arts, and the music of his country whereas most of the African filmmakers know the sounds and the rhythms of a particular music, but they don't know in which era it was created.

FRANÇOISE PFAFF: *Do the African filmmakers suffer from cultural alienation?*
OUSMANE SEMBÈNE: It is a lack of knowledge, a not-knowing and not an alienation. For the filmmakers to be able to express themselves and to speak and tell stories about their people it's necessary to acquire a certain knowledge of their history. In this regard I often ask myself, why we need artists. . . .

FRANÇOISE PFAFF: *Why do we need artists in your opinion?*
OUSMANE SEMBÈNE: There are different kind of artists: There are those who celebrate the ruling power and there are those who criticize it. The one who is in power needs the artists to comfort him and to dazzle his people. He doesn't like those who are disturbing and often gives them a rough time. By the way, one can notice that whenever the established power starts to oppress an artist, the people lose their liberty too. The people also need artists. But why do these people, who don't even have the power to buy a blackboard for their schools, need artists? And in

whose name is a Sembène boasting about the right to speak in the name of his people? These are the questions that I ask myself, but I don't try to find the answer.

FRANÇOISE PFAFF: *The artist can help his people to remember, as in the case of* Camp de Thiaroye. *As far as I'm concerned, I had absolutely no idea of the events that are related in the film, because in France they obviously don't appear in the history books that we used in school. Maybe one of the tasks an artist has is to reflect and perpetuate the collective memory.*
OUSMANE SEMBÈNE: But do we always consider the artist and the collective memory in this sense? In the past a traditional artist, a classic storyteller, a griot for example, was his own author, producer, and actor. In the evening all the people gathered to hear him. What he said was quite clear. One could bribe and corrupt him to denigrate someone in particular, but whenever he entered the circle, in the middle of his audience, nobody could touch him. He was the master of everything. He also imitated the voices of all the animals. When he started to denigrate a man or a women, he tried hard to imitate the voice of these people so that his audience could understand who he was talking about. Even a king had to play this game and to accept that he was being imitated.

FRANÇOISE PFAFF: *How do you connect this to the function of a contemporary artist?*
OUSMANE SEMBÈNE: I don't know. I have lots of ready-made theories I am always asking myself. I often relate an adventure that happened to me some years ago in Cameroon that surprised me a lot. When I presented the film *The Mandat* they told me that a police superintendent wanted to see me in the hotel where I was staying. I met him and he offered me a drink. Than he asked me how I managed to find out the story of the film *The Mandat*. I told him that it happened in Senegal. He told me that he had witnessed similar events in Cameroon. For him it was something diabolical.

FRANÇOISE PFAFF: *So you were something like a medium?*
OUSMANE SEMBÈNE: No, it's by coincidence that sometimes films become true in reality. I know that after people saw the film in Conakry,

a lot of things changed at the post office and in the market. Some people said: "Be careful, don't play the trick of *Mandat* on me!"

FRANÇOISE PFAFF: *So your film was so significant that it entered the everyday speech?*
OUSMANE SEMBÈNE: Yes, at least to a certain point. And it is a film that you see and you want to see it again. I presented *The Mandat* in 1991 to high-school pupils from Dakar. The film was followed by a discussion and the pupils between fifteen and twenty years old thought that the film was recently released because it treats subjects that are still very present.

FRANÇOISE PFAFF: *On the other hand,* Camp de Thiaroye *takes place in a very precise moment in history. How did you come to choose this subject?*
OUSMANE SEMBÈNE: I love to draw parallels between history and modernity. If it's possible I would make a film about history followed by one about modernity. I think that the artist is a contemporary being, but he is also the connection between a past and the future.

FRANÇOISE PFAFF: *Unlike* Camp de Thiaroye, Guelwaar *takes place in a contemporary reality. How did you get the idea to make* Guelwaar? *Can you make a few comments about this film?*
OUSMANE SEMBÈNE: *Guelwaar* is based on a true story. One day, when I came back from a journey, my assistant Clarence Delgado gave me an article that he had cut out from the newspaper. I read it and put it into a file. Then I made *Camp de Thiaroye*. I wrote and made quite a lot of things. One morning, the story of the article emerged just like that onto the surface. The story had taken place in the region of Thiès that I know very well from my writing of *Le bouts de bois de Dieu*. I read and read the news item again and I said to myself: "This is an interesting story!" Then I started to write the screenplay of the film which unfolds in 1992. The plot is very simple: It's a nowadays error of administration. One day a Muslim family makes a mistake with the corpse of a family member. Instead of burying the Muslim corpse, they accidently take the body of a Catholic and bury it in the Muslim cemetery.

FRANÇOISE PFAFF: *How can such an error occur?*
OUSMANE SEMBÈNE: Two men died in a hospital on the same day. They took them to the mortuary. The Muslim family came first to recover their corpse and they buried it. The Catholic family came to the hospital one or two days later, after the preparations. As they went to verify, they noticed that the body in the mortuary was not their own. What did they do? Search for the right one or let it be? This faithful Catholic family started to search for the corpse of their family member. The police also investigated with the deputy mayor and the prefect. They discovered quite soon that the body of the Catholic man had been buried in the Muslim cemetery and they decided to recover it. Now, we also have the dubious side of the events, that of the politicians. In Africa you never die a natural death, and it is in these circumstances that the artist has left his mark. In fact, the one who died, Guelwaar, didn't die of a natural cause at all. He had been killed. Why had he been killed? Because it is now over thirty years that they have bothered us with the "aide alimentaire." You can help somebody for one or two days but you can not help a whole nation for over thirty years. The elders had gathered and instructed Guelwaar, who always had a big mouth, to announce this message in the course of a popular meeting where donations should be distributed. He did so and was killed.

FRANÇOISE PFAFF: *Did the elders delegate the power to him?*
OUSMANE SEMBÈNE: No, not the power. They instructed him to speak for them and to proclaim that they are humiliated, that they are fed up with the "aide alimentaire" and that the politicians and others are all lying.

FRANÇOISE PFAFF: *So, it's a film that is about both an administrative error as well as a problem of consciousness in connection with aide alimentaire?*
OUSMANE SEMBÈNE: It's your job to analyze that.

FRANÇOISE PFAFF: *How does* Guelwaar *end?*
OUSMANE SEMBÈNE: They find Guelwaar's body. At the end of the film we find ourselves in the present time where the young people are also fed up. They don't want to live and to grow up begging.

FRANÇOISE PFAFF: *So there are a series of flashbacks which is quite unusual in your cinema.*

OUSMANE SEMBÈNE: There are a series of flashbacks to capture the present reality and the parallel life of Guelwaar. There is the story, the search for the corpse up to the Muslim cemetery. In the meantime there are a series of reminiscences of Guelwaar to understand better how he was acting. That means that we have a present time and a past time. I reconstruct the personality through flashbacks and return to the present.

FRANÇOISE PFAFF: *How do they find out that Guelwaar was murdered?*
OUSMANE SEMBÈNE: You have to see the film. At the end of *Guelwaar* the living and the dead merge and the new generation refuses begging by taking the initiative. On their way back from the Muslim cemetery, the young people intercept a lorry that is going to distribute aid. They scatter the grains on the ground and let the truck, which is transporting Guelwaar's body, circulate around. The elders and the priest hesitate to walk over the grains. Will they do the same and also walk over the grains?

FRANÇOISE PFAFF: *Is that how the film ends?*
OUSMANE SEMBÈNE: That's it!

FRANÇOISE PFAFF: *How did you produce the film? Did you do it alone or with foreign coproducers?*
OUSMANE SEMBÈNE: I have a coproducer, Jacque Perrin. He runs the production office "Galaté" in Paris.

FRANÇOISE PFAFF: *Have you worked with African film studios as you did in the case of* Camp de Thiaroye?
OUSMANE SEMBÈNE: No, with French studios, because it was there that I had the possibilities.

FRANÇOISE PFAFF: *You came to Toronto and you met with Afro-Canadian filmmakers. What do you think about their films?*
OUSMANE SEMBÈNE: To be frank, I haven't seen their films, but I think that if the encounter makes it possible for Africans and Afro-Canadians to interchange ideas, that's a good thing. We need such ideas on both sides.

FRANÇOISE PFAFF: *Do the Afro-Canadians know Africa or is it still a myth for them?*

OUSMANE SEMBÈNE: Some of them know Africa. Why talk about myths? It is good to have dreams. The problem is not if they know or if they ignore. They were not born in Africa, it's not their fault. One cannot have a poor opinion about them if they are constructing an idealized image of Africa for themselves, that's normal. In the course of this encounter, which I hope to be fruitful, it is our duty to show them the African realities. It's the same as some Africans who think that the Blacks in America are living in the middle of paradise. They have seen *Dallas* on TV and for them America is paradise. Anyone who lives in America is rich and has millions of dollars. For the moment you cannot remove these ideas from their mind.

FRANÇOISE PFAFF: *So, it's by this kind of encounter that you show them the reality of contemporary Africa?*
OUSMANE SEMBÈNE: I don't show them the reality of contemporary Africa. Together we will try to figure out how to shape our future. We shouldn't stay any longer on the periphery of history. Europe is no longer our dreamland. We are in the position to generate a new culture, and if we don't shape this new culture, it's our death. I think that the encounter with people from the diaspora is as enriching for us as Africa is for them.

FRANÇOISE PFAFF: *How do you see the future of African cinema?*
OUSMANE SEMBÈNE: There will be a future, there is no doubt about it. Africa will not regress anymore. There may be bad films, but there will always be a developed film industry. The content of these films will be a different matter. We could easily succumb to the shortcomings of commerce.

FRANÇOISE PFAFF: *What you say there is interesting, because I have the impression that* Camp de Thiaroye *is more commercial than your preceding films.*
OUSMANE SEMBÈNE: What do you mean by commercial?

FRANÇOISE PFAFF: *The narrative style as well as the way it is structured has a more western touch than your preceding films.*
OUSMANE SEMBÈNE: Ah? Maybe!

FRANÇOISE PFAFF: *Did you intend it to be this way?*
OUSMANE SEMBÈNE: Maybe you will get another impression when you see *Guelwaar*. I think that in a film about soldiers the acting should not be slow. Generally, soldiers are well disciplined, they are not the ones who drag along. Even a soldier who comes from Africa will be perfectly in time after five or ten years in the army. So, I think it would have been very inappropriate to treat them like the characters in *Emitai, Xala*, or other films. I tried to figure out their life context, the context in which they were living. It is the trumpet that structures the day of the soldiers.

FRANÇOISE PFAFF: *So it's this kind of rhythm that you have tried to respect in* Camp de Thiaroye. *What will you do after* Guelwaar? *Do you already have an idea for a new film or will you return to writing?*
OUSMANE SEMBÈNE: Right now, I am writing and sketching out a novel. I won't tell you anything about the subject. You have to wait until it's finished.

FRANÇOISE PFAFF: *And your film about* Samory. *Is it for later?*
OUSMANE SEMBÈNE: I am not obliged to do this film.

FRANÇOISE PFAFF: *Let's come back to* Camp de Thiaroye. *Was it successful on an international level?*
OUSMANE SEMBÈNE: Yes, only France didn't want it. I don't care about that. For the moment it won a prize in the Festival of Venice and another at the Festival of Ouagadougou.

FRANÇOISE PFAFF: *The Senegalese cinema, which was rich and very prolific at a certain point, seems to be stagnated. Besides your films there is nothing much to see. Why?*
OUSMANE SEMBÈNE: I cannot speak for others. The only thing I know is that the Senegalese government has invested a lot and for a long time in the domain of the cinema. However, it's not the money that generates creativity. This is a problem of individuals.

FRANÇOISE PFAFF: *Isn't the Senegalese government investing anymore in the cinema?*
OUSMANE SEMBÈNE: They will start again. It's important to bet on a good horse. The people believe that making films is an easy thing and

everybody thinks that he can be a filmmaker from one day to the other. It's only at the end that one can realize that money has been invested for nothing.

FRANÇOISE PFAFF: *There were also some financial scandals in the Senegalese cinema. Is this one of the reasons that the government stopped investing in the cinema?*

OUSMANE SEMBÈNE: There were scandals, but in 1992 the government started to invest in our cinema again. On the other hand, Madame Annette Mbay took the initiative to organize a yearly festival of Senegalese film in Dakar, the RECIDAK. I think that by that means it will be possible to moralize the profession of filmmaking.

FRANÇOISE PFAFF: *Recent films like* Yaaba, Le Choix, *and* Camp de Thiaroye *are coproductions. Does this present a viable solution for the African cinema?*

OUSMANE SEMBÈNE: I think so. It's a pity that we have not developed another partnership, a partnership between Africans. That's what I tried to do with *Camp de Thiaroye*. It's possible that in the following years until the end of this century this process of cooperation will develop between Africans.

FRANÇOISE PFAFF: *But a coproduction also involves making profits. Does this mean a shift from a mainly didactic cinema to a more profitable and more commercial cinema?*

OUSMANE SEMBÈNE: Let's see the films to come and then we can judge them later.

FRANÇOISE PFAFF: *In spite of its diversity and the improved technical quality, the African cinema is still not recognized at the international festivals. Meanwhile the U.S. company California Newsreel is distributing a certain number of African films on video. Several African filmmakers, however, rise up against the minimization of their works on the video format, and the lack of control they have with regard to a possible piracy of the video cassettes. What is your position with regard to this subject? Do you contemplate the distribution of your films on video format?*

OUSMANE SEMBÈNE: Me, I am mainly in favor of the cinema. I really prefer wide-screen, because if I see my films on video, I feel sick. I would not like my films to be distributed on video. I don't like the video. I don't say that I will never use it; I only say that I prefer cinemascope. I still hope that the people are going to visit the movie theatres, but it is very difficult.

FRANÇOISE PFAFF: *Do you want to work one day together with a member of the Diaspora, with an Afro-American filmmaker for example?*
OUSMANE SEMBÈNE: Yes, if there is a story that is interesting for both of us.

FRANÇOISE PFAFF: *So, that has to be a story that you have written together?*
OUSMANE SEMBÈNE: Oh, yes.

FRANÇOISE PFAFF: *Would you work with someone like Spike Lee?*
OUSMANE SEMBÈNE: With Spike Lee or anyone else. First there has to be a story. Then Spike Lee has his temperament and I have mine. We would have to see how it turns out.

FRANÇOISE PFAFF: *Which Afro-American films do people usually watch in Senegal?*
OUSMANE SEMBÈNE: The films of Spike Lee, who provides us with a lot of information about the situation of Afro-Americans, especially after the events in Los Angeles. I think that Spike Lee's films are not bad, and he is an interesting filmmaker-personality.

FRANÇOISE PFAFF: *Do you think that he will be able to guard this personality in spite of the commercial touch of his latest films?*
OUSMANE SEMBÈNE: You cinema critics, you are always puristic. But how to capture the people? The people are not going to cinema like they go to a religious mass. So you don't have to transform a cinema into a mosque or any other ideological chapel. I think that people go to cinema partly for entertainment, which does not mean that there is no reflection but you cannot present them a catechism. It's a new style and Spike Lee's films are successful in Africa.

FRANÇOISE PFAFF: *Is this new style closer to the western commercial cinema canon than to the films with a message?*

OUSMANE SEMBÈNE: The western cinema canon has nothing to do with that at all. The question is how to reach the people of your country. I don't like American coffee, but does this mean that I have to dislike all coffee? Italy does not produce any coffee, but it makes the best coffee in the world. If you go to Ivory Coast where they grow coffee, you will drink Nescafe. So, where can we take reference? There is no canon/reference point, not for the one side nor for the other side. The point is to sell and better your product according to the rules of the market.

FRANÇOISE PFAFF: *Do you have to submit yourself to that, like Spike Lee, if you want to continue making films?*

OUSMANE SEMBÈNE: I don't have to submit myself to that, rather I need to have control over my decisions and submit the market to my wishes and desires. The point isn't that I submit myself.

FRANÇOISE PFAFF: *That's a good conclusion, thank you.*

Interview with Ousmane Sembène about *Guelwaar*

BERND WOLPERT/1995

BW: *The story that you tell in* Guelwaar *starts with an administration error. Was this incident based on an actual event or was it completely invented by your (artistic) imagination?*

OS: It really happened. Only recently did I hear that something similar happened again. The dead bodies of two women with the same name, of the same age and from two villages only ten miles apart, were mistaken for each other. One of the two women had already been buried when the parents of the other woman noticed the error as they came to pick up the body. They therefore decided not to bring the body into their own village, but their daughter had already been buried. Thus, the two women were buried in graves next to each other.

BW: *The character of Guelwaar is not just made up but refers to a politician, Almany Samori Touré, who lived near Diouala in the late nineteenth century.*

OS: He was a resistance fighter and lived in the late nineteenth century. He fought for eighteen years for his people against the French, the Germans, and the English.

BW: *What did he achieve?*

OS: He wanted to strength the identity of his people and defend their autonomy. But you really compare the two men. Touré was a real leader.

From *EZEF*, http://www.gep.de/ezef/Guelwaar-2006.pdf. Translated from the German by Gabi Schneider. Reprinted by permission.

But he was not a born leader. He became one by hard work. His fate is very moving. He was a young man, approximately twenty years old, when his mother was arrested and enslaved.

This happened in 1882/83 and thus in the time when slavery came to an end in Europe. After he had found the African king Cissé, he visited him and told him: "Take me as your slave and free my mother." But the king kept him and his mother as well. He stayed there for seven years. He was trained to become a fighter and became very famous. And since he had a strong sense of justice, the rest of the fighters helped him and his mother to flee. He returned to his village, and the village elders declared him leader of the militia. Since he was very intelligent, he succeeded in gaining the support of the common people.

In this way he succeeded in changing the society in which he lived. Within ten years he had founded his own state and had become its leader. Parts of what is today Guinea, Senegal, Mali, and Burkina Faso formed the state. He ruled like a king, and with his own big army, he fought against the armies of the colonial empires who began invading the region from 1885 onwards.

BW: *The film analyses the origin and the course of the conflict in a very traditional way. Since the people involved in the conflict were not interested in finding explanations as to what caused it—only the police officer tries to do so—their own mistakes are systematically hushed up and those of the others exaggerated. The film demonstrates and analyses this with the stylistic device of satire. Do you want to hold the mirror up to your audience with your film?*
OS: Yes, I prefer the mirror, because so far the Africans have proved to be very prudish when confronted with their idiosyncracies and mistakes.

BW: *The film refrains from a confrontation of good and evil. Instead, it denounces the ignorance and double standards, the hypocrisy and arrogance of those in power. Even the hero Guelwaar does not escape criticism. Is this how you perceive reality? Is this the perspective of an old wise man, who is no stranger to anything and has seen and experienced it all before, or is it a narrative device employed in order to reach and convince the audience more easily.*
OS: The latter is the case. We are neither all good nor all evil. Everybody takes what they want and nobody cares about anybody else.

In Africa we are not any better or worse than the people elsewhere. But there is no virtue in misery and poverty.

BW: *Straight at the start of the final credits you characterize the story of the film as a "legend of the 21st century." Surely, this refers first and foremost to the attitude of the young people, who, at the end of the film, throw the food, which was to be used to bribe the village, from the vehicles and drive over it with their carts. This scene, as well as the celebrations held by the people in order to express their thanks for the aid received from Europe shown earlier on in the film, explicitly criticizes aid. Do you think that it is only the helpers that gain from aid?*

OS: Africa has received aid from Europe for the last thirty-five years. But the misery has become deeper and deeper and the Europeans send money again and again. But this money then ends up in bank accounts in Switzerland. Therefore one has to wonder whether it is partly because the Africans heavily rely on the aid to be continued forever and ever.

If a person falls over next to you, you help him get up again, of course. And if your neighbor's house catches fire, you help him to extinguish. And you also help him to rebuild the house again. But after that, you will have to work and earn money yourself again. And the neighbor will have to complete the rebuilding of his house on his own. But in Africa this does not happen. People rely on being helped here. You have governments in Africa that are paid far too high salaries in comparison to the productivity of their country. In Senegal a member of parliament earns between 80,000 and 100,000 Franc-CFA per month. A farmer's family of five earns about 150,000 Francs a year. Who profits from aid, the bourgoisie or the farmers? And when the bourgois African complains about poverty, he speaks about himself and not about the farmers! The aid given to the Africans is therefore extremely bad for Africa's development. You have to realize that those who rule cannot rule without outside help. And the debts, which exist because of this situation, do no good at all. At the moment you can witness the recolonialization of francophone West Africa—a recolonialization by the most legal means you can imagine. Private French companies, for instance, begin to control the big cities' water and energy supplies communication and TV stations. And what is left? Nothing.

BW: *The film does not end in the abstract rejection of aid. Guelwaar himself makes it too easy for himself. This becomes very clear when Guelwaar's widow starts talking to Guelwaar's clothes, his "cover," because his dead body has disappeared. This is one of the most impressive scenes of the film for me.*
OS: Yes it is very intimate. This is Africa naked.

BW: *His wife accuses him of not having done anything for his family all his life in this necessarily one-sided dialogue. What is to be done, then?*
OS: I did nothing but let someone die in a very mythological way. Because every people needs a hero. Remember Bertholt Brecht's statement: Unhappy the land that is in need of heroes.

BW: *I think that another strength of the film is that there is no returning to tradition.*
OS: No, it just does not exist. The past does not return. Africa's past needs to be historically classified, to be seen in a historical context. When did something happen? Before slavery? During slavery? Before or during colonization? To which epoch, as far as human history is concerned, does this correspond? If we look at the history of all humankind we cannot help but realize that black leaders took part in the selling of their brothers. During colonial times black people participated in the conquest of their own countries, even in the conquest of their fathers and mothers. This is a historical fact.

BW: *Let's talk about something different now: Can Islam and Christianity on their own safeguard the peaceful coexistence of people? Or do we, first and foremost, need a strong, secular state, who will have to guarantee peace—as it is personified in the character of the police officer in your film.*
OS: In West Africa all states are secular. But there is a subtracultural basis, which allows Africa to absorb all religions. We could observe that in 1992, for instance, when the Pope came to Dahomey in Benin he met the traditional chiefs there, the fetishists, the representatives of African religions, which are developing, changing, and expanding at the moment. The Catholic religion has thus been transformed (in a syncretic way). The same has happened to Islam. What I cannot understand at all, is the Africans' great belief in Gods. It is their strength but also their weakness. But that's what Africa is like. I am interested in it, but I can neither

explain nor understand it. They believe in everything. They blend everything. They are Catholic or whatever, but it doesn't get them any further. And then there is also the Western way of life as a reference frame—that is one of the big problems Africa is facing at the moment.

BW: *I would like to come back to the role of the secular state once more. Is it the secular state's role to safeguard peace or will the religious communities manage to coexist peacefully without its interference? That is, at least, what the Imam and the priest stand for, isn't it?*
OS: They do not need the state to get along with each other. In small states religious and political responsibilities overlap sometimes. And when the laws of the state or the Sharia law don't get them any further, they consult tradition. It's as if you try to separate hot and cold water in a jug.

BW: *Catholics and Muslims are normally quite hostile to each other; however, as soon as they start fearing that fetishists are at work, they hold together.*
OS: They have not become best friends. The Imam broke the rules of his religion in order to get the body, but he did not do that out of magnanimity, but because he didn't want to have a Catholic body on his graveyard. When the Christians approach the graveyard with the coffin and the crucifix on top of it, he stops them. However, people are not as strict as that everywhere in Senegal. The North is different from the South. In Casamance, for instance, each village has only one graveyard for everyone. And on All Saints' Day the Catholics remember all of the dead, Muslims included.

Another example off these big contradictions in Africa is the following: Sometimes the fetishists ask their clients to bring a bone from the graveyard, when they are asked to treat a disease. They do not mind whether it is the bone of a Christian or a Muslim, however. It is difficult to get one's head round Africa at the moment. A lot of African heads of state, who attain good qualifications from European universities, appoint fetishists and maributs as their advisors.

BW: *How do you explain that?*
OS: If I could explain it, I would have made a good film about this issue.

BW: *The message of this film, as well as of your previous films, does not only address people in Senegal. In which countries has* Guelwaar *been shown already? And how did the public react?*

OS: I showed my films in all francophone countries. I will soon travel to Cameroon and Gabun in order to talk about cinema and culture there.

One of the difficulties I am confronted with in Africa is, however, that people here think that artists can solve problems. Therefore people come and ask questions because they think that you can solve problems with a film, a picture, or music. That is why sometimes instead of answering their questions I ask them, "Why do you need artists? In a situation like this, in all these financial and economic difficulties, why do you need art? I am not elected, nobody voted for me. Nevertheless I spend all my time answering questions, talking about Africa. When doing so, I make mistakes, of course, and I am sometimes even ignorant. But the people listen to me and talk to me. And as soon as they find out that I am making a film, they bring their news to me into the bush and tell me what happened to them and their neighbors. They have got the film I want to make in their minds, already. And they tell me what to show in my film and what to say.

BW: *Are your films shown in mainstream cinemas or are you invited to special events to show your films? Where are regular showings?*

OS: There are distribution companies in Senegal, Burkina Faso, the Ivory Coast, and Mali. But in other countries it is more difficult. I run a distribution company in Cameroon, Chad, and Central Africa. But Africa is huge. Only here in Zurich does Africa appear to be as small as Switzerland perhaps!

Ousmane Sembène

DAVID MURPHY/1995

MURPHY: *Your first novel,* Black Docker, *deals with the African community in Marseilles during the 1950s. The Jamaican writer, Claude McKay, also deals with the black community in Marseilles during an earlier period, the 1920s, in his novel,* Banjo. *Had you read this book before writing* Black Docker?

SEMBÈNE: No, I hadn't read it. I still haven't read it either. I don't think it was available during the colonial period. I know people have written comparisons of the two books but I myself haven't read it.

MURPHY: *During this period, did you identify more with the work of black writers from the United States like Richard Wright, James Baldwin, Ralph Ellison, than with the works of African writers who wrote about a mythical Africa of the past?*

SEMBÈNE: But I *am* African. Why would I go looking for something in the United States? I don't have to search for an identity. I'm an African. For me, Africa is the centre of the world. The United States and Europe are on the periphery of my world. I was born in Africa not in the ghettos of a big American city like the blacks of the diaspora.

MURPHY: *The reason why I asked the question is that you have often said that you wanted to create a different image of Africa from the one put forward by Negritude writers. But the story of your first novel is set in France, in a racially mixed community, and it deals with problems between blacks and whites.*

Interview conducted 30 November 1995. From *Sembène: Imagining Alternatives in Film and Fiction* by David Murphy (Trenton, NJ: Africa World Press, 2003). Reprinted by permission by David Murphy.

This is a subject that black American writers often deal with. I was simply wondering if these writers had influenced you.

SEMBÈNE: You know, I never think about things like that. That's your job. Of course, there were other writers who didn't have the same conception of Africa as me. They spoke a bit naïvely about the mythical side of things. But I just write and that's all there is to it. I don't think about other writers. I'm the centre of my world.

MURPHY: *In* Black Docker, *Diaw Falla is unable to legitimate his position as a self-educated, African writer. Is the novel, with its* mise en abyme *of an African writing his first novel, an attempt to address the problems you faced at the outset of your literary career?*

SEMBÈNE: You know, there are no races: yellow, black, white, none of them exists. During the 1950s, I tried to fight against the colonial regime. At the time, nobody believed that an African could master science. The French wouldn't allow Africans to become physicists, etc. At the time, we wanted to claim our human rights.

MURPHY: *You are often referred to as a committed writer but we can see that from the start of your career, with the* mise en abyme *in* Black Docker, *you were already concerned with the form of your work. Does it bother you as an artist that criticism often deals with the themes of your books without looking at the structure or the aesthetic aspect, which are the means by which an artist transmits his message?*

SEMBÈNE: But that's their problem. I'm not interested in all that. When I write a book, it's finished for me. I don't want to spend my time thinking about why I did this or that.

MURPHY: *In your first two books,* Black Docker *and* O Pays, mon beau peuple!, *the female characters seem to be a lot more passive than the ones we find in your later works. Did you find it difficult to write female roles at first?*

SEMBÈNE: It's because of questions like that that I don't like giving interviews. You academics are what I call "chronophages." Do you know what I mean by that? "When did you do this or that?" What's more, you're all disciples of Freud as well. I don't ask myself questions like that.

MURPHY: *The image you present of women in your society is fairly complex. The women in your work are often aware of their inferior position but their education has taught them to be submissive, and the rivalry between women prevents solidarity from developing. How do you see the evolution of women's role in society here in Senegal?*
SEMBÈNE: But the African woman has more freedom than the European woman! You ask the question because Europeans think that the African woman is oppressed. In Africa, women and men have separate powers in strictly defined areas.

MURPHY: *It might be true that the African woman has more freedom than it is thought in Europe. But for example, in* Taaw, *we see Yaye Dabo repudiate her husband and she is shocked by her own behaviour. It goes against her education.*
SEMBÈNE: Listen, the mother exists. She feels certain things. Her children are more important to her than anything else. She wants them to succeed. In your country [Ireland], people have been killing each other for thirty years. Think of all those widows or those women who have lost children. You see, mothers are the same in every part of the world.

MURPHY: *During the 1950s, you lived in France. When exactly did you return to Africa?*
SEMBÈNE: I returned after independence.

MURPHY: *Were* Tribal Scars *and* L'Harmattan *written in Africa? And in which order did you write them?*
SEMBÈNE: I can't remember which year they were published.

MURPHY: *1962 and 1963.*
SEMBÈNE: Yes, I wrote them after my return to Africa.

MURPHY: *Did you write* Tribal Scars *as a collection with a specific structure? Or did you just group together stories that you had written over a certain period, or that might have been published in journals perhaps?*
SEMBÈNE: I'm always writing. I'm always in the middle of writing something. Even now, I have stories at home that I haven't published.

MURPHY: *But were the choices for first and last story deliberate? "In the Face of History" sets the reader thinking about questions of form straight away by referring to the two meanings of "histoire." Then,* Tribal Scars *or* The Voltaique *gives us all those different versions of the history of scarification, and at the end, the narrator asks the reader for his opinion.*
SEMBÈNE: The history of scarification was a subject that I had researched heavily when I was working on a book about slavery that was never published. I noticed that the slaves that made it to the Caribbean had no marks on their faces. The slaves had no scars. So, I talked with a lot of people and I discovered that the whole phenomenon [of scarification] was limited to the coastal regions of Africa. In the beginning, people scarred their faces to avoid becoming slaves. But people don't want to believe me. They give mythical and symbolic explanations.

MURPHY: *The Negritude school saw itself as the voice of tradition. Was* Tribal Scars *an attempt to appropriate tradition for your own ends?*
SEMBÈNE: It's more than just an attempt. I do appropriate it.

MURPHY: *You wanted to situate Africa within history rather than in the mythical world of tradition?*
SEMBÈNE: But Africa has always existed within history. For me, Africa is the centre of the world!

MURPHY: *Yes, but what I mean is that you wanted to explain African traditions in a more concrete way: to escape from the mythical Africa, to show people that Africa is at the centre of the world, if you like! To explain to Africans how they reached this point in their history.*
SEMBÈNE: Yes, it was necessary to show people that they had to share responsibility for their own history. To show them that slavery existed here and that Africans helped to enslave other Africans. We must assume responsibility for our history.

MURPHY: *Since* Tribal Scars, *you've mainly written shorter works, short stories and especially novellas. The novella is a genre in which the story is sketched, where not everything is said, and which often casts an ironic and disillusioned eye on its subject. There's quite a contrast here with the epic elements of novels such as* O Pays, mon beau peuple! *and* God's Bits of Wood.

Is this a reflection of the move from the optimism of independence to the pessimism and disappointment of post-independence?
SEMBÈNE: But who says the novella is ironic and disillusioned? That's what you say. I just write and that's it.

MURPHY: *Yes, but you must accept that your first novels, and* God's Bits of Wood *in particular, have an epic side that we don't find in your later work.*
SEMBÈNE: I write. I make films. I don't think about questions like that. That's the critic's job.

MURPHY: *You often seem to structure your films and fiction around the notion of silence. For example,* The Promised Land *and* Guelwaar *give a voice to two dead characters. The dead cannot speak but the artist can speak for them. I'm thinking also about Pays in* Camp de Thiaroye *who cannot express his suffering, or Thierno in* Niiwam *who has to keep quiet in order to keep his terrible secret. How do you explain this paradox of silence and language in your art?*
SEMBÈNE: Language is like that. Sometimes you don't need to speak to explain something.

MURPHY: *But language seems to be linked to power in your work.*
SEMBÈNE: You don't need to speak to hold power. Power exists. I try to present the world as I see it.

MURPHY: *You might think that I'm trying to flatter you but I think that your work contains a serious reflection on questions of form, a reflection that is neglected by the critics. Critics constantly write about your commitment but you don't write political pamphlets. You've said yourself in interviews that you don't write a "slogan literature."*
SEMBÈNE: You know, African critics constantly speak about commitment without even knowing what it means. African critics all want to carry out the revolution by proxy. Do you know Maguèye Kassé from the university [of Dakar]? He's held two conferences on my work in the university and they never stopped talking about commitment. Maybe the European critic could be useful in introducing a deeper reflection on the question of form. You just don't get that here. I don't write a literature of political slogans. European criticism is more developed in

this area. Yes, I'm an artist, and as an artist, what interests me is to remain as close to my people as possible.

MURPHY: *In the preface to* White Genesis, *the narrator claims that he was asked not to recount this story of incest. Is it the aim of your work to create a discourse around subjects like religion, politics, tradition, subjects that often seem to pass uncontested?*
SEMBÈNE: These things are all part of life. We need to talk about them. I made a film of *White Genesis* but I ended up censoring it myself. The film lasts twenty-two minutes. We showed it to the public and the debate lasted three hours. The film denounces incest, a subject that people don't like to talk about in any country. But people must keep talking to each other.

MURPHY: *In Africa, tradition is often quoted to defend certain conservative values. But in your work, you try to open up traditions to more positive readings that are useful in contemporary Africa. Are you attempting to go against the arguments of traditionalists when you present traditional characters such as the griot, the wise man Kocc Barma, the* ceddo *warrior, as "oppositional figures"?*
SEMBÈNE: Yes. You see, there are good and bad elements in tradition. I'm no expert on Kocc Barma or his era but, if I'm not wrong, it was the era of the slave trade. Do you see what I mean?

MURPHY: *You're trying to point out elements of tradition that are practical within modern Africa? You're giving an alternative version of African traditions?*
SEMBÈNE: Exactly. I did the same thing in *Ceddo*. I admit that the film is not historical but it's *my* version. You know, the Wolof are the most bastardised ethnic group in Senegal. They're always looking towards the West or Mecca. They're not interested in Africa.

MURPHY: *Do you consider Samory Touré, with whom you have been preoccupied for so long now, as an oppositional figure?*
SEMBÈNE: That's not just my interpretation. They're facts. I was intrigued by this character who had fought the French for eighteen years without ever leaving West Africa. I wanted to find out about his methods, his motivation. I'm trying to find out why certain people resisted longer than others. The Wolof resisted for a while and then surrendered.

MURPHY: *Will the film [about Samory] ever be made?*
SEMBÈNE: It's a dream. You have to dream.

MURPHY: *The question of African languages, and in your case Wolof, has always played an important role in your work. Why didn't you continue to write in Wolof after the publication of* Ceddo?
SEMBÈNE: The language question is primarily a political matter. Above all, Africans are pragmatic. A Wolof says to himself, "I have to learn French to get a job." That's how it works. It's economic factors that determine these things. Why write in Wolof if the book will be banned? Senghor was illiterate in his own language. The word "ceddo" comes from pulaar and there is germination [i.e. a double "d", not a single "d" as Senghor argued]. There were African linguists working with us on the newspaper *Kaddu* and Senghor had an Austrian linguist as his adviser. We were right. Why listen to a European? This was an African matter, the word comes from pulaar.

MURPHY: *But the censorship of* Ceddo *wasn't simply to do with linguistics, was it? Was it not also linked to your controversial interpretation of Senegalese history?*
SEMBÈNE: Not really. The film was released before the birth of the fundamentalist movement. It was before the Islamic revolution in Iran. You know, the Shah of Iran wanted a copy of the film and I turned him down. Then, when Khomeini took over, I offered them a copy and they turned me down! That's history for you.

MURPHY: *What happened to the newspaper,* Kaddu, *that you mentioned earlier?*
SEMBÈNE: We were losing money. I put in a lot of my money to allow the newspaper to survive but it couldn't go on forever.

MURPHY: *Do you think that the language question is still important?*
SEMBÈNE: You know, Francophone Africa was the most colonised part of Africa. Most of the African civil servants were educated in schools set up to train people for the colonial service. If we hadn't gained independence, these people would have become colonial officials. Here in Senegal, we have a national languages week. That reminds me of my

childhood during the colonial era when there was a colonial week. Throughout the year, we learned about French history and culture, and then we had one week of local culture. It's the same thing nowadays.

MURPHY: *In principle, cinema should allow you to reach a wider public, the people you can't reach through your books, but unfortunately one rarely sees African films in Africa. How can the situation be improved?*
SEMBÈNE: There is no cultural policy in Africa. Politicians think it's enough to eat and shit and everything's alright! On the radio the other day, I heard that the World Bank/IMF said that it might be a good idea to develop culture in Africa as that might help the economy! When I was in your country, I began by reading Irish plays. What's that guy's name? Oh, well. Anyway, you've been killing each other in Ireland for twenty-five years but you're proud of a writer like Joyce. Culture is something that unites a people. The problem with cinema is that it's an industry. It's controlled by the Americans. I make films designed to make you think. You have to make the public think. Not all the time, but . . .

MURPHY: *Is it true that, in the past, you used to go into small villages in the bush to screen your films?*
SEMBÈNE: I still do. The others [his staff at Filmi Doomireew] showed some films on 25, 26, and 27 [November 1995] while I was in Cameroon. We show them free in the villages. We ask for 200 CFA in the schools so that we can break even. It's important for me to see how people "read" my films. It's a pity we're not going into the bush again soon. You should see how people react to films. In other African countries, I'd already be in prison by now but here the people love me too much. Once I crashed into a car driven by a white man. It was my fault but the people didn't want to know. I had to go and see the white man afterwards to pay for the damage. The people go too far sometimes. I only work for my people.

MURPHY: *Ritual plays a vital role in your cinematic work: we see the rituals of fetishism and consumerism in* Xala. *Is this one of the organising principles of your cinema?*
SEMBÈNE: Yes, ritual is very important. In Europe, it's practically disappeared. Each people needs its own rituals.

MURPHY: *You've often said that cinema is the modern art form that is closest to the art of the* griot, *with its mixture of gesture, ritual, and words.*
SEMBÈNE: Yes, my people recognise themselves through rituals. Europeans find this hard to understand. When you lose your own rituals, you lose a part of your soul.

MURPHY: *Your most recent film,* Guelwaar, *denounces the institutionalisation of a dependence mindset in Africa. And that was twelve years after you had denounced dependence on the former coloniser in* The Last of the Empire. *So, what do you think of the current situation in Africa?*
SEMBÈNE: It's worse! But I'm still optimistic. You have to be optimistic.

MURPHY: *What do you think of Axelle Kabou's argument: that Africa is "refusing development"?*
SEMBÈNE: She's right. A lot of people have criticised her but I've always defended her. I don't know her and I don't want to meet her. But she said something that had to be said and I respect her for that.

MURPHY: *So Africans are refusing development?*
SEMBÈNE: Careful! It's the politicians who are refusing development.

MURPHY: *Axelle Kabou thinks that the absence of a genuine African unity is one of the major causes of the current state of the continent. Do you agree?*
SEMBÈNE: I think we should start by creating regional structures. It's a necessary step in the development of Africa.

MURPHY: *The fall of the communist regimes of the former USSR and of Eastern and Central Europe has put an end to the stand-off between East and West. What do you think about the current state of the world?*
SEMBÈNE: Liberalism will never replace communism. Africa needs communism. Capitalism doesn't work, just look at the United States. It's the most individualistic country in the world. In Europe, you think it's enough to be wealthy and everything's alright. Communism is the only system that can help Africa. The Soviet Union trained mechanics and artisans that Africa needed: its demise is a loss for Africa. Communism is the only hope for Africa.

Still the Fire in the Belly: The Confessions of Ousmane Sembène

MAMADOU NIANG / 2000

MAMADOU NIANG: *I'm curious about the way you shuttle between the novel and filmmaking. It is not usual for writers, and it shouldn't be easy for you who put almost all of your novels on the screen. How does Sembène "the writer" get to filmmaking, and how does Sembène "the filmmaker" get back to writing?*

OUSMANE SEMBÈNE: Well! I must confess it's not always easy. A screenplay is a book written in telegraphic form, and the dialogues have to respect a carefully planned timing. You cannot be verbose. You must resort to mimics, body language, eye contact, the movements of actors, etc. . . . I think they are separate trades, but they're not incompatible for me, I'm used to it since I've been doing it for over thirty years.

MN: *Is it conceivable that the novelist filmmaker Sembène would take to the screen a novel or a screenplay written by someone else?*

OS: No! I don't think so. I could be interested in a book, and with the accord of the writer, develop a screenplay, but it would be an adaptation.

MN: *There are directors who are not writers, who are not auteurs. They're called in to direct someone else's idea.*

From the African Film Festival's 2001 website, http://www.africanfilmny.org/network/news/Fniang.html. Reprinted by permission of Mamadou Niang.

OS: People have different talents. Some have a visual intelligence, but lack the imaginative thinking that writing requires. But this separation has more to do with the parts of the world where "filmmaking" is an industry. We're talking about specialization here, where in Europe or in America you may have four persons working on a screenplay, before the studio even names a director. But that's an enrichment; that's a luxury. There are no written rules. Nothing is absolute in this business.

MN: *So, then you could work in that context?*
OS: Yes, one can be both a woodcutter and a sculptor at once.

MN: *Of all your writing and films, has there been a time you would call a defining moment throughout your long career, a moment of fulfillment, of triumph?*
OS: I've loved everything I've done at the moment I am doing it. It's the next thing that obsesses me. I'm not in the habit of psychoanalyzing myself, but I'm taken totally by the task at hand. Once the work is completed, which I hope is of the highest quality I can deliver, then it belongs to the public. It's no longer mine.

MN: *But I bet you've had moments of great satisfaction.*
OS: Oh yes! After I've put that final touch, it's a satisfying feeling. Writing, or making a film is many, many months of adventure. It is a gratifying moment when you put the final dot, and sign the release for the publication of a novel, or when you finish mixing sound for a film and see the audience coming into the theater. See, I'm a craftsman, not an artist. I take pleasure in the work I do, but it is a process, pruning, carving, trimming . . . writing, rewriting. It's work that needs to be done well. Never an extraordinary jubilation, but always a happy feeling.

MN: *I imagine that the filmmaker Sembène is more popular than the writer Sembène. Does it frustrates you that most people in Africa only know the filmmaker, or do you think that the public appreciates both equally?*
OS: I am generally happy about the way my work is received. But I wished that our peoples in Africa spent more time reading, and then go to the movies. Reading and movies are both means of intellectual and cultural nourishment. I've always said that cinema in Africa is an

evening class, a "continuing education" at this stage of its development in our societies. But we must make good films which address our struggles. There's no point in making films to simply entertain or bore people with protest films about labor rallies. Our films must for an hour and a half or two entertain, but also inspire and make the headlines of conversations in the workplace, and in the homes.

Reading is a privilege. It's a solitary project. People who read a lot, who strive for knowledge, are persons of great mind. Other people's thoughts help us better access our own. I wish my people were the biggest readers in mankind and the best moviegoers. I've always thought that reading and cinema should be considered in legislative debates involving quality of life and sustainable development issues. They play a major influence in how we live, and what we do. Beauty belongs to everyone. We all like things beautiful.

MN: *Do you have the same expectations when you finish a novel, as when you wrap a film?*

OS: No. Each work has a life of its own, and makes its own way to the public. Today, it looks like each work has its own audience.

MN: *Is there a distinction between Sembène the filmmaker and Sembène the writer?*

OS: Yes, they are different. But it's like you want to separate the cold from the hot water you poured in the same sink. The two approaches are distinct. I am pursuing two different forms, but it's the same "Sembène."

Further, using multiple mediums I felt was a necessity. I've always tried to explore how to make my work more accessible to people. How as an artist, a witness of my time, and member of my society, I can bring my contribution like the tailor, the shoemaker, like anyone else. And I always ask myself: Why does society need artists? What do we need artists for?

MN: *Why?*

OS: I ask you . . . it's an interesting question!

Here is a mass of people asking to be entertained, enlightened, educated, and informed; they want to be given something to think about. And on top of that they ask for accountability, although we're not elected. In my own situation, my people are very demanding of me and of my work. Sometimes they even tell me what I should or should not do. On one hand, they have elected presidents, ministers, representatives, who should account for what they do, and on another hand, I am posted in their mind—an invisible official of a different sort, whom they wait for and ask what's next? For them, the artist is the psychic who can see it, and bring light. That's why we need artists.

MN: *Which makes the artist's role as equally important as the politician's.*
OS: We see what is not generally perceptible or that people are hiding. When people fight to get a law enacted, after they've won and think they got a good law passed, the artist's role is to violate that certainty. We ought to go further, and that law, transformed under the artist's vision, is no longer fitting. Artists are nonconformists. It is not to say that artists can be politicians; it is incompatible. An artist who practices politics is artistically dead. We may have democratic and political ideals, and we must, but shouldn't get involved in militantism or party politics. Ideologies and religion are conformists.

MN: *In their respective capacities, who plays the most important role in society, the artist or the politician?*
OS: I think the artist plays a larger role. An honest politician is only but an administrator, a facilitator. Period. The politician does not produce anything.

Let me tell you a folksy image: art helps people refuel their egos so they can better face their anguish and the iniquities of society. Men can face adversity and deal with injustice only when they're fraught with their culture. When we talk about defending your country, we're not talking geography. We're talking about defending your mother, your father, your wife, your children, we're talking about your heritage. You are performing an act of culture, safeguarding your dignity, your pride. Fighting for your independence is nothing but an act of culture. Politicians transform people into alimentary canals, evaluate them in tons of rice, corn, wheat, hospital beds, and school desks. Culture does not answer to arithmetics. From birth to death, it's within man, its guiding companion. It is not palpable, and art helps enlighten it.

MN: *The politician you're talking about, is he not the practitioner as we know it today . . . Couldn't there be somewhere in the artist's imagination a certain political practice which restores a dignified political action?*
OS: All right, okay . . . It's the perpetual fantasy. Descartes spoke of the city where the artist would be king, but I'm reminded of an Arab proverb: When a great king was asked, if he were to sacrifice someone, who would that be? His answer was the artist. Then he was asked, if he were to save someone, who would be the last person on earth? His answer was the artist.

MN: *You wrote the novel* Guelwaar *after having made the film. This is a common practice in Hollywood, where a blockbuster is always turned into a check-out-counter item. Did you glance at Tinseltown?*
OS: Oh, no. I am far from Hollywood . . . I like *Guelwaar*. Though the film came to me first, I also like the book. It's not to say it is my favorite. But the book is richer, fuller than the film. With this book I tried to experiment with an approach which could serve to teach students in screen writing at the school we want to set up in Dakar, to train and produce a number of writers. Screenplay is a difficult practice, a tedious process.

Now, *Guelwaar* is based on a true story. Someone died, and relatives, when they arranged for burial, learned that his remains had been mixed up at the mortuary . . . Also true are the issues I dramatized, namely the issue of aid to African countries. I know many people who resent these forms of assistance. Officers and officials who beat people who can't pay their taxes also exist. Conflicts between Muslims and Christians, although being swept under the rug, are rampant. To lace all this in an interesting story for film is different from putting it in a book. But the book enables me to get further. This case was an experiment. It's not Hollywood; the West is not my point of reference. Sure, we learn from Europe, and we must, but only organization and technology. For the rest, I am the center of the universe; Africa is my universe. I need no lesson from the West, neither moral nor how to conduct my life.

MN: *When Pierre-Henri Thioune took the podium in* Guelwaar, *the movie, and in his language, Wolof, addressed the rally, and denounced aid and its paralyzing consequences, which he said, "leads to permanent dependance," his electrifying speech was so riveting and convincing that it was enough to get him killed. In the book, in French, I did not find the same compelling charisma. I felt the force and the quality of the delivery in his own language was lost in French. Do you feel frustrated at not being able to render in European languages the full drama of your characters?*

OS: This is an obvious limitation. It is a problem of a cultural nature. I write first in Wolof, then I translate into French. It's a drawback for African writers practicing in European languages. I don't have a solution to this dilemma, and we must adapt.

In Japan, I saw American actors speaking Japanese, quite amazing, considering that English, or American English is almost the universal lingua franca. You're right, but if you're in a different cultural universe you must reach out. You're Wolof, and your reaction is quite understandable—hearing your mother tongue from an eloquent speaker isn't quite the same as reading the same words in French. In the book this section is in italics, it's a moot warning, but we should not be purists by dwelling on these issues.

MN: *But what about the larger question of national languages. We keep postponing the advent of our languages into officialdom. You had the bitter experience of having your film kept from release in Senegal for ten years, because the president who had strong French sensibilities didn't like the way you spelled "Ceddo." You also lead a roaring fight to establish curriculums in Wolof. What has changed since?*

OS: But that's another matter! Ask the presidents. We are ready, but the authorities in command aren't ready. We know what to do if legislation is enacted. But officials who lack vision aren't hurried. But in the case of Senegal there's another problem. Non-Wolof populations do not like the idea of erecting Wolof as the universal language, but the language is spoken by at least 80 percent of Senegalese. So the result is that we keep locking ourselves in the European logic, preferring the colonial language. I don't understand why.

MN: *Are your audiences abroad missing a lot because of the language barrier?*

OS: You're deprived of many things when you're not familiar with a culture. African cultures are not esoteric, but people don't know them.

If you dubbed a Chinese or a Japanese film even in Wolof, I would still miss a lots of things. I'm not well acquainted with Asian cultures.

MN: *So does this impediment require you to make a special effort on the image work, to make it more expressive to compensate for language.*
OS: Even the image has limitations. Literature is the best solution. Books are better translated than pictures. Subtitles do not give the substance of a film, which is inseparable from the dialogue. It's a compression, but it's the best of the existing possibilities. Dubbing is something else. I made *Guelwaar* in two versions, Wolof and French. These are our contradictions, but it is best received this way. It's interesting in a sense that we could sometime dub our films in various African languages—Swahili, Bambara, Ibo, and so on. But here we're dealing with technical matters, not artistic ones.

MN: *And we are limited with technical matters?*
OS: We are not limited. We lack cultural policies in our nations. We have no limitations; I refute the idea of an Africa that is limited. What we lack are visionary leaders, people who have coherent policies. Our leaders know nothing other than the politics of food rationing, sustenance. Period. But man doesn't live on bread alone. Look at the continent; only artists are succeeding in organizing themselves. With the FESPACO and FEPACI we have formed the largest independent association in all of Africa. Artists who gather every two years, striving to establish a viable institution. And we are the most independent and the most anarchist on the planet. And my role as the elder is to encourage everyone, especially the young, because it's tough. Whether they succeed or fail, it is important that they hang tight.

MN: *Man doesn't live on bread alone, but is there enough bread around? With the astounding finances required to make a film in a continent beset by shortages of all kinds, isn't it an incongruity?*
OS: Africans are not miserable! We have bad leaders; the elite class, intellectuals, people in government, they're the wicked. They're the ones who beg, bow down, and keep humiliating us. Africans do not panhandle to the West. What they call crises are not crises. It's like the normal evolutionary process of a developing human body. It's illness of

infancy . . . What is thirty years of independence compared to a hundred years of colonization and centuries of slavery?

MN: *In a great number of African films one can see the influence of theater, African theater. Is it an esthetic choice or simply the evolution of a form of artistic expression?*
OS: We must be very careful on this. Francophone countries in Africa have a mediocre theater; there is not really a culture of theater in Senegal, the Ivory Coast, etc. . . . But theater found fertile grounds in English-speaking countries. Nigeria has a prolific theater tradition. Under apartheid, South Africans found theater and music their most forceful means of artistic expression; there it is a vital art form. In these countries, including Ghana, cinema is a natural extension of the art form.

MN: *After thirty years of filmmaking on the continent, with more than a hundred films produced, can we say that the African filmmaker can pretend to having a career in films?*
OS: No, too soon. I can't even myself speak of a career. Thirty years is nothing. Filmmaking needs an industry, and our structures are too precarious. The desire, the material, the artistic possibilities are abundant, but we severely lack the necessary tools. We do not control the means and the medium. They're in the hands of whites. Egypt has a film industry. South Africa is on its way to building one. But, for the most part, we depend on Europe. But this too will change. We've begun collecting equipment and building outfits in Ouaga . . . It will happen.

MN: *Despite the help of white Europeans?*
OS: Listen! Let me tell you something. In war, wherever you get the gun, what matters is that you know how to point it towards the enemy and shoot. Is that clear?

MN: *But the aid that you castigate . . . It's easy for Ousmane Sembène, who's already established a solid international reputation, to speak like this.*
OS: It's crazy how they plug it into our heads. But that's not aid. These are contractual arrangements. We are bound by agreements. When we make a film with French and European agencies, they get a piece. They have their rights when the picture is completed, and they use it to their

own ends, in addition to cataloguing it in their libraries as if their own. On another hand, when I make a film with their participation, I contribute to the development of their film industry by hiring their men and women. They don't help me! Nobody helps me! I'm not a beggar.

MN: *Does European money influence the artistic creation of African filmmakers?*
OS: It depends on the individual. I have the final cut on my works, and I don't want to talk about others.

MN: *International aid is a major theme in* Guelwaar . . . *How corrosive is it to your judgment?*
OS: It's terrible, worse . . . It's like feeding a person everyday with sweets or honey. Go ask the doctor what it does to the body. I think that as Kocch Barma says, "If you want to kill a good and noble person, give him all he needs, whenever he needs it." He'll end up losing all senses of real life, not being able to accomplish anything for himself. It deters effort; the desire to find for one's own is lost; he is a monster among us; all he says is thanks, thanks, and thanks. Kocch Barma has denounced this before my parent's time. There are people in real need, but society, if organized, could and should take care of them. You must help your neighbor whose house was destroyed by fire; but foreign aid from western donor nations, disguised under the name of "International Cooperation" must stop. How many millions of dollars the U.S. has handed Africa for thirty-five years, and where is the money? Where are the results of those investments? No roads, no hospitals, no schools, no universities . . . But, yes, a corrupt bourgeois elite getting richer and never has enough.

MN: *You're also a harsh critic of the grieving brain drain afflicting Africa. The exodus of the educated to Europe and America . . .*
OS: There are different kinds of exodus. "When the goat doesn't find enough to browse on the grass, she'll break the cord and get away": It's a saying from our ancestors. They knew then . . .

But Barthelemy the westernized, in *Guelwaar*, arriving from Paris to just bury his father, and looking down on every thing African—in his confrontations with the officer he shows the worst of a colonized mind. Barthelemy has deserted. He has nothing to do with those who left for lack of space to develop themselves. With a characteristic selfishness, he refuses to face the struggle, leaving to gentler lands with a diploma, which his people helped pay for during his first ten years of education. And these people return only to exploit their folks.

MN: *You include in your schedule a great number of public appearances, to attend speaking engagements and talk about culture and film in Africa. You have become a de facto ambassador of African culture.*
OS: I think we must go back further. I think for us in Africa and in the Third World, artists are cultural ambassadors. It's a new Africa that's being created, in a slow and difficult birth. People throughout the world know only the pictures of misery and suffering that are distilled on television by non-Africans. Those are real and serious, but there is another side of Africa—the Africa which is struggling every day and winning, the Africa fighting to reassemble an illustrious past that was stolen, an Africa not losing faith. Our Africa is not the one represented by our leaders; it is not a bum begging around as they make the rest of the world believe. And we must get out and show them. Yes, we are self-appointed emissaries with the desire to represent the best, the worst, the great, and the meager of Africa. For me, it's a duty and a cultural tradition.

MN: *Twenty-six years ago, you embarrassed African Americans when you came the first time to the U.S. to show your films. They did not expect to see, told by an African, stories of African kings and chiefs who participated in the slave trade or tales of corrupt head-of-states and dictators who oppress their own people. Do audiences you now meet have a better appreciation of your work?*
OS: They have changed. A generation ago, they thought that there was an abstract African ideal to believe in, to help alleviate the denials they suffered in America. But I didn't come to talk about an ideal Africa, to present a model nation. And I think they understood that to love Africa, one must understand it, knowing that many things in our history were not pretty, that Africans have been accomplices, partners in the slave trade.

MN: *And which Africa, the one before that period, or colonial Africa?*
OS: I believe we have been able to establish a dialogue, and they understood that I am interested in exchanges and confrontations that

help define a project for my society. I have seen the arrival of a new wave of African American filmmakers and directors. I'm happy about that and have a number of friends among them.

MN: *In two of your most recent works,* Guelwaar *and* Niwam, *the heroes, the most compelling characters are corpses, dead bodies. What's behind these metaphors?*

OS: Death is a problem only for the living. Those stories are real happenstance. They're both true stories. But I am more interested in the living and how they endure—how they will continue to build their future. The dead help strengthen and unite. Guelwaar is an unknown local hero whose death becomes a national tragedy and made him a hero postmortem. In *Niwam,* we don't know the dead—an infant—but know everything about his father. Birago Diop, the storyteller, once wrote that "the dead are not dead . . ." In my films, men fight and resist; death doesn't stop the struggle, the course of history. Now, what's happening in Liberia, Rwanda, Casamance is death by politics; they're assassinations.

MN: *You've become a target of a certain class of younger filmmakers. What do they chide you about?*

OS: In Africa, we've lost our sense of history; the last to arrive always thinks he is first. But in our context this is exacerbated by neocolonial elements. France, especially the French left, has always elected and adopted an African artist one at a time to be exhibited as a figurehead and as the best among the rest of us. But as far as I am concerned I prefer to remain the unifier. I find it legitimate that we do not all have the same preoccupations, but I don't have to justify or explain anything. Life is like a river: it ebbs and it flows.

MN: *In* Guelwaar, *once again, as in* Ceddo, Emitai, *and in most of your twelve films you display a genuine respect for female strength. Nogoye Marie is elevated as a symbol of endurance and wisdom.*

OS: If we do not praise and dignify our women's heroism, which I see as preeminent, Africa is not going to be liberated. Let's be clear about this: If we do not accord women their rightful place, there will be no liberation. Women work a whole lot more than men do, and if work was in and of itself liberating, women who farm fields daily would have long been liberated. Women's emancipation doesn't only depend on labor. If we do not wake up and appreciate justly the role of women and share responsibilities, we will lose. But I think there's a gender revolution going on in Africa anyway, and we will have to conform.

MN: *Given all these considerate, if not flattering remarks about women, how come you haven't met any to make do with. You've been a single for a long time!*

OS: [laughs] I'm no model. I'm married with the creative process. I have female friends and they understand the life I live, that I want to stay independent. I like my freedom—freedom to wake up whenever I please, to go to bed whenever I please, and to write as late as I please in total tranquility. I tell my friends, an artist is not a good husband—he may be an excellent lover.

I have not succeeded in bridging the incompatibility between living with a partner and the nature of my work which has no timetable. But I wish that what would be remembered of me would be about my contribution to my community. Society isn't always right, and all I do is to just sail along with society.

Interview with Ousmane Sembène

SAMBA GADJIGO/2004

After more than three years of work, Ousmane Sembène has just completed the final touches on his feature film *Moolaadé*. This film, selected for the Cannes Film Festival (Un Certain Regard section) will be presented to the press on May 14, then to the general public on May 15. A few hours after the completion of the film, on April 11, Mr. Sembène granted me this interview that I conducted in Rabat.

GADJIGO: *Mr. Sembène, you have just finished the subtitling of your film* Moolaadé *at the Cinematographic Center of Morocco, in Rabat. Could you tell what this film means to you in particular—to your career, your everyday struggle?*

SEMBÈNE: No, I don't know what this finished product means as an object. I can tell you that, based on its content, the film is the second in a trilogy that, for me, embodies the heroism in daily life. One finds that nowadays war is rampant in Africa, especially south of the Sahara. There's also our life; life continues, after all, with our daily actions that are forgotten by the masses. The people don't retain them. They want to convince us that we "vegetate." But yet, this underground struggle, this struggle of the people, similar to the struggles of all other peoples, that's what I call heroism in daily life. These are the heroes to whom no country, no nation gives any medals . . . They never get a statue built. That, for me, is the symbolism of this trilogy. I have already made two, *Faat-Kine*, this one now *Moolaadé*, and I am preparing for the third. In respect to

---

From *Rabat* (April 11, 2004). Reprinted by permission of Samba Gadjigo.

Moolaadé, it's a film that takes place in a rural space, a village symbolic of a green Africa. This Africa, while living its life, is in contact with "the others." So we have some exterior influences which allow the African to gather a better knowledge of himself. In *Moolaadé*, there are two values in conflict with each other: One the traditional, which is the female genital excision. This goes a long way back, before Jesus, before Mohammed, to the times of Herodotus. It's a tradition. It was instituted as a value in order to, in my opinion, continue the subjugation of women . . . The other value, as old as human existence: the right to give protection to those who are weaker. When these two values meet, cross, multiply, clash, you see the symbolism of our society: modern elements and elements that form part of our cultural foundation. On top of these add the elements that belong to the superstructure, notably religion. These are the waters in which this group, this film, sails.

GADJIGO: *You have said that* Moolaadé *was the most African of all of your films. Could you tell more about that?*
SEMBÈNE: I said it in the sense that, in this film, we are within the African cultural foundation. Certainly, with some elements from the outside, but the whole film takes place inside a language, a culture, and its metaphors and symbols. We witness the arrival of two foreign elements. One is an ex-military man. He has, in the name of humanity, participated in all the peacekeeping forces. The other is an exile in Europe (for his own interests), who is the son of the village chief. To me, this is the most African film.

GADJIGO: *From the time you wrote your first novel,* The Black Docker *(1956), in which the first chapter was called "The Mother," you have a given a very particular emphasis to women, to the heroism of the African woman. Why does this heroism recur, as a leitmotif, throughout your work?*
SEMBÈNE: I think that Africa is maternal. The African male is very maternal; he loves his mother; he swears on his mother. When someone insults his father, the man can take it; but once his mother's honor has been hurt, the man feels he's not worthy of life if he doesn't defend his mother. According to our traditions, a man has no intrinsic value; he receives his value from his mother. This concept goes back to before Islam: the good wife, the good mother, the submissive mother who knows

how to look after her husband and family. The mother embodies our society . . . I continue to think that African society is very maternal. Maybe we have inherited from our pre-Islamic matriarchy. That said, to me, every man loves a woman. We love them. Besides, more than 50 percent of the African population are women. More than half of the 800,000,000 that we are. This is a force that we must be able to mobilize for our own development. There's no one that works as hard as the rural woman.

GADJIGO: *Out of the fifty-odd African countries, today more than thirty-eight practice the excision. Then, why the choice of Burkina Faso and Djerisso when you could have also made the film somewhere else. Why Djerisso?*
SEMBÈNE: I could have done it somewhere else, but I would not have had this setting that I searched for and didn't find except here. I simply looked for a village that responded to my creative desire. Why shouldn't I paint a rose black? I traveled thousands of kilometers. I went to Burkina Faso, Mali, Guinea, and Guinea Bissau. But when I saw this village I told myself: this is the village! But there's more: this hedgehog-like mosque in the middle of the village, its unique architecture in the sub-Saharan region. This architecture wasn't inspired by outside influences. we owe it to the termite ants, to the anthills, the symbol of *Moolaadé*. That's why I chose Djerisso.

GADJIGO: *You have often said: "To me, creation is like the kora (musical instrument of twenty-one strings), it has many threads. I play like I hear it, and the essential thing is that I am free." What pleasures did you derive from the production of* Moolaadé?
SEMBÈNE: The experience is not complete yet. I worked with a team that included people from Morocco, Ivory Coast, Benin, Mali, Burkina Faso, France, and Senegal. Now that we have just finished the film I wait to see the reaction of my people to it. It won't belong to me anymore after that. The joys, the difficulties, the tribulations, and the pleasure that I tasted during its making will leave me at the first screening of the film. Despite my age, I only think about the future, and I would wish it to be a timeless film.

GADJIGO: *Had you wanted to do the postproduction work in Europe, in France, you would have been able to. So why Rabat, why Morocco?*

SEMBÈNE: It's not my first Moroccan experience. I already did all the postproduction work of *Faat-Kine* in Morocco—editing, sound, etc. . . My pride is in being able to say that this film, *Moolaadé*, was born on the continent and from the continent. That is my personal pride. Maybe I will be able to show African filmmakers, the younger ones, that we can create everything we need within the continent. We are a chosen land. We are not a rich land: we are a chosen land. It's said that the first men were born in Africa; they talk about Lucy. They tell us also about Egypt: the conflict that we have with the Maghreb and the European world. Cheikh Anta Diop, in his book with which I agree, shows that all civilizations originate from the Egypt of the Pharaohs, which was a black civilization. The same with the excision, it comes from a black goddess. When Herodotus saw her, it was the first time the subject of excision came up. It was the fourth or fifth century BC. On this continent, we have Egyptian values, those from Zimbabwe, those born in Nigeria. But what is the origin of the breakdown that we're experiencing now? We must ask ourselves this question. Not to cry about the past, but I think that we can recreate these values from our current African perspective. We have a lot of history. It's our patrimony; we must reseize it and tell ourselves that we can do it. But it's a psychological problem.

GADJIGO: *You've been part of worker's unions. You have fought at the dock in Marseille, during the Indo-China war; you have actively participated in the demonstrations against the colonial war in Algeria and you were in the ranks during the Korean War. But why, at a given moment, did you decide to take your battle to the cultural terrain, to the arts?*

SEMBÈNE: That I don't know. I can't respond. My father was a simple fisherman; my grandfather was a simple fisherman. All his life, my father only lived to fish. He liked to repeat to me often that he would never work for a white man. All his experience was in fishing. In my family, I was the first to go to school.

GADJIGO: *Yes, however, at the CGT library in Marseille you discovered the great writers. Later, you yourself decided to go into writing and then into filmmaking.*

SEMBÈNE: No, no! In respect to writing, it was only on the political action level. Because in these libraries, at that time, when I was young, the books told me about the Africa of banana trees, the exotic Africa, the good Blacks, the black child who never grows old. I knew of stories in which people fought; they were not passive. So, I said, "No, it's not like that where I come from. True, in Africa there are coconut trees, banana boats; but above all there are men. We are not ants." And now, as for how and why . . . I leave you to your Freudian disease . . .

GADJIGO: *Freud, perhaps. But I am convinced that at a given moment you made a conscious choice and decided to turn more towards art rather than throw yourself towards the political arena.*

SEMBÈNE: Ah, politics . . . Yes, but it's the emptiest choice. Culture is political, but it's another type of politics. You're not involved in culture to be chosen. You're not involved in its politics to say, "I am." In art, you are political, but you say, "We are. We are" and not, "I am." At each stage of life, the people create their own culture, they mark their era, and advance! So, when I discovered culture, I made use of that. Politics. Not the politician's politics, to become deputy, cabinet head, or something else; but to speak in the name of my people. And it's there that I see a contradiction. With what purpose have you come to interview me, to speak about my work? I am not elected, I don't owe you the vote. The reward that one has, as an artist, is when people come to express their encouragement.

GADJIGO: *In 1975, at the University of Indiana at Bloomington, you gave a lecture entitled "Man Is Culture." During that whole week that I worked with you, you were always searching for, I would say, the "right word" to express what is, for you, African culture.*

SEMBÈNE: But I was speaking to whom? In this area there are those who speak Mandingue, but there are also people who don't speak Mandingue but that also speak French. It's by that exact word that I am going to be able to situate them and show them what's going on. Here, it's not about academic French, academic English . . . it's about language used in everyday life. It could be also that this worry about the exact word comes to me through literature; the worry of being heard well, understood properly.

GADJIGO: *You have often said that cinema is somewhat mathematic, unlike literature. It's also, at the same time, an art and an industry. Where does African cinema sit today? What direction is it taking?*

SEMBÈNE: I can't tell you. But one thing is certain: we are close to our success. How, when? I have no idea! Will the path be straight, twisted, uphill, downhill? But we are forced to succeed. Because, in this century, a people who cannot speak of itself is bound to disappear. A whole continent, 800,000,000 people disappear? No! We cannot and we should not.

GADJIGO: *We have gone through the experience of slavery; we have gone through colonization; now it's the experience of globalization and neocolonization. Every time, the people of Africa arise every time from their wounds. Ousmane Sembène, where do we get our strength from?*

SEMBÈNE: I don't know, I can't say. But, we must pay a lot of attention to what you have just said. Until now Africa has always risen, but this new century is the most dangerous century; this present phase is the most dangerous one for the continent. Slavery was blessed by the Church and accepted by the Europeans. You can find it in the Bible, the Koran, and even the Talmud. With colonization, it was Europe that divided Africa for its riches. In the eighteenth and nineteenth centuries, the Europeans got together again several times to carve up Africa. France, Italy, England, Germany divided and shared Africa. Even during slavery each of these countries had their area on the African coast. Now, Europe is in the process of uniting, of regrouping—this same Europe that divided us, that same France who, in 1789, spoke of liberty, of man's rights, for them, but not for the Africans. They continued to practice slavery and then colonization. Globalization isn't so. Once again we find ourselves squeezed for our primary riches that Europe wants. We are, one more time, the object of the battles. What is thought nowadays in Africa is even more worrisome. Since 1960, Africans have killed more Africans than a hundred years of slavery and colonization. Now people speak of globalization, and it's enough to just take our area called "francophone." Our leaders, I'd say almost all of them, have houses in Europe, ready to retire to Europe as soon as the smallest problem comes up in their country. We are not concerned by globalization; we are not even in tow. The problem is more mental than economic. When Africans cannot exchange between themselves, between neighboring countries, that is a problem right there. They speak about the market constituted by the European Union, about 250,000,000 people. In Africa we are a potential market of more than 900,000,000! The economic laws and laws of physics are the same everywhere, in all cultures, all languages.

GADJIGO: *Since 1960, you have also fought for the rehabilitation of our national languages. In the '70s, with some other people, you created* Kaddu, *a newspaper in Wolof. Very recently, this year,* Doomi Golo, *by Boubacar Boris Diop, became the first novel ever published in Wolof. In private radio people are doing extraordinary work in Wolof, Pular, Soninke, Bambara . . . If the political will existed today, couldn't we generalize the teaching of our languages?*

SEMBÈNE: You say "if." You, a professor of French, tell me what "if" means. Our leaders don't want to. Imagine for a moment that south of the Sahara, an African language became the official language of the country. The majority of our leaders would not lead anymore. It's the farmers who are going to lead, because the current leaders don't speak their mother tongue.

GADJIGO: *We have spoken earlier about the trilogy. You have made* Faat-Kine *(2000),* Moolaadé *(2004). What will the third be?*

SEMBÈNE: This time it takes place in the city, it has to do with our government. The title of this next film is *The Brotherhood of Rats*.

GADJIGO: *Thank you!*

The Power of Female Solidarity: An Interview with Ousmane Sembène

JARED RAPFOGEL AND RICHARD PORTON/2004

IN A CAREER STRETCHING from 1966's *Black Girl* to his most recent film, *Moolaadé*, the eighty-one-year-old Senegalese director Ousmane Sembène has established himself not only as one of the giants of African cinema but as one of the world's great political filmmakers. Trained as a dockworker until being drafted into the French army during World War II, and later a trade-union activist in Marseilles, Sembène began his career as a novelist (his many books include *Le docker noir* and *God's Bits of Wood*), before turning to film in 1966 with the short *Borom Sarret*. This was followed by the feature, *Le Noire de . . .* (*Black Girl*, 1966), a portrait of a young Senegalese woman working as a domestic in the home of a middle-class French family. Sembène has since made eight feature films, which have ranged widely in terms of setting and period, from urban to rural and from the nineteenth century to World War II to the present day, but his political commitment, acute social observation, and cinematic sophistication have remained constant.

Three of Sembène's films are period pieces—*Emitai* and *Camp de Thiaroye* are both set during World War II, the first portraying the standoff that occurs when French soldiers attempt to conscript the residents of a small village and confiscate its rice, the second charting the smoldering discontent of a regiment of African soldiers who return from fighting

From *Cineaste* (Winter 2004). Reprinted by permission.

for the French only to find that they're treated by their colonial masters more as prisoners than as war heroes; while *Ceddo* (Sembène's masterpiece) brings to life a more distant epoch, depicting a power struggle between Muslims and Catholics in a village in nineteenth-century Senegal. But because of the centrality of colonialism in these films, a historical phenomenon whose legacy is still at the heart of the African experience, it is clear that they are as much about the present as about the past (the two are explicitly interwoven in *Ceddo* in breath-taking fashion when, at one of the most wrenching, dramatic points of the narrative, the images are accompanied by a soundtrack of African-American spirituals, collapsing centuries of history into one moment, and providing a vivid example of the cinematic mastery with which Sembène is able to create a distancing effect that, far from undercutting the power of the sequence, amplifies it).

The rest of the films take place in present-day Senegal (or, in *Moolaadé,* Burkina Faso, representing an unspecified African nation), and function rather like contemporary histories. *Xala,* in particular, embellishes many of the themes found in the period films, tracing the effects of colonialism and imperialism by focusing on the emergence of the black bourgeoisie. The story of an ambitious black businessman who takes a third, much younger wife, but finds himself unable to consummate this new marriage, *Xala* is one of the best demonstrations of Sembène's powers of social and political observation, as well as his satirical finesse.

Sembène's work is radical formally as well as politically, but he may be nearly alone among political filmmakers in striking a delicate but confident balance between this radicalism and a broad accessibility. Indeed, the two are so closely wedded as to be almost indistinguishable. One of the most striking features of his work is the declamatory, antinaturalistic acting style of his performers—they deliver their lines slowly and clearly, reciting them rather than embodying them, almost as if they are taking part in a ritual. While most critics interpret this (not without justification) as a Brechtian distancing device, it fulfills a more straightforward, practical function as well, aiding in the comprehension of a diverse and multilingual African audience.

A quality of ritual is invoked in other ways as well, above all through the strict unity of time and space which structures nearly all of Sembène's films, most explicitly in *Mandabi, Emitai, Ceddo, Camp de*

Thiaroye, *Guelwaar*, and now *Moolaadé*. These films all take place in highly circumscribed location; over the course of just a day or two, and the result is a remarkable immediacy, a sense of presence, which imbues their themes with a profound weight and urgency. This emphasis on a particular place and span of time provides the anchor that, throughout most of Western cinema, is conventionally achieved by the presence of a central protagonist or a small group of central characters. The absence of such figures may be the most radical, unfamiliar aspect of Sembène's films—though many of his movies feature characters who distinguish themselves in varying degrees from the others, the emphasis is always on the community (his last film, *Faat Kiné*, was perhaps the exception to this rule). And films such as *Emitai* and *Ceddo* take this approach to an extreme—there are truly no distinctive characters in these films, no one whose perspective or experience is privileged. The community itself is the central character, redirecting our attention to the social and communal rather than the individual, the psychological.

In fact, if there is a single thread linking each film in Sembène's ouevre, it is that they all portray a crisis that arises within a community, tracing its progress and eventual resolution (more often than not a tragic one). In *Emitai*, it is the standoff between the soldiers and the women of the village who refuse to provide their rice; in *Ceddo*, the kidnapping of a princess by a bandit; in *Guelwaar*, the accidental burying of a Catholic political activist in a Muslim cemetery; and now, in *Moolaadé*, the protection one woman, Collé Ardo Gallo Sy, provides to four young girls who have refused to submit to the traditional ritual of female circumcision.

Moolaadé is distinctive within Sembène's body of work primarily for being, more explicitly than in the past, directed towards an audience of Africans of all nations, and (without ever underestimating the force of the opposition or the difficulty of defeating it) for expressing a relative optimism, a conviction that change is possible, that suffering is not in vain. Filmed in Burkina Faso, in a village chosen by Sembène for its ability to suggest similar villages throughout Africa, *Moolaadé* aspires to cross national and cultural boundaries, a universalism justified by the ubiquity of the practice of female circumcision (or genital excision, as it is referred to in Africa) across the continent. Sembène has conceived the film as a catalyst for discussion of this destructive tradition, and the film's rousing last act, in which a large segment of the community's female population is radicalized, joining Collé in her opposition to the village's conservative leaders, seems explicitly intended to encourage indignation and, ideally, action.

Moolaadé is anything but a simplistic work of rabble-rousing, though, with its nuanced attitude towards the forces of globalization and capitalism (embodied by the roving salesman, Mercenaire, a figure of great ambiguity), and towards the institution of polygamy (the fact that the strong willed, self-confident, authoritative Collé is her ineffectual husband's second, rather than first wife, complicates the way we see her). But the film's greatest strength may be its multifaceted view of the complex interweaving of tradition and modernity in contemporary African culture. Despite Sembène's devotion to denouncing female genital excision, this abusive ritual is counterbalanced by the valuable, positive tradition of the moolaadé, the inviolable principle of asylum that Collé invokes in order to protect the young girls.

On the other hand, one of the most unambiguous forces of positive social change in *Moolaadé* is, surprisingly, the media, as represented by the radios that the village leaders confiscate and destroy in a desperate attempt to quell the women's rebelliousness. It is strange, from a Western perspective, to find the media presented in such a positive light. But this is only one of many paradoxes that run throughout Sembène's vision of the contemporary African experience, an experience that is inherently contradictory, Sembène suggests, precisely because it is the site of a confrontation between different cultures, technologies, and attitudes.

Cineaste interviewed Sembène in October 2004 on the eve of *Moolaadé*'s American premiere at the New York Film Festival. Samba Gadjigo of Mount Holyoke College provided simultaneous translation.—Jared Rapfogel

CINEASTE: *There have been other films dealing with the question of female genital excision, primarily documentaries such as Pratibha Parmar's* Warrior Marks *(which offended some African viewers), as well as fiction films made by Africans (e.g., Cheick Oumar Sissoko's* Finzan*). Are you familiar with these films and, if so, were you deliberately trying to do something different in your films?*

OUSMANE SEMBÈNE: I've seen all of the films made by Africans because we see each other all the time. Without being rude, I thought I could approach this subject in a different way. And, of course, I primarily had an African public in mind while making this film. I didn't want to put the practice of excision center stage, but instead wanted to put men and women, and their responses to the practice, in the foreground. I wanted to highlight the contradictions entailed by two values: the *Moolaadé*, which is the right to asylum and protection and society's demand that the girls submit to excision. Those are two conflicting values. I wanted to emphasize that the men justify excision by referring to Islamic tradition, which provides a dramatic structure for the film. This leads to discussions in open forums when I screen the film for African audiences. Hundreds of people attend these evening screenings. Sometimes we have disagreements, and we often then screen the film again the next evening and continue the discussions.

CINEASTE: *I read that you've not only screened* Moolaadé *to audiences in Senegal, but have also held screenings in other African countries.*
SEMBÈNE: I have already taken the film to other African countries and conducted discussions. It's not only the case with *Moolaadé*; I've done this with all of my films. For me, cinema is a kind of evening school. Of course, a new Africa is being born, and the precondition for this change is a rupture with the African past and a connection with the West. The artist has the duty to try to explain these changes.

CINEASTE: *In more specific terms, what has been the response of audiences to the critique of genital excision in the film? Have people shared their own feelings and experiences?*
SEMBÈNE: Sometimes we manage to convert men to our viewpoint although it's usually women who agree with us. And, among the actors in the film, some agree with the practice of excision and some are opposed. But no can give a proper explanation of why excision should be allowed because the origin of that practice dates back to time immemorial; no one can tell you when it started. Of course, there are some African states that have passed legislation condemning excision, which I think is very courageous. While there are some states that haven't had the courage to take this step, everyone comes when you screen a film—it's an open forum. Some people claim that *Moolaadé* is a very violent film.

But I don't believe that even my own research has uncovered all of the devastation wrought by excision.

CINEASTE: Moolaadé *and* Faat Kiné *seem more optimistic than many of your previous films. Does this reflect your vision of how things are changing in Africa?*
SEMBÈNE: In *Faat Kiné,* when you consider the context of Senegalese society, you have a single woman's struggle. She discovers the power of money and the value of freedom. The only solution she can have to her problems is a personal and individualistic one. This encourages her to work harder to solve her problems, because her goal is to earn enough money to send her children to study abroad. Whereas, in *Moolaadé,* although it's also a personal problem—Collé tries to shield her child from excision—she also invokes the ancient tradition to offer other children sanctuary. You probably notice that, in *Moolaadé,* Collé never acts; she always *reacts* to events. But whenever she reacts, she moves forward with the other characters. On the individual level, she is the only woman being flogged at one point in the film. Yet the other characters react with her. I deliberately made a decision to make both women the same age. It's just that one woman—Faat Kiné—deals with life in an urban setting and the other is in a rural, traditional setting.

CINEASTE: *But perhaps the point is that, although both women have their individual struggles, they both seem to achieve some measure of success when contrasted with some of your earlier films that ended quite bleakly.*
SEMBÈNE: I wouldn't characterize the endings of my other films as bleak. While working within the context of my mileu, I'm trying to create what I'd term "militant cinema." My main activity is to attend screenings in villages and conduct conversations with spectators in those villages. I try to convince people that we should take responsibility for our own predicaments. When dealing with the specific context of *Moolaadé,* I also think we should bear responsibility for the situation depicted in the film. But, of course, once I have screened my films, it becomes a public event and everyone is free to make up their mind and draw any conclusions that they would like to from a work of art.

CINEASTE: *You have said, in conjunction with* Moolaadé, *that "when women progress society progresses." Your belief in women as the most progressive members of society seems to be one motif that runs through your work from early films like* Black Girl *and* Tauw *to the present.*

SEMBÈNE: Well, you could also say that this is an undercurrent in the work of most African musicians. But when you look at my films chronologically, the historical epochs are quite different.

CINEASTE: *Of course, in* Moolaadé *there is perhaps the paradoxical fact that Collé is one of several wives. There is an inter-interesting dynamic set up, given that she's a very headstrong and dynamic woman, but, being the second wife, has to defer to the first wife.*

SEMBÈNE: That's your vision of the film. When I say *you*, I'm not talking about you personally. I mean that it's a Eurocentric interpretation. The first wife is really the person who's in power when the husband's not there; even when he is there, she sometimes predominates. And in every polygamous arrangement, the second wife, who can be the husband's preferred wife, can also have quite a bit of autonomy. But, yes, you're right; Collé must take orders from the first wife. I'll just give you an example. In the film, the first wife says to the second, "If I did not agree to your marriage, you wouldn't have spent one day in this house." Similarly, the third wife must negotiate with the first two wives. You have to understand the internal dynamics of this family. Collé cannot do anything without the agreement of the first wife.

CINEASTE: *But perhaps there's another interesting complication. Although the idea of polygamy might be difficult for Westerners to accept, there's a suggestion in* Moolaadé*—and it's also true in other films such as* Mandabi*—that the multiple wives achieve a kind of group strength can even overwhelm the men at times.*

SEMBÈNE: You have to understand how these women were raised. There's a real hierarchy—the senior wife, the second wife, and the junior wife. Then the man is the supreme master, so to speak. But, when I say that the man is the supreme master, it is because he *believes* this. In actuality, the first wife, not the husband, wields the power. People don't say this, but it's something that's unspoken.

That's why, in the context of polygamy in my society, I just see the man as a progenitor—the only role he has is to make babies *[laughs]*. He has to satisfy his own sexual appetites, but he also has to satisfy the three women's sexual needs. He's just a sex machine, so to speak *[laughs]*. Of course, in this situation there's inevitably some sort of rivalry between the three wives because they're often denied sexual satisfaction. And when the man is around, no matter what he's done during the previous night, he has to perform sexually. To help him perform, the woman feeds him food that functions as an aphrodisiac. Since the women know more about these aphrodisiacs than men do, they share their secrets.

CINEASTE: *Unlike some of the other films made on the subject, you highlight both the positive aspects of tradition (the* Moolaadé*) as well as the negative (excision). You present a very nuanced portrait of tensions within the community.*
SEMBÈNE: In any case, this is how I saw it. Take the practice of *Moolaadé*, for example. There are a lot of young Africans who have not heard of it, who are not aware of that tradition. Yet that form of protection and right of asylum has always existed in our society. When you're in a mosque, for example, no one can come and snatch you away. That's a value everyone knew about. For example, if I was abusing my child and he sought protection, I wouldn't have the right to lay my hand on him after that. There are some villages that still abide by these rules, but it's a tradition that's been forgotten in the big African cities.

CINEASTE: *The film is also nuanced by light of the fact that not all of the women oppose excision and not all of the men support it. The complexities of the debate are not overlooked.*
SEMBÈNE: I didn't want to make a film that could be reduced to propaganda—a banner, so to speak. It has to be nuanced and leave room for reflection. You also have to understand that mothers often take their children to surgeons to have the operation performed—with the silent complicity of men of my age.

My main purpose is to trigger discussion so that the practice will be abolished. You'll notice in the film that, when Collé displays her scars, it means that she's had a C-section. I'm trying to put the problem in a modern context so that audiences can understand how she got to that point. Millions of women still die in childbirth as a result of this practice. There are now many young girls who flee the villages for urban areas in order to escape the consequences.

There are many mothers who want to shield their daughters from excision. They have to take this responsibility on themselves; no one else will do it for them. They of course need support.

To give you one example: Two weeks ago in Burkina Faso, a woman received a jail sentence for practicing excision. It may seem normal for people to have to abide by the law, but for us in Africa this represents a milestone. The surgeon who performs the operation is usually a women in her seventies, while the trial lawyers are usually in their forties. Given the respect for elders in our society, an elderly woman usually receives enormous deference. Being able to put an elderly woman like this on trial signals a big change in our society. When I showed the film in Burkina Faso, the country's first lady attended and presided over the screening; many of the women's organizations were also there.

CINEASTE: *Most of your films make use of a remarkable unity of time and space. They almost all take place in a single location over the course of a day or two. Is there a reason you've chosen this approach?*

SEMBÈNE: It's mainly economic—it's cheaper to do it this way. Given the mathematics of cinema—the costs accrued when you change sets or change the lighting, it's easier to do it this way. I have to ration everything.

CINEASTE: *While it would be wrong to put words in your mouth, it creates both immediacy and a ritualistic sense.*

SEMBÈNE: Yes, you're right! I'm not in Hollywood and I am looking for an alternative approach that will allow me to tell a lively story.

CINEASTE: *One thing that makes your films, including* Moolaadé, *unique—and is distinctive within world cinema—is the emphasis on the community rather then individuals. They're radical films inasmuch as there's really no central character and this is of course even more apparent in earlier movies such as* Emitai *and* Ceddo.

SEMBÈNE: Given the current situation in Africa, I don't think you can feature one main character in a story. I'm not making epics dealing with warriors, but am more concerned with daily life. I think this communal approach to filmmaking enables my audiences to understand the films better when we're engaged in discussions. With a communal approach, people can see themselves on screen. You can't take a character like, for example, Faat Kiné and single her out; it doesn't work. That's the result of my own analysis of the current situation in Africa.

CINEASTE: *We agree, but so many filmmakers seem to feel that you're obliged to have a single protagonist for the audience to "relate" to. They assume that this strategy brings audiences "into" the film and I wonder if you're consciously going against the grain of the dominant psychological, interiorized approach to narrative.*

SEMBÈNE: You can start with one individual, but when you get to the reaction to that individual's actions it becomes, for me, a community-based narrative. We are not alone within our communities; there's not one political party or one trade union to consider. There are instead people with differences and points in common.

CINEASTE: *Does this tendency refer back to the tradition of the griot, the storyteller who's responsible for transmitting values to the community?*

SEMBÈNE: That's what I would like to accomplish. In our culture, the griot is traditionally a sacred character but he has now become a very banal individual. He used to be a very respected figure and he didn't just sing praises to his society but was a guardian of the past and of the truth. Since he was a master of the spoken word, he was a trustee of society's secrets.

CINEASTE: *This point also highlights an aspect of your films that is rare in Western cinema. So many of the films feature crises being worked out verbally through communal debate.*

SEMBÈNE: Africa still needs that. Even though it's undergoing change, I wish it could preserve those values. Unfortunately, in the cities, as I mentioned before, these values are fading away. Most of our leaders are mimicking the West.

CINEASTE: *Taking up that point: some years ago, you launched a scathing attack on the neocolonial elite in* Xala. *Do you think this critique is still pertinent to the situation in Senegal today?*

SEMBÈNE: I don't want to make any sweeping generalizations, but, within the Francophone countries at least, I think the situation is worse than it was in the Sixties and Seventies. During the last forty years, more Africans killed each other than were killed by outsiders during the previous hundred years. I'm talking about wars, not deaths by disease. Nowadays, the leadership is even more alienated from the people than the leaders of the previous generation. That's the dangerous situation we're faced with now. And I'm going to deal with this topic in my next film, *The Brotherhood of the Rats.* [holds up script] Even though the situation is worse, you have to bear witness. As far as many issues go, we've actually regressed over the years. Tradition has just become a value people use to escape reality. People merely invoke tradition in order to go backwards.

CINEASTE: *To return to* Moolaadé, *do you see some hope in the development in an indigenous African media? The Western left often views the media as a means of deception, but your film goes against the grain of Marxism in the West by viewing it as a source of consciousness-raising (particularly since the women's radios that are seized appear to represent to major source of enlightenment).*
SEMBÈNE: My view is that, without the media, there's no future. It's not the media itself that are of importance—it's the content. I'm dealing with the issue of globalization. In reference to the Western left that you mention, hasn't it become backward and lost ground in recent years in its fight with the mainstream?

CINEASTE: *Yes, that's true.*
SEMBÈNE: In Africa, we have a lot of independent radio stations. But our leaders don't like these independent radio stations! Yet now we have radio stations broadcasting in all of the African languages. This is important because of the many African languages and the great geographical distances on the continent. If you speak two or three languages, you can listen to several stations dealing with different topics. For Africans, radio and television are very important tools.

CINEASTE: *Is this related to the fact that you shot the film in Burkina Faso? Are you making more of an effort to address the problems of African nations outside of Senegal? Is "Pan-Africanism" still a viable goal?*
SEMBÈNE: I was working with technicians from France, Senegal, Benin, and other countries. But it was difficult to the extent that they're all from

cities and the place we were shooting in Burkina Faso didn't have electricity or running water. And there were a lot of mosquitoes—I can attest to that! In addition to French, the actors spoke Bambara. It's not a majority language or a lingua franca, but most people in West Africa speak it.

It's too easy to speak of Pan-Africanism. Marcus Garvey and Du Bois in the United States introduced the notion of Pan-Africanism. To put in a nutshell, Africa is a vast continent. It's in the interest of Africans, however, to have regional ties because the countries complement each other, both economically and culturally.

Of course, African unity is the ultimate goal. But at the time when the concept of Pan-Africanism was formulated, there were no independent states in Africa—except perhaps Ethiopia. Now that we've had independent states for forty years, we haven't made one steps of progress towards Pan-Africanism. All of our heads of state talk about Pan-Africanism, but they all want to preserve their thrones as in monarchies. No one wants to share political power. As far as the Francophone countries go, those leaders spend more time with the French President than they do among themselves. How can you talk about Pan-Africanism in this context? Does Bush hold meetings about his national interests in China? Of course not. We can't even talk about globalization yet in Africa; we're on the periphery of the world. We have raw materials in our soil, but this doesn't make us wealthy; it makes other nations wealthy. If you look at the raw data of the United Nations, there are about 800 million people in Africa—three-fourths live on less than a dollar a day.

CINEASTE: *This problem was of course the theme of one of your most powerful films in recent years*—Guelwaar.

SEMBÈNE: Yes, you're right. But, again, the role of the artist is to raise issues and trigger discussion.

CINEASTE: *How much faith do you have in the possibility that these movies will bring about change?*

SEMBÈNE: I realize that I'm not able to change my society single-handedly. But I have the impression, when I bring students food for thought and conduct discussions with them, that I'm doing my part. I was recently in central Africa, screening *Moolaadé* in the South of

Cameroon. In the North, they are Muslims and practice excision. I wouldn't have been able to show the film there—even my friends dissuaded me from doing that. I couldn't have changed anyone's mind there; it's just like the elderly man in the movie who doesn't want the women to listen to the radio because he's afraid that they're being fed subversive ideas. Yet I don't think that Africa can afford to live in isolation nowadays, closed in upon itself.

Ousmane Sembène

BONNIE GREER/2005

OUSMANE SEMBÈNE, the Senegalese-born "father of African cinema," talked to Bonnie Greer about film-making in Africa, his European experiences and why Live 8 is fake, before receiving the fellowship of the BFI. Here's a full transcript.

BONNIE GREER: *Before I start, I'd like to say that I am a huge fan of this gentleman, so I am really nervous. But I am going to do my best. There will be simultaneous translation by Mr. Samba Gadjigo, Mr. Sembène's biographer and himself an eminent professor of French at Mount Holyoke College in Massachusetts.* Moolaadé *is the second film in a trilogy, and you call it a trilogy about the heroism of daily life. Could you expand on that, please?*
OUSMANE SEMBÈNE: We are talking here about the African continent, and it is a continent going through a crisis. Nobody can deny that we have a lot of wars going on; brothers killing brothers; we have a lot of diseases and catastrophes. But on the other hand, we have a majority of individuals, both men and women, who are struggling on a daily basis in a heroic way and the outcome of whose struggle leaves no doubt. This is a struggle whose purpose is not to seize power, and I think the strength of our entire society rests on that struggle. And it is because of this struggle that the entire continent is still standing up. So I've tried in my own way to sing the praises of those heroes, because I am also a witness to that daily struggle. In the traditional society which I come from, when

From *The Guardian* (June 5, 2005). Reprinted by permission of Bonnie Greer.

you look at our societies, whether you're talking about the Mandinka, Bambara, or Fulani, we have the tradition of the storyteller called the griot and also other kinds of storytellers. Their role was to record memories of daily actions and events. At night, people would gather around them and they would tell those stories that they had recorded. I think there are parallels between myself and these storytellers, because in that traditional society, the storyteller was his own writer, director, actor, and musician. And I think his role was very important in cementing society. Now, with new technologies and the tools that we have acquired, I think we can take inspiration from them and do some work.

BG: *You have said that* Moolaadé *is your most African film. Can you expand on that?*

OS: When I made such a statement, I was referring to its narrative structure and aesthetic. But then, ultimately, it's up to my people to judge whether or not I have come close to telling their reality. What makes the difference between this film and the others I've made is that I already know what the people are saying in the rural areas. I think it is up to you, brought here in the west by the contingencies of history, it is up to you to understand and to see what is African in this film. And I think your appreciation and judgment is going to help me improve my future work. Right now, I am very, very obsessed, because right now, *Moolaadé* is enjoying some measure of success. So what am I going to do with my next film? Since the setting for the next film is going to be an urban area, how am I going to talk about African cities? Of course when I talk about African cities, there is no difference between a building in London or Abidjan or anywhere in the world. But what is important is to wonder, the men or the women who live in that building, what kind of life are they living? It's not enough to have all kinds of gadgets. This is what I'm working on right now.

BG: *I adore the title of the latest film in the trilogy,* Brotherhood of Rats. *I love it because you're talking about a very important subject: it's about the cities and the complicity or not of African governments in some of the troubles afflicting African states.*

OS: I think that's just part of my job. If I center that film on an urban area, how can I show it to people who live in the rural area? How can

I make this film in such a way that a peasant in my village in Casamance can understand what's going on? And how can I now really raise my voice against all the embezzling that's going on in the cities? Here I am talking about people of this new generation. I am making this film for the young people who are here in this room, and who are going back home: how can I inspire them?

BG: *What do you think of the cinema numerique, the digital cinema?*
OS: For us, everything is good. I think that every tool that we can appropriate and use is good for us. What counts here actually is the result of the battle of the sexes, the war between husbands and wives.

BG: *I want to go back a little bit to the early days—your life was formidable even before you began to make cinema. You were in the war, you fought for freedom in Algeria, you were a dockworker in Marseilles, you hurt your back and then decided to take a less strenuous job and investigate some of the literature of the African and diasporic world, particularly Claude McKay, the great Jamaican novelist and member of the Harlem Renaissance, and his idea about the docks in Marseilles and the languages of the African diaspora.*
OS: I am really unable to talk about my life—I don't know my life. I've traveled a lot and this is the life that I have lived, but that doesn't mean that I know myself.

BG: *All right then, women?*
OS: I love all women. Can you show me one man who doesn't love women?

BG: *Well, you are in England. I was struck, and the reason why I wanted to show* Ceddo, *although you didn't want me to show* Ceddo, *is because of the moment in it where a strong woman is putting a line in the ground. So I want to ask, first about the idea of women in African cinema, especially in your cinema, and how important they are for you?*
OS: Here we are talking about past civilizations. When I was growing up, married women, of their own accord, always tied a belt around their waists. I think it's a symbol of their loyalty, their fidelity. It didn't have anything to do with the men. So when she takes off her belt and shakes it, she was putting her own life and honor on the line. So for husbands

like myself, when they shake their belts and tell us not to cross the line, none of us would be able to do it. And it is only on those occasions that the community recognizes the woman's right to kill. Of course you can rape the body, but you can never go against that rule. So one has to die for that rule to be broken. But here we are talking about what I call medieval Africa, and of course now things have changed. Right now, women wear belts that are gold or leather or whatever, but that doesn't mean that they are more loyal.

BG: *Madame [Fatoumata] Coulibaly [who played the lead role of Colle in* Moolaadé*], how was it for you, playing in this movie?*

FATOUMATA COULIBALY: Thank you first of all, and I think that it shows that you have a strong interest in African films. Even before I was called upon to act in this film, I was already working in Malian radio and TV. My job was working in programs designed for women and children, and centered on the family. I traveled a lot into rural areas, and I talked to the women and everybody there. And I tried to touch on all the issues relevant to their lives. During that work, I noticed that many young girls died following the female genital mutilations (FGM), through hemorrhaging. So I did some research in the rural areas. When I decided to conceive of a program without consulting my boss, I ran into a lot of problems.

I myself made a documentary film which was broadcast only once on Malian television, and of course people hid the tape and said that it was lost. That's when our administration decided to silence any dialogue about FGM. In spite of that, of course, I wanted to continue that kind of work. In my work I also collaborated with an NGO composed of women. We would go to the rural areas, and we would try to educate them about hygiene and the family, in their own languages, not in French or English. We brought together the village chief and every man, woman, and child—everybody came to those meetings. Of course, we don't start head-on with FGM; we would strategically beat around the bush for a while and then only come to the issue that is important to us. Because in our society, talking about sex is still a taboo, and of course many village chiefs don't want to hear about that issue. "You are trying to deviate us from our way of life, our traditions." And of course the argument they give is that these traditions date back to before our birth, and actually they accuse us of being funded by the outside world to subvert their way of life. But with persistence we would come back and get our message across.

Sometimes we used dolls to show the body parts of a woman in childbirth, we show them the pain and suffering of a woman who has been excised. Of course when we show those things graphically, they hide their faces. But we always managed to find a strategy, through jokes and whatnot, to bring them to look and take responsibility and face what we are showing them as a reflection of their own bodies. Of course, the position I hold in Mali—I am very popular—so that helped me in my job. After a while I can see that they are not closing their eyes anymore and they face the body from which a baby is emerging. Of course we do all this with the complicity of a midwife. People ask us questions and we engage in dialogue. We also talk about all the consequences of excision, and I think that has yielded some positive results in abandoning FGM. And so afterward, when Mr. Sembène was casting in Bamako—at the time, he did not know how involved I was in the struggle against FGM—I was honored, privileged, and lucky to be chosen to play this lead role. I'll tell you, this is just the beginning of my struggle, and I want you all to join and support me so that we can reach a positive result.

BG: *This leads me to the two most interesting lines in the film. One, the last words of Colle's husband, "It takes more than a pair of balls to make a man," but the strongest sentence is when Mercenaire says, "Africa is a bitch." I'd like you to elaborate.*

OS: Mercenaire says, "Africa is a bitch," because he's completely in despair: he was shocked at what he was witnessing. Maybe it's me who put my words into his mouth.

BG: *That's what I would like you to speak about.*

OS: Because I love Africa, that's why I call it a bitch. When you love something . . . I think there is no contradiction between loving Africa and calling it a bitch. I am saying it out of desperation. And the other sentence you refer to is a phrase that is used a lot in Africa, in many languages. Actually, when you look at the Bambara version, it is rendered as "It takes more than a pair of trousers to make a man." But since I wanted to make it a more powerful statement, I made it "It takes more than a pair of balls to make a man." In the Bambara, the metaphor of trousers is important because a male child cannot wear trousers before circumcision. Circumcision is a symbol of entry into manhood. So that's why I was playing with those two metaphors; but I decided to use "pair of balls."

BG: *You've said that Africa is matriarchal, the idea of the woman as the strong force in Africa. But for us in the west, polygamy is not an acceptable or pleasant practice. Yet you sort of nuance it, the way you nuanced several customs like the excision and the protection, so in the film it is a polygamous situation, yet the women are very much in control. So is this the African language of cinema, is this an African aesthetic?*

OS: As far as I am concerned, Africa is a woman. As far as I can tell, and maybe my knowledge is very limited, I really don't think that two thousand years of Christianity has brought anything to humanity. When you look at African education, the basis of all African education is this idea of femininity that I'm talking about. Whether you are talking about me or my father, usually, women just give us the illusion that we are in control. Actually, even our virility depends on the gaze and the control of women. Without women, we cannot do anything. I think it's a good thing.

BG: *One, almost final question, and this is a political and philosophical question, about pan-Africanism. You've been a great fighter for the liberation, through cinema, of African consciousness, African thought, African people. People in the diaspora, as many of us are in this room—I am myself a sixty-year-old, so I understand, but for the generation after me, and the generation after them, does pan-Africanism necessarily speak to them? Does it have any meaning at all today?*

OS: For me, anything that unites is useful. Anything that can bring understanding and peace is important. And for me, there was a phase in which pan-Africanism was a political action. At the beginning of the last century, London was the center of pan-Africanism. Actually, the first time I visited London was for a meeting about pan-Africanism. In the 1920s, Africa was not the center of pan-Africanism; the center was in the diaspora. And it was during those early years, around the twenties, that we saw the first educated Africans. After the first world war, it became stronger and all the people who came from all horizons knew each other. And we met and talked about independence: Chou En-Lai from China, George Padmore, W. E. B. Du Bois—those were the people engaged in the struggle. After independence, we preserved the idea of pan-Africanism for the unity of the continent. For me, that is very important.

BG: *But today?*

OS: Nowadays, with the kind of policies that our leaders are engaged in, and here I am specifically talking about the French-speaking parts of Africa, they are the most alienated individuals I have ever seen. I think it is France that is really leading the job of dividing Africa. Most of our presidents have dual nationalities, French and African. When the going gets tough, they run away to Paris and all our decisions are made in Paris. I think in that context it's very difficult to talk about pan-Africanism. Of course, it's just plain rhetoric. Why don't they abolish political borders in Africa? What is stopping them from developing education in Africa? And again, when talking about the francophone countries, there are a lot of states where the annual budget is secured only with the intervention of France. So that's why I think in that context it is difficult. But I don't think we should give up. I am positive that one day we will become independent.

The toughest fight we engaged in was the struggle against apartheid, and many people in Europe joined, supported that fight, and some of them were gunned down. I think what we need is goodwill because now our struggle is harder because it is an economic struggle. And now Europe is organizing itself. So I think there needs to be a rupture between Africa and Europe, and all the international laws being conceived here in the west have to be revisited and changed. Just one case in point, now European countries are running into problems with China because of T-shirts. What did China do? China's flooding their markets with T-shirts. But last century, France and England bombed Shanghai—they took weapons and invaded them. They can no longer do that because China has organized itself; and Vietnam has organized itself. That is what we lack back in Africa: we have been subjugated so much that all we can do is beg, and some even think what we are going through is a comedy.

Then there is the issue of cotton. During slavery, negroes were in the cotton fields. Everybody knew about that. Now that they are not forcing us to make cotton, we make cotton and they don't want it. What should we do? I mean, even our leaders have failed to build factories to transform that cotton for our clothing. We could make any kind of material that would be even better than what is made here, but we wait for everything to come from European industry. They are selling us rags. And everywhere you go in Africa, in the big cities, you would think that you were in a Salvation Army store. They have even created an NGO whose role is to sell us secondhand clothes. I think the youth need to hear these stories. The struggle continues.

BG: *That leads beautifully into my next question. What do you think of the big campaigns going on now in Britain: Make Poverty History, Live 8, Hear Africa 05? Big initiatives to make people aware and to maybe give money.*
OS: I think they're fake, and I think African heads of state who buy into that idea are liars. The only way for us to come out of poverty is to work hard. Poverty means begging throughout the world. I know your prime minister is spearheading that kind of campaign. A few years ago, the British army was in Sierra Leone—were they there to fight against poverty? It's a mistake, it's a lie. But it's up to Africans to know that, and I think we have to start that revolution back home.

BG: *Well, let's see if that hits the newspapers tomorrow. How much do you want to bet it won't? My last question, I saw you on French television, on a program called* Rideau Rouge. *You were speaking with a young filmmaker from Burkina Faso, and you said, "African filmmakers have to be less modest," and then you went into a discussion about the future of African cinema. Can you elaborate on those two things?*
OS: I think cinema is needed throughout Africa, because we are lagging behind in the knowledge of our own history. I think we need to create a culture that is our own. I think that images are very fascinating and very important to that end. But right now, cinema is only in the hands of filmmakers because most of our leaders are afraid of cinema. Europeans are very smart in that matter—every night they are colonizing our minds, and they are imposing on us their own model of society and ways of doing it. And many of our men dress in English suits, with British ties. Our first ladies are called the duty-free ladies and they use only European perfumes and only wear labels.

INDEX

CONVERSATIONS WITH FILMMAKERS SERIES
PETER BRUNETTE, GENERAL EDITOR

The collected interviews with notable modern directors, including

Robert Aldrich • Woody Allen • Pedro Almodóvar • Robert Altman
Theo Angelopolous • Michelangelo Antonioni • Ingmar Bergman
Bernardo Bertolucci • Tim Burton • Jane Campion • Frank Capra
Charlie Chaplin • The Coen Brothers • Francis Ford Coppola • George Cukor
Brian De Palma • Clint Eastwood • Federico Fellini • John Ford
Terry Gilliam • Jean-Luc Godard • Peter Greenaway • Howard Hawks
Alfred Hitchcock • John Huston • Jim Jarmusch • Elia Kazan • Buster Keaton
Stanley Kubrick • Akira Kurosawa • Fritz Lang • Spike Lee • Mike Leigh
George Lucas • Sidney Lumet • Joseph L. Mankiewicz • Sam Peckinpah
Roman Polanski • Michael Powell • Satyajit Ray • Jean Renoir • Martin Ritt
Carlos Saura • John Sayles • Martin Scorsese • Ridley Scott • Steven
Soderbergh • Steven Spielberg • George Stevens • Oliver Stone
Quentin Tarantino • Andrei Tarkovsky • Lars von Trier • François Truffaut
Liv Ullmann • Orson Welles • Billy Wilder • John Woo • Zhang Yimou
Fred Zinnemann